Edward A. Pollard

The Second Year of the War

Edward A. Pollard

**The Second Year of the War**

ISBN/EAN: 9783337825911

Printed in Europe, USA, Canada, Australia, Japan

Cover: Foto ©Andreas Hilbeck / pixelio.de

More available books at **www.hansebooks.com**

THE

# Second Year of the War.

BY

EDWARD A. POLLARD.

AUTHOR OF "BLACK DIAMONDS," ETC.

"Durate! et vosmet rebus secundis servate."—ENEID.

# PREFACE.

In presenting a second volume of a popular History of the Southern War for Independence, the author gratefully acknowledges the kind reception by the Southern public of his first volume, the generous notices of the independent Press of the Confederacy, and the encouragement of friends. He has no disposition to entreat criticism or importune its charities. But he would be incapable of gratitude, if he was not sensible of the marks of public generosity which have been given to a work which made no pretensions to severe or legitimate history and ventured upon no solicitations of literary success.

He can afford no better vindication of the character and objects of his work than by quoting here what was prefixed to one of the editions of his first volume:

"Every candid mind must be sensible of the futility of attempting a high order of historical composition in the treatment of recent and incomplete events; but it does not follow that the cotemporary annal, the popular narrative and other inferiour degrees of history can have no value and interest, because they cannot compete in accuracy with the future retrospect of events. The vulgar notion of history is that it is a record intended for posterity. The author contends that history has an office to perform in the present, and that one of the greatest values of cotemporary annals is to vindicate in good time to the world the fame and reputation of nations."

"With this object constantly in view, the author has composed this work. He will accomplish his object, and be rewarded with a complete satisfaction, if his unpretending book shall have the effect of promoting more extensive inquiries; enlightening the present; vindicating the principles of a great contest to the cotemporary world; and putting before the living generation in a convenient form of literature, and at an early and opportune time, the name and deeds of our people."

*Richmond, July,* 1863.

# CONTENTS.

## CHAPTER I.

The New Orleans Disaster...Its Consequences and Effects...Dispatches of the European Commissioners...Butler "the Beast"...Public Opinion in Europe...The Atrocities of the Massachusetts Tyrant...Execution of Mumford...Lesson of New Orleans...Spirit of Resistance in the South...Change in the Fortunes of the Confederacy...Two Leading Causes for it...The Richmond "Examiner"...The Conscription Law...Governor Brown of Georgia...Re-organization of the Army...Abandonment of our Frontier Defences...The Policy of Concentration...Governor Rector's Appeal...First Movements of the Summer Campaign in Virginia...The Retreat from Yorktown...Evacuation of Norfolk...Destruction of the "Virginia"...Commodore Tatnall's Report...Secretary Mallory's Visit to Norfolk...The Engagement of Williamsburg...The Affair of Barhamsville...McClellan's Investment of the Lines of the Chickahominy...Alarm in Richmond...The Water Avenue of the James...The Panic in Official Circles...Consternation in the President's House...Correspondence between President Davis and the Legislature of Virginia...Noble Resolutions of the Legislature...Response of the Citizens of Richmond...The Bombardment of Drewry's Bluff...The Mass Meeting at the City Hall...Renewal of Public Confidence...The Occasions of This...JACKSON'S CAMPAIGN IN THE VALLEY...The Engagement of McDowell...The Surprise at Front Royal...Banks' Retreat Down the Valley...The Engagements of Port Republic...Results of the Campaign...Death of Turner Ashby...Sufferings of the People of the Valley of the Shenandoah...MEMOIR OF TURNER ASHBY.

PAGE 17

## CHAPTER II.

The Situation of Richmond...Its Strategic Importance...What the Yankees Had Done to Secure Richmond...THE BATTLE OF SEVEN PINES...Miscarriage of Gen. Johnston's Plans...THE BATTLES OF THE CHICKAHOMINY...Storming of the Enemy's Entrenchments...McClellan Driven from his Northern Line of Defences...The Situation on the Other Side of the Chickahominy...Magruder's Comment...The Affair of Savage Station....The Battle of Frazier's Farm...A Terrible Crisis...Battle of Malvern Hill...The Enemy in Communication with his Gunboats....The Failure to Cut him off....Glory and Fruits of Our Victory....Misrepresentations of the Yankees...Safety of Richmond...The War in Other Parts of the Confederacy...The Engagement of Secessionville...The Campaign of the West...The Evacuation of Corinth...More Yankee Falsehoods...Capture of Memphis...The Prize of the Mississippi...Statistics of its Navigation...Siege of Vicksburg...Heroism of "the Queen City"...Morgan's Raid into Kentucky...The Tennessee and Virginia Frontier...Prospects in the West...Plan of Campaign there. . . . . . . . . . PAGE 57

## CHAPTER III.

Effect of McClellan's Defeat in the North...Call for more Troops...Why the North was not Easily Dispirited...The War as a Money Job...*Note:* General Washington's Opinion of New England...The Yankee Finances...Exasperation of Hostilities...The Yankee Idea of a "Vigourous Prosecution of the War"... Ascendancy of the Radicals...War Measures at Washington...Anti-Slavery Aspects of the War...Brutality of the Yankees...The Insensibility of Europe... Yankee Chaplains in Virginia...Seizures of Private Property...Pope's Orders in Virginia...Steinwehr's Order Respecting Hostages...The Character and Services of General John Pope...The "Army of Virginia"...Irruption of the Northern Spoilsmen...The Yankee Trade in Counterfeit Confederate Notes... Pope's "Chasing the Rebel Hordes"...Movement Against Pope by "Stonewall" Jackson...BATTLE OF CEDAR MOUNTAIN...McClellan Recalled from the Peninsula...The Third Grand Army of the North...Jackson's Surprise of the Enemy at Manassas...A Rapid and Masterly Movement...Change of the Situation...Attack by the Enemy upon Bristow Station and at Manassas Junction...Marshalling of the Hosts...Longstreet's Passage of Thoroughfare Gap... The Plans of General Lee...Spirit of our Troops...Their Painful Marches... THE SECOND BATTLE OF MANASSAS...A Terrible Bayonet Charge—Rout of the Enemy...A Hideous Battle-Feld...General Lee and the Summer Campaign of Virginia...Jackson's Share in it...Extent of the Great Victory of Manassas... Excitement in Washington...The Yankee Army Falls Back Upon Alexandria and Washington...Review of the Situation...Rapid Change in our Military Fortunes...What the South had Accomplished...Comparison of Material Strength Between North and South...Humiliating Result to the Warlike Reputation of the North. . . . . . . . . PAGE 83

## CHAPTER IV.

Rescue of Virginia from the Invader...Gen. Loring's Campaign in the Kanawha Valley...A Novel Theatre of the War...Gen. Lee's Passage of the Potomac...His Plans...Disposition of our Forces...McClellan again at the Head of the Yankee Army...THE BATTLE OF BOONSBORO'...THE CAPTURE OF HARPER'S FERRY—Its Fruits...THE BATTLE OF SHARPSBURG...Great Superiority of the Enemy's Numbers...Fury of the Battle...The Bridge of Antietam...A Drawn Battle...Spectacles of Carnage...The Unburied Dead...General Lee Retires into Virginia...McClellan's Pretence of Victory...The Affair of Shepherdstown...Charges against McClellan...His Disgrace...Review of the Maryland Campaign—Misrepresentations of Gen. Lee's Objects...His Retreat...Comment of the New York "Tribune"...The Cold Reception of the Confederates in Maryland...Excuses for the Timidity of the Marylanders... What was Accomplished by the Summer Campaign of 1862...The Outburst

CONTENTS. vii

of Applause in Europe...Tribute from the London "Times"—Public Opinion in England...Distinction between the People and the Government—The Mask of England...OUR FOREIGN RELATIONS IN THE WAR....A Historical Parallel of Secession...Two Remarks on the "Neutrality" of Europe...The Yankee Blockade and the Treaty of Paris—The Confederate Privateers—Temper of the South...Fruits of the Blockade. . . . . . PAGE 128

## CHAPTER V.

Movements in the West...The Splendid Programme of the Yankees...Kentucky the Critical Point...Gen. Kirby Smith's Advance into Kentucky...THE BATTLE OF RICHMOND...Reception of the Confederates in Lexington...Expectation of an Attack on Cincinnati...Gen. Bragg's Plans...Smith's Movement to Bragg's Lines...Escape of the Yankee Forces from Cumberland Gap...Affair of Munfordsville...Gen. Bragg between the Enemy and the Ohio...An Opportunity for a Decisive Blow...Buell's Escape to Louisville...The Inauguration of Governor at Frankfort...An Idle Ceremony...Probable Surprise of Gen. Bragg...THE BATTLE OF PERRYVILLE...Its Immediate Results in our Favour...Bragg's Failure to Concentrate his Forces...His Resolution of Retreat...Scenes of the Retreat from Kentucky...Errours of the Campaign...A Lame Excuse...Public Sentiment in Kentucky—The Demoralization of that State...The Lessons of Submission. . . . . . PAGE 149

## CHAPTER VI.

Our Lines in the Southwest...General Breckenridge's Attack on Baton Rouge...Destruction of the Ram Arkansas...Gen. Price's Reverse at Iuka...Desperate Fighting...THE BATTLE OF CORINTH...Van Dorn's Hasty Exultations...The Massacre of College Hill...Wild and Terrible Courage of the Confederates...Our Forces Beaten Back...Our Lines of Retreat Secured...The Military Prospects of the South Overshadowed...THE DEPARTMENT OF THE TRANS-MISSISSIPPI...Romance of the War in Missouri...Schofield's Order Calling Out the Militia...Atrocities of the Yankee Rule in Missouri...Robbery Without "Red Tape"...The Guerilla Campaign...The Affair of Kirksville...Execution of Col. McCullough...The Affair of Lone Jack...Timely Reinforcement of Lexington by the Yankees...The Palmyra Massacre...The Question of Retaliation with the South...THE MILITARY AND POLITICAL SITUATION...Survey of the Military Situation...Capture of Galveston by the Yankees...The Enemy's Naval Power...His Iron Clads...Importance of Founderies in the South...Prospect in the Southwest...Prospect in Tennessee...Prospect in Virginia...Stuart's Raid into Pennsylvania...Souvenirs of Southern Chivalry...The "Soft-mannered Rebels"...Political Complexion of the War in the North...Lincoln's "Emancipation Proclamation"...History of Yankee Legislation in the War...Political Errour of the Emancipation Proclamation—Its Effect on the South...The Decay of European Sympathy with the Abolitionists...What the War Accomplished for Negro Slavery in the South...Yankee Falsehoods and Bravados in Europe...Delusion of Conquering the South by Starvation.. Caricatures in the New York Pictorials...The Noble Eloquence of Hunger and Rags...Manners in the South...Yankee Warfare...The Desolation of Virginia...The Lessons of Harsh Necessity...Improvement of the Civil Administration of the Confederacy...Ordnance, Manufacturing Resources, Quartermasters' Supplies, &c. . . . . . . . . . PAGE 167

## CHAPTER VII.

The Heroism of Virginia...Her Battle-Fields...Burnside's Plan of Campaign...Calculations of his Movement upon Fredericksburg...Failure to Surprise Gen. Lee...THE BATTLE OF FREDERICKSBURG...The Enemy Crossing the River...Their Bombardment of the Town...Scenes of Distress...The Battle on the Right Wing...The Story of Marye's Heights...Repulse of the Enemy... The Old Lesson of Barren Victory...Death of Gen. Cobb...Death of General Gregg...Romance of the Story of Fredericksburg...Her Noble Women...Yankee Sacking of the Town...A Specimen of Yankee Warfare in North Carolina...Designs of the Enemy in this State:..The Engagements of Kinston... Glance at other Theatres of the War...Gen. Hindman's Victory at Prairie Grove...Achievements of our Cavalry in the West...The Affair of Hartsville... Col. Clarkson's Expedition...Condition of Events at the Close of the Year 1862. . . . . . . . . . . PAGE 192

## CHAPTER VIII.

The Eastern Portion of Tennessee...Its Military Importance...Composition of Bragg's Army—THE BATTLE OF MURFREESBORO'...The Right Wing of the Enemy Routed—Bragg's Exultations...The Assault of the 2d January..."The Bloody Crossing of Stone River"...The Confederates Fall Back to Tullahoma...Review of the Battle Field of Murfreesboro'...Repulse of the Enemy at Vicksburg....THE RE-CAPTURE OF GALVESTON....The Midnight March... Capture of "the Harriet Lane"...Arkansas Post Taken by the Yankees...Its Advantages...The Affair of the Rams in Charleston Harbour...Naval Structure of the Confederacy...Capture of the Yankee Gunboat "Queen of the West"... Heroism of George Wood...Capture of "the Indianola"...The War on the Water...The Confederate Cruisers...Prowess of "the Alabama."

PAGE 211

## CHAPTER IX.

An Extraordinary Lull in the War...An Affair with the Enemy on the Blackwater...Raids in the West...Van Dorn's Captures...THE MEETING OF CONGRESS...Character of This Body...Its Dullness and Servility...Mr. Foote and the Cabinet...Two Popular Themes of Confidence...Party Contention in the North...Successes of the Democrats There...Analysis of the Party Politics of the North...The Interest of New England in the War...How the War Affected the Northwestern Portions of the United States...Mr. Foote's Resolutions Respecting the Northwestern States...How They Were Received by the Southern Public...New War Measures at Washington...Lincoln a Dictator...Prospect of Foreign Interference...Action of the Emperor Napoleon... Suffering of the Working Classes in England...The Delusions of an Early Peace...The Tasks Before Congress...Prostrate Condition of the Confederate

CONTENTS.    ix

Finances...President Davis' Blunder...The Errours of Our Financial System...
The Wealth of the South...The Impressment Law of Congress...Scarcity of
Supplies...Inflated Prices...Speculation and Extortion in the Confederacy...
Three Remarks About These...The Verdict of History. . . PAGE 235

## CHAPTER X.

Character of Military Events of the Spring of 1863...Repulse of the Enemy at Fort McAllister...THE SIEGE OF VICKSBURG...The Yazoo Pass Expedition...Confederate Success at Fort Pemberton...The Enemy's Canals or "Cut Offs"...Their Failure...BOMBARDMENT OF PORT HUDSON...Destruction of "The Mississippi"...A Funeral Pyre...Happy Effects of our Victory...A Review of the Line of Inland Hostilities...Hooker's Hesitation on the Rappahannock...The Assignment of Confederate Commands West of the Mississippi...The Affair of Kelly's Ford...Death of Major Pelham...NAVAL ATTACK ON CHARLESTON...Destruction of "The Keokuk"...Scenery of the Bombardment...Extent of the Confederate Success...Events in Tennessee and Kentucky...Pegram's Reverse...The Situation of Hostilities at the close of April 1862.
PAGE 250

## CHAPTER XI.

Close of the Second Year of the War...Propriety of an Outline of Some Succeeding Events...Cavalry Enterprises of the Enemy...The Raids in Mississippi and Virginia...SKETCH OF THE BATTLES OF THE RAPPAHANNOCK...The Enemy's Plan of Attack...The Fight at Chancellorsville...The Splendid Charge of "Stonewall" Jackson...The Fight at Fredericksburg...The Fight at Salem Church...Summary of our Victory...DEATH OF "STONEWALL" JACKSON...His Character and Services. . . . . . . . . PAGE 268

## CHAPTER XII.

A Period of Disasters...DEPARTMENT OF THE MISSISSIPPI...Grant's March Upon Vicksburg...Its Steps and Incidents...The Engagement of Port Gibson...The Evacuation of Jackson...The Battle of Baker's Creek...Pemberton's Declarations as to the Defence of Vicksburg...A Grand Assault upon "the Heroic City"...Its Repulse...*The Final Surrender of Vicksburg*...How the Public Mind of the South was Shocked...Consequences of the Disaster...How it Involved Affairs on the Lower Mississippi...Other Theatres of the War...THE CAMPAIGN IN PENNSYLVANIA AND MARYLAND...Hooker Manœuvred out of Virginia...The Recapture of Winchester...The Second Invasion of the Northern Territory...The Alarm of the North...General Lee's Object in the Invasion of Maryland and Pennsylvania...His Essays at Conciliation...The Errour of Such Policy...The Advance of his Lines into Pennsylvania...The Battle of Gettysburg...The Three Days' Engagements...Death of Barksdale...Pickett's Splendid Charge on the Batteries...Repulse of the Confederates...Anxiety and Alarm in Richmond...Lee's Safe Retreat into Virginia...Mystery of his Movement...Recovery of the Confidence of the South * * * * * Review of the Present Aspects of the War...Comparison Between the Disasters of

1862 and those of 1863...The Vitals of the Confederacy yet Untouched... Review of the Civil Administration...President Davis, his Cabinet and his Favourites...His Private Quarrels...His Deference to European Opinion... Decline of the Finances of the Confederacy...Reasons of this Decline—The Confederate Brokers...The Blockade-Runners...The Disaffections of Property-Holders...The Spirit of the Army...The Moral Resolution of the Confederacy...How the Enemy has Strengthened it...The Prospects of the Future.
PAGE 283

## CHAPTER XIII.
### REVIEW—POLITICAL IDEAS IN THE NORTH, &c.

The Dogma of Numerical Majorities...Its Date in the Yankee Mind... Demoralization of the Idea of the Sovereignty of Numbers...Experience of Minorities in American Politics...Source of the Doctrine of "CONSOLIDATION"...The Slavery Question the Logical Result of Consolidation...Another Aspect of Consolidation in the Tariff...Summary of the Legislation on the Tariff...A Yankee Picture of the Poverty of the South....John C. Calhoun... President Davis' Opinion of his School of Politics..."Nullification," as a Union Measure...Mr. Webster's "Four Exhaustive Propositions"...The True Interpretation of the Present Struggle of the South...The Northern Idea of the Sovereignty of Numbers...Its Results in this War...President Lincoln's Office...The Revenge of the Yankee Congress Upon the People...The Easy Surrender of their Liberties by the Yankees...Lincoln and Cromwell...Explanation of the Political Subserviency in the North...Superficial Political Education of the Yankee...His "Civilization"...The Moral Nature of the Yankee Unmasked by the War...His New Political System...Burnside's "Death Order"...A Bid for Confederate Scalps....A New Interpretation of the War... The North as a Parasite...The Foundations of the National Independence of the South...Present Aspects of the War...Its External Condition and Morals... The Spirit of the South and the Promises of the Future.   .   . PAGE 309

# THE SECOND YEAR OF THE WAR.

## CHAPTER I.

The New Orleans Disaster...Its Consequences and Effects...Dispatches of the European Commissioners...Butler "the Beast"...Public Opinion in Europe...The Atrocities of the Massachusetts Tyrant...Execution of Mumford...Lesson of New Orleans...Spirit of Resistance in the South...Change in the Fortunes of the Confederacy...Two Leading Causes for it...The Richmond "Examiner"...The Conscription Law...Governor Brown of Georgia...Re-organization of the Army...Abandonment of our Frontier Defences...The Policy of Concentration...Governor Rector's Appeal...First Movements of the Summer Campaign in Virginia...The Retreat from Yorktown...Evacuation of Norfolk...Destruction of the "Virginia"...Commodore Tatnall's Report...Secretary Mallory's Visit to Norfolk...The Engagement of Williamsburg...The Affair of Barhamsville...McClellan's Investment of the Lines of the Chickahominy...Alarm in Richmond...The Water Avenue of the James...The Panic in Official Circles...Consternation in the President's House...Correspondence between President Davis and the Legislature of Virginia...Noble Resolutions of the Legislature...Response of the Citizens of Richmond...The Bombardment of Drewry's Bluff...The Mass Meeting at the City Hall...Renewal of Public Confidence...The Occasions of This...JACKSON'S CAMPAIGN IN THE VALLEY...The Engagement of McDowell...The Surprise at Front Royal...Banks' Retreat Down the Valley...The Engagements of Port Republic...Results of the Campaign...Death of Turner Ashby...Sufferings of the People of the Valley of the Shenandoah...MEMOIR OF TURNER ASHBY.

The fall of New Orleans was one of the most extraordinary triumphs which the enemy had obtained. It was the crowning stroke of that extraordinary campaign of the winter and spring of the year 1862, in which, by the improvidence of the Southern authorities and a false military policy which divided their armies and weakened them by undue dispersion, they had lost much of their territory, most of the prestige of their arms, and had fallen upon a train of disasters well calculated to affect the general public, both at home and abroad. The close of this campaign, so ill-starred to the Confederacy, found it with scarcely more than three entire States—Texas, Alabama and Georgia. Large portions of the territories of Virginia, the Carolinas and Florida were occupied by the enemy; he had broken our line of defences in Tennessee, and held important positions on the Upper Mississippi; and now, by the capture of New Orleans, he had secured the great Southern depot of the trade of the immense central valley of the continent, obtained command of an extent of territory accessible by his gunboats greater than the entire country before lost to the Confederacy, and had good reason to hope, by the junction of his fleets on the Mississippi, to open its navigation, and give to the West an outlet to the ocean.

The conquests of the Federal arms made in the winter and spring of 1862, were not without their effect in Europe, and presented to the nations in that part of the world a sombre picture of the Confederacy. The dispatches of our ministers at the courts of England and France declared that the prospect of recognition, of which they had formerly given such warm and sanguine assurances, had been overclouded by the disaster at New Orleans. Mr. Slidell, wrote from Paris that the French government declared that "if New Orleans had not fallen, our recognition could not have been much longer delayed." He added, however, that he had been assured that "even after that disaster, if we obtained decided successes in Virginia and Tennessee, or could hold the enemy at bay a month or two, the same result would follow"—a promise, to the breach of which and to the unhappy expectations which it excited, we shall hereafter have occasion to refer. Mr. Mason, our minister at London, also referred to the opinion that at the time of the enemy's capture of New Orleans, our recognition was on the eve of accomplishment.

The immediate sufferers of the disaster at New Orleans were the people of that city. It was aptly rewarded for its easy submission by the scourge of a tyrant. The corrupt and merciless master of this great emporium, General Butler of Massachusetts, was a man who found no merit in submission, unless such as grovelled in the dust and paid personal court and pecuniary tribute to himself. The rule of this vulgar and drunken man excited the horrour and disgust of the civilized world, and secured for him in the South the popular soubriquet of "the Beast." His order which stigmatized as prostitutes the ladies of New Orleans, who betrayed in the streets or from the balconies their indignation against the invaders of their city, while it made him the hero of the hour in the North with a people who admired the coarse spirit of the bully, drew upon him the execrations of all humane and honourable people. In the British Parliament, Lord Palmerston declared the proclamation to be "infamous," and the condemnation of the indecent and dirty edict was echoed by the press of Europe.*

The acts of the tyrant of New Orleans surpassed all former

---

t * The "Order 28," which has stigmatized its brutal author throughout Christendom, was at first refused publication by all the newspapers in New Orleans. It was then copied on sheets of paper and surreptitiously posted on many of the principal corners of the streets in the immediate neighbourhood of the St. Charles Hotel. The next day all of the newspaper offices were ordered to be closed for disobedience of orders. On this becoming known, the *True Delta* paper published the order, and the other newspapers timidly submitted to the *force* of circumstances, and published it also. The natural excitement and indignation that followed throughout the community is indescribable. Several lady subscribers sent to the newspaper offices and indignantly and positively forbade that such papers should longer be left at their dwellings. Mayor Monroe, with a party of influential citizens, at once called on the Beast and endeavored to obtain some qualification of the order; but they could get no satisfaction and were rudely dismissed. Mayor Monroe then wrote an indignant and reproachful communication to Butler, and again pressed him for a modification of the hateful order. Butler then sent for the Mayor. Mayor Monroe replied, "Tell General Butler my office is at the City Hotel, where he can see me, if desirable." Butler retorted, that unless the Mayor came at once to his headquarters, he would send an armed force to arrest and bring him there. Further opposition being useless, the Mayor, chief of police, and several friends, then went to the St. Charles Hotel, where they found the Beast in a towering rage. Butler claimed to be much insulted at the conduct of the Mayor, and without ceremony or delay, sent Mr. Monroe and those who accompanied him to prison. In a few days they were all shipped down to Fort Jackson.

atrocities and outrages of the war. In frequent instances, citizens, accused by Butler of contumacious disloyalty, were confined at hard labour, with balls and chains attached to their limbs; and sometimes this degrading punishment was inflicted upon men whose only offence was that of selling medicines to the sick soldiers of the Confederacy. Helpless women were torn from their homes and confined in prison. One of these—a Mrs. Phillips—was accused of laughing as the funeral train of a Yankee officer passed her doors; she was seized, and, with an ingenious and devilish cruelty, her sentence was pronounced by Butler—imprisonment on an island of barren sand under a tropical sun. Various pretexts were invented for plundering the inhabitants of the conquered city: men were forced to elect between starvation by the confiscation of all their property and taking an oath of allegiance to the invaders of their country; fines were levied at pleasure, and recusants threatened with ball and chain.

The conduct of the negroes in New Orleans became intolerable to their owners. They were fed, clothed and quartered by the Yankees, who fraternized with them generally in a shameful way. The planters in the neighbourhood of the city were required to share their crops with the commanding General, his brother, Andrew J. Butler, and other officers; and when this partnership was refused, the plantations were robbed of everything susceptible of removal, and the slaves taken from their owners and compelled to work under the bayonets of Yankee guards.

It would occupy many pages to detail what the people of New Orleans suffered at the hands of the invaders whom they had so easily admitted into their city, in insult, wrongs, confiscation of property, seizure of private dwellings and brazen robbery. The Yankee officers, from colonel to lieutenant, as the caprice of each might dictate, seized and took possession of gentlemen's houses, broke into their wine rooms, forced open the wardrobes of ladies and gentlemen, and either used or sent away from the city the clothing of whole families.

Some of the private residences of respectable citizens were appropriated to the vilest uses, the officials who had engaged them making them the private shops of the most infamous female characters.

But while Butler was thus apparently occupied with the oppression of "rebels," he was too much of a Yankee to be lost to the opportunity of making his pecuniary fortunes out of the exigencies which he had created. The banker and broker of the corrupt operations in which he was engaged, was his own brother, who bought confiscated property, shipped large consignments from New Orleans, to be paid for in cotton, and speculated largely in powder, saltpetre, muskets and other war material sold to the Confederacy, surreptitiously sent out from the city and covered by permits for provisions. Of the trade in provisions for cotton, Butler received his share of the gains, while the robbery was covered up by the pretence of consumption in New Orleans "to prevent starvation," or by reported actual issue to troops. The Yankee General did not hesitate to deal in the very life-blood of his own soldiers.

The rule of Butler in New Orleans is especially memorable for the deliberate murder of William B. Mumford, a citizen of the Confederate States, against whom the tyrant had invented the extraordinary charge that he had insulted the flag of the United States. The fact was that before the city had surrendered, Mumford had taken down from the mint the enemy's flag. The ensign was wrongfully there; the city had not surrendered; and even in its worst aspects, the act of Mumford was simply one of war, not deserving death, still less the death of a felon. The horrible crime of murdering in cold blood an unresisting and non-combatant captive, was completed by Butler on the 7th of June. On that day Mumford, the martyr, was publicly executed on the gallows. The Massachusetts coward and tyrant had no ear or heart for the pitiful pleadings made to save the life of his captive, especially by his unhappy wife, who in her supplications for mercy was rudely repulsed, and at times answered with drunken jokes and taunts. The execution took place in the sight of thousands of panic-stricken citizens. None spoke but the martyr himself. His voice was loud and clear. Looking up at the stars and stripes which floated high over the scene before him, he remarked that he had fought under that flag twice, but it had become hateful to him, and he had torn it and trailed it in the dust. "I consider," said the brave young man, "that the manner of my death will be no disgrace to my wife and child; my country will honour them."

The experience of New Orleans gave a valuable lesson to the South. It exhibited the consequences of submission to the enemy in confiscation, brutality, military domination, insult, universal poverty, the beggary of thousands, the triumph of the vilest individuals in the community, the abasement of the honest and industrious, and the outlawry of the slaves. The spirit of resistance in the South was fortified by the enemy's exhibitions of triumph, and the resolution gained ground that it was much better to consign the cities of the Confederacy to the flames than to surrender them to the enemy. A time was approaching when Yankee gunboats was to lose their prestige of terror; when cities were no longer to be abandoned or surrendered on the approach of a foe; and when the freemen of the South were to be taught how, by a spirit above fear and ready for all sacrifice, they might defy the most potent agencies of modern warfare.

With the bright month of May a new era was dawning on the fortunes of the Confederacy. This happy change of fortune was due not only to the improved resolution of the South. It is in a great degree to be attributed to two leading causes in the military administration. These were, first, the conscription law, with the consequent re-organization of the army; and, secondly, the abandonment of our plan of frontier defence, which made way for the superiour and more fortunate policy of the concentration of our forces in the interiour.

The first suggestion of a conscription law was made by the Richmond *Examiner*—a bold and vigilant leader of the newspaper press of the Confederacy. It was met with violent opposition from the administration, with the clamor of demagogical presses that the suggestion conveyed a reflection upon the patriotism of the country, and with the fashionable nonsense that it was a confession calculated to give aid and comfort to the enemy. But the early advocates of conscription enjoyed the singular triumph of converting public opinion completely to their side, and forcing the government at a future period to the confession that the system which it had at first frowned upon had proved the salvation of the country.

At the beginning of the war we had nothing that deserved the title of a military system. There was no lack of zeal or determination in the South; but the organization of the army was defective, its discipline was retarded by bad laws, and at a time that the forces of the enemy in Virginia had reached the highest state of efficiency, our own army was passing through successive stages of disorganization to dissolution. The army of the enemy was superior to our own in every respect, except courage and good cause; they had every guaranty of success that numbers, discipline, complete organization and perfect equipments could effect.

The military system of the South dates from the passage of the conscription law. To this measure must be attributed that solidity in the organization of our army and that efficiency which challenged the admiration of the world. The beneficial effects of this enactment were soon manifest as well to ourselves as to the world. It distributed over the Confederacy the levies in proportion to the inhabitants of each State and county. It centralized the organization of the army. And it introduced a regular system of recruiting, which guarantied that the efficiency of the army would not be impaired by the lapse of time and the loss of health and life incident to warfare.

The conscription law came not a moment too soon. The acts of Congress providing for re-enlistments had failed to effect the desired object.* Without decadence of the real valour of our people or their invincible determination to achieve their independence, the spirit of volunteering had died out, and the resolution of our soldiers already in the field was not sufficient to resist the prospects, cherished for months amid the sufferings and monotony of the camps, of returning to their homes. The exigency was critical, and even vital. In a period of thirty days the terms of service of one hundred and forty-eight regiments expired. There was good reason to believe that a large majority of the men had not re-enlisted, and of those who had re-enlisted, a very large majority had entered companies which could never be assembled, or if assembled, could not be prepared for the field in time to meet the invasion actually commenced.

The first act of conscription was passed on the 16th of April, 1862. It was afterwards enlarged by another act, (27th September), giving the Executive the power to call into service persons between the ages of thirty-five and forty-five. Although the rush of volunteers had comparatively ceased, and the ardour of the individual did not suffice for the proffer of self-devotion, yet the sentiments and convictions of the mass recognized as the most sacred obligation the stern duty of defending, if needs be, with their entire numbers, their imperilled liberty, fortune and honour. The conscription law was, generally, cheerfully acquiesced in. In every State one or more camps of instruction, for the reception and training of conscripts, was established; and to each State an officer, styled a commandant of conscripts, was appointed, charged with the supervision of the enrollment and instruction of the new levies.

The execution of the conscription law was unfortunately resisted for a time by Governor Brown of Georgia. The correspondence between him and the President on the subject, which was printed and hawked in pamphlet form through the country, was a curiosity. It was illustrated copiously by Mr. Brown with citations from the Virginia and Kentucky resolutions of 1798 and exhumed opinions of members of the old Federal Convention of 1787. In the most vital periods of the country's destiny, and in the fierce tumults of a revolution, the people of the South were refreshed with exhumations from the politicians of 1787, and the usual amount of clap-trap about our "forefathers," and the old political system that had rotted over our heads.

The beneficial effect of the conscription law in the re-organization of our army was assisted by some other acts of legislation. That re-organization was advanced by the appointment of Lieutenant Generals, some commanding separate departments, and others heading army corps under a General in the field. The policy of organizing the brigades with troops and Generals from the several States was pursued, as opportunities offered, without detriment to the public service. The greater satisfaction of the men from each State, when collected together, the generous emulation for glory to their State, and the fair apportionment of officers assured to each State according to its contribution of defenders to the country, overbalanced the inconvenience of separating regiments or companies previously associated, and the liability to State jealousies. Military courts were organized to secure the prompt administration of the military law, to check desertion and straggling, to restrain license of all kinds, and to advance temperance, discipline and subordination.

But it was not only the re-organization and improved morale of the army that came to the aid of the declining fortunes of the South in the war.

The disasters on the Mississippi frontier and in other directions had constrained the government to adopt the policy of concentrating its forces in the interiour of Virginia. The object of all war is to reach a decisive point of the campaign, and this object was realized by a policy which it is true the government had not adopted at the instance of reason, but which had been imposed upon it by the force of disaster. There were childish complaints that certain districts and points on the frontier had been abandoned by the Confederates for the purpose of a concentration of troops in Virginia. An inflammatory appeal was made by Governor Rector of Arkansas to the States of the Trans-Mississippi, representing that the government had deserted them in transferring its troops to other portions of the Confederacy, and suggesting that they should form a new association for their safety. But the appeal was severely rebuked by public sentiment. The complaint of Governor Rector cost him his election, and the display of the demagogue consigned him to the reproaches of the public.

Such complaints were alike selfish and senseless, and in most cases nothing more than the utterances of a demagogical, short-sighted and selfish spirit, which would have preferred the apparent security of its own particular State or section to the fortunes of the whole Confederacy. The fact was, that there was cause of intelligent congratulation, even in those districts from which the Confederate troops had been withdrawn to make a decisive battle, that we had at last reached a crisis, the decision of which might reverse all our past misfortunes and achieve results in which every State of the Confederacy would have a share.

But the first movements of the famous summer campaign in Virginia that was to change the fortunes of the war and adorn our arms, were not auspicious. The designs of some of these movements were not properly appreciated at the time, and some of the incidents that attended them were real disasters.

We have seen that by the happy boldness of General Magruder in keeping the enemy in check on the line between Yorktown, on York river, and Mulberry Island, on James river, the advance of the grand Federal army, destined for the capture of Richmond, was stayed until our forces were rescued by the consummate strategy of Gen. Johnston from the pressure of enveloping armies, who arrived in time to reinforce our lines on the Peninsula. It became necessary, however, in the judgment of that commander, to fall back in the direction of Richmond. It was easily seen by General Johnston that at Yorktown there was no prospect of a general action, as the attack on either side would have to be made under disadvantages which neither army was willing to risk. The Yankees were in superiour force, besides their additional strength in their gunboats, and in falling back so as to invest the line of the Chickahominy, General Johnston expected to force the enemy to more equal terms. The difficulty was to match the strength of the enemy on the water; and the best practical equivalent for this was considered to be the open field, where gunboats being out of the question, the position of our troops would be the same as if at Yorktown they had had a force of gunboats exactly equal to that of the enemy, thus neutralizing his advantage in respect of naval armament.

The retreat from Yorktown produced uneasiness in the public mind, and naturally shook the confidence of the many who were in ignorance of the plans of the cautious and taciturn strategist at the head of our forces in Virginia. It involved our surrender of Norfolk, with all the advantages of its contiguous navy-yard and dock. And it was accompanied by a disaster which, in so far as it was supposed to be unnecessary and wanton, occasioned an amount of grief and rage in the Confederacy such as had not yet been exhibited in the war.

This memorable disaster was the destruction of the famous mailed steamer Virginia—"the iron diadem of the South." This vessel, which had obtained for us our first triumph on the water, was an object of pride, and almost of affection, to the people of the South. She was popularly said to be worth fifty thousand troops in the field. Nor was this estimate excessive, when it is recollected that she protected Norfolk, the navy-yard and James river; that no fleet of transports could safely land its troops, designed to attack those places, at any point from Cape Henry to the upper James, as far as she could ascend; that her presence at Norfolk had annihilated the land and water blockade at Newport News, passed the control of the James river into our hands, and protected the right flank of our army on the Peninsula.

The Virginia was destroyed under the immediate orders of her commander, Commodore Tatnall, on the morning of the

11th of May, in the vicinity of Craney Island. According to his statement, he had been betrayed into the necessity of destroying his vessel by firing her magazine, by the deceitful representations of his pilots, who at first assured him that they could take the ship, with a draft of eighteen feet of water, within forty miles of Richmond, and after having lifted her so as to unfit her for action, then declared that they could not get her above the Jamestown flats, up to which point the shore on each side was occupied by the enemy. It is proper to add, that this statement of facts was contested by the pilots, who resented the reflections made upon their loyalty or courage. Whatever may have been the merits of this controversy, it is certain that the vessel was destroyed in great haste by Commodore Tatnall, who, in the dead hour of night, aroused from his slumbers and acquainted with the decision of his pilots, ordered the ship to be put ashore, landed his crew in the vicinity of Craney Island, and blew to the four winds of heaven the only naval structure that guarded the water approach to Richmond.

The destruction of the Virginia was a sharp and unexpected blow to the confidence of the people of the South in their government. How far the government was implicated in this foolish and desperate act, was never openly acknowledged or exactly ascertained; but, despite the pains of official concealment, there are certain well-attested facts which indicate that in the destruction of this great war-ship, the authorities at Richmond were not guiltless. These facts properly belong to the history of one of the most unhappy events that had occurred since the commencement of the war.

The Virginia was destroyed at 5 A. M. of the 11th of May. During the morning of the same day a prominent politician in the streets of Richmond was observed to be very much dejected; he remarked that it was an evil day for the Confederacy. On being questioned by his intimate friends, he declared to them that the Government had determined upon, or assented to, the destruction of the Virginia, and that he had learned this from the highest sources of authority in the capital. At this time the news of the explosion of the Virginia could not have possibly reached Richmond; there was no telegraphic communication between the scene of her destruction and the city, and the evidence appears to be complete, that the Government had at least a prevision of the destruction of this vessel, or had assented to the general policy of the act, trusting, perhaps, to acquit itself of the responsibility for it on the unworthy plea that it had given no *express* orders in the matter.

Again, it is well-known that for at least a week prior to the destruction of the Virginia, the evacuation of Norfolk had been determined upon; that during this time the removal of stores was daily progressing; and that Mr. Mallory, the Secretary of the Navy, had within this period, himself, visited Norfolk to look after the public interests. The evacuation of this port clearly involved the question, what disposition was to be made of the Virginia. If the Government made no decision of a question, which for a week stared it in the face, it certainly was very strangely neglectful of the public interest. If Mr. Mallory visited Norfolk when the evacuation was going on, and never thought of the Virginia, or thinking of her, kept dumb, never even giving so much as an *official nod* as to what disposition should be made of her, he must have been more stupid than the people who laughed at him in Richmond, or the members of Congress who nicknamed without mercy, thought him to be.

It is also not a little singular that when a court of inquiry had found that the destruction of the Virginia was unnecessary and improper, Mr. Mallory should have waived the calling of a court martial, forgotten what was due to the public interest on such a finding as that made by the preliminary court, and expressed himself satisfied to let the matter rest. The fact is indisputable, that the court martial, which afterwards sat in the case, was called at the demand of Commodore Tatnall himself. It resulted in his acquittal.

The evacuation of Norfolk was the occasion of great distress to its population. But it was the part of a wise policy, that our military lines should be contracted and that the troops of Gen. Huger should be consolidated with the army before Richmond.

The retreat from Yorktown to the Chickahominy was marked by spirited incidents and by one important engagement. McClellan becoming, through an accident, aware of the movement of Gen. Johnston, immediately pursued our columns, which recoiled on him at Williamsburg, on the 5th of May, and drove back his army. During the whole of that day, Gen. Longstreet's division, which brought up the rear, was engaged with the enemy from sunrise to sunset. The day was marked by signal successes, for we captured three hundred and fifty prisoners, took nine pieces of artillery, and left on the field, in killed and wounded, at least three thousand of the enemy. During the night, our army resumed its movement towards Richmond, and half an hour after sunrise it had evacuated the town, under the necessity of leaving our killed and wounded in the hands of the enemy.

The following day, the insolence of the enemy was again checked on the route of our retreat. On the 7th of May he attempted a landing, under cover of his gunboats, at Barhamsville, near West Point. The attempt was ineffectual. The Yankees were driven back, after they had assaulted our position three different times—the last time being forced to the cover of their gunboats by the brave Texans of Gen. Whiting's division who, in the face of an artillery fire, pressed the fugitives so closely that many were driven into the river and drowned.

The investment of the lines of the Chickahominy brought the two opposing armies within sight of Richmond. After a desultory military experience, a useless and inglorious march to Manassas, a long delay on the banks of the Potomac and Chesapeake, and a vague abandonment of these lines for operations on the Peninsula, McClellan, who was the "Napoleon" of the Democratic party of the North, but a slow and contemptible blunderer in the estimation of the Republicans, found himself, by the fortune of circumstances, within sight of the steeples and spires of the long-sought Capital of the Confederacy.

The proximity of the enemy was an occasion of great anxiety to the people of Richmond, and the visible tremour of the Confederate authorities in that city was not a spectacle calculated either to nerve the army or assure the citizens. The fact is, that the Confederate authorities had shamefully neglected the defences of Richmond, and were now making preparations to leave it, which were called prudential, but which naturally inspired a panic such as had never before been witnessed in the history of the war. The destruction of the Virginia had left the water avenue to Richmond almost undefended. The City Council had for months been urging upon the Confederate Government the necessity of obstructing the river, and failing to induce them to hurry on the work, had, with patriotic zeal, undertaken it themselves. A newspaper in Richmond—the *Examiner*—had in good time pointed out the necessity of obstructing the river with stone, but the counsel was treated with such conceit and harshness by the government, that it was only at the risk of its existence that that paper continued for weeks to point out the insecurity of Richmond and the omissions of its authorities. The government was at last aroused to a sense of danger only to fall to work in ridiculous haste, and with the blindness of alarm. The appearance of the Yankee gunboats in James River was the signal for Mr. Secretary Mallory to show his alacrity in meeting the enemy by an advertisement for "timber" to construct new naval defences. The only obstruction between the city and the dread Monitor and the gunboats was a half-finished fort at Drewry's Bluff, which mounted four guns. Some of the Confederate officers had taken a "gunboat panic," for the line of stone obstructions in the river was not yet complete. They seized upon schooners at the wharves loaded with plaster of paris, guano, and other valuable cargoes, carried them to points where they supposed the passage of the river was to be contested, and in some instances sunk them in the wrong places.

There is no doubt that about this time the authorities of the Confederate States had nigh despaired of the safety of Richmond. The most urgent appeals had been made to Congress by the press and the people to continue its session in Richmond while the crisis impended. But its members refused to give this mark of confidence to the government, or to make any sacrifice of their selfish considerations for the moral encouragement of their constituents. They had adjourned in haste and left Richmond, regarding only the safety of their persons or the convenience of their homes.

Nor was the Executive more determined. In the President's mansion about this time all was consternation and dismay. A letter written by one of his family at a time when Richmond was thought to be imminently threatened, and intercepted by the enemy, afforded excessive merriment to the Yankees, and made a painful exhibition to the South of the weakness and fears of those entrusted with its fortunes. This letter, written with refreshing simplicity of heart, overflowed with pitiful sympathy for the President, and amused the enemy with references to the sore anxieties of "Uncle Jeff," and to the prospect of his sinking under the misfortunes of his administration. The authenticity of this letter was never called into question: it is a painful and delicate historical evidence, but one to which, in the interests of truth, allusion should not be spared.*

---

\* The following is a portion of the letter referred to. The reflections which it makes upon the courage of our noble, suffering soldiers were probably hasty, and may be spared here:

\* \* \* "When I think of the dark gloom that now hovers over our "country, I am ready to sink with despair. There is a probability of Gen'l "Jackson's army falling back on Richmond, and in view of this, no lady is "allowed to go up on the railroad to Gordonsville for fear, if allowed to one, "that many others would wish to do it, which would incommode the army."

"General Johnston is falling back from the Peninsula, or Yorktown, and "Uncle Jeff. thinks *we had better go to a safer place than Richmond.*

It is true that President Davis, when invited by the Legislature of Virginia to express his intentions towards Richmond,

"We have not decided yet where we shall go, but I think to North Carolina,
"to some far-off country town, or, perhaps, to South Carolina. If Johnston
"falls back as far as Richmond, all our troops from Gordonsville and "Swift
"Run Gap" will also fall back to this place, and make one desperate stand
"against McClellan. If you will look at the map, you will see that the
"Yankees are approaching Richmond from three different directions—from
"Fredericksburg, Harrisonburg, and Yorktown. Oh! God, defend this peo-
"ple with thy powerful arm, is my constant prayer. Oh, mother, Uncle Jeff.
"is miserable. He tries to be cheerful, and bear up against such a continua-
"tion of troubles, but, oh, I fear he cannot live long, if he does not get some
"rest and quiet.
"Our reverses distressed him so much, and he is so weak and feeble, it
"makes my heart ache to look at him. He knows that he ought to send his
"wife and children away, and yet he cannot bear to part with them, and we
"all dread to leave him too. Varina and I had a hard cry about it to-day.
"Oh! what a blow the fall of New Orleans was. It liked to have set us all
"crazy here. Everybody looks depressed, and the cause of the Confederacy
"looks drooping and sinking; but if God is with us, who can be against us?
"Our troops are not doing as well as we expected * * * * * * * The
"regiments that are most apt to run are from North Carolina and Tennes-
"see. I am thankful to say that the Mississippi and Louisiana troops behave
"gloriously whenever called on to fight.
"Uncle Jeff. thinks you are safe at home, as *there will be no resistance at
"Vicksburg*, and the Yankees will hardly occupy it; and, even if they did,
"the army would gain nothing by marching into the country, and a few
"soldiers would be afraid to go so far into the interior.
"P. S. We all leave here to-morrow morning for Raleigh. Three gun-
"boats are in James River, on their way to the city, and may probably reach
"here in a few hours; so we have no longer any time to delay. *I only hope
"that we have not delayed too long already.* I shall then be cut off from all
"communication with ———, and I expect to have no longer any peace."
"I will write again from Raleigh, and Fanny must write me a letter and
"direct it to Raleigh; perhaps I may get it. I am afraid that Richmond
"will fall into the hands of the enemy, as there is no way to keep back the
"gunboats. James River is so high that all obstructions are in danger of
"being washed away; so that there is no help for the city. She will either
"submit or else be shelled, and I think the latter alternative will be
"resorted to.
"Uncle Jeff. was confirmed last Tuesday in St. Paul's Church by Bishop
"Johns. He was baptized at home in the morning before church.
"Do try to get a letter to me some way. Direct some to Raleigh and some
"to Richmond. Yours, ever devotedly,
———."

had declared that he entertained the prospect of holding it. But his reply was full of embarrassment. While he declared his intention not to surrender the city, he at the same time suggested the fanciful possibility, that even with the loss of Richmond our struggle for independence might be protracted for many years in the mountains of Virginia. In the meantime, the acts of the Confederate officials gave visible and unmistakable signs of their sense of the insecurity of the capital. They added to the public alarm by preparations to remove the archives. They ran off their wives and children into the country. They gave the public every reason to believe that Richmond was to become the prey of the enemy, and the catastrophe was awaited with lively alarm, or dull and melancholy expectation.

In the early weeks of May the capital of the Confederacy presented many strange and humiliating spectacles. The air was filled with those rumours of treason and disloyalty which seem invariably to grow out of a sense of insecurity. Men who had been loudest in their professions of resistance and self-devotion when the Yankees were at a distance, were now engaged in secreting their property, and a few openly flattered themselves that they had not committed themselves in the war in a way to incur the enemy's resentment. Some of them had their cellars packed with manufactured tobacco. The railroad trains were crowded with refugees. At every extortioner's shop on Main Street, even including the book-stores, an array of packing trunks invited attention, and suggested the necessity of flight from Richmond. At the railroad depots were to be seen piles of baggage, awaiting transportation. But the most abundant and humiliating signs of the panic were to be seen in the number of pine boxes about the departments ticketed "Columbia, South Carolina," and which contained the most valuable of the public archives.

In this condition of the public mind, a new appeal was made to it. When it was ascertained that the Monitor, Galena, and Aristook, were about to head for Richmond, the Legislature of

Virginia passed resolutions calling upon the Confederate authorities to defend it to the last extremity, and to make choice of its destruction rather than that of surrender to the enemy. This resolution was worthy of the noble State of Virginia, and of a people who were the descendants of Washington's cotemporaries, of Hampden's friends, and of King John's Barons. Its terms were too explicit to admit of any doubt in their construction, or any wavering on the part of the Confederate authorities. They expressed the desire that Richmond should be defended to the last extremity, and declared that "the President be assured, that whatever destruction or loss of property of the State or individuals shall thereby result, will be cheerfully submitted to."

The resolutions of the Legislature were responded to in meetings of citizens. The magical effects of the spirit which they created will long be remembered in Richmond. The Confederate authorities were stimulated by the brave lesson; inert and speculative patriotism was aroused to exertion; mutual inspiration of courage and devotion passed from heart to heart through the community, and with the restoration of public confidence, came at last vigorous preparations. The James was rapidly filled up, the works at Drewry's Bluff were strengthened, and a steady defiance offered to the Yankee gunboats, which had appeared within a few miles of the city at a moment when the last gap in our river obstructions was filled up by a scuttled schooner.

On the 15th of May, the fleet of Yankee gunboats in the James opened an attack on our batteries at Drewry's Bluff. The sound of the guns was heard in the streets of Richmond, and various and uncertain reports of the fortunes of the contest agitated the public. In the midst of the excitement, an extraordinary scene occurred in the city. A meeting of citizens had been called at the City Hall on an accidental occasion, and at the enthusiastic call of the crowd, impromptu addresses were made by the Governor of Virginia and the Mayor of the city. Each of these officials pledged his faith that Richmond should never be surrendered. Gov. Letcher declared, with a peculiar warmth of expression, that if the demand was made upon him, with the alternative to surrender or be shelled, he should reply, "bombard and be d——d." Mayor Mayo was not less determined in the language which he addressed to the citizens. He told them that even if they were to require him to surrender the Capital of Virginia and of the Confederacy, he would, sooner than comply, resign the mayoralty; and that, despite his age, he still had the nerve and strength to shoulder a musket in defence of the city founded by one of his ancestors. These fervid declarations were responded to by the citizens with wild and ringing shouts. Nor were these the demonstrations of a mob. Among those who so enthusiastically approved the resolution of consigning Richmond to the flames rather than to the possession of the enemy, were some of the most wealthy and respectable citizens of the place, whose stakes of property in the city were large, and whose beautiful homes were exposed to the shot and shell of the malignant foe.

The night brought the news of a signal victory. Our batteries, under the skillful command of Capt. Farrand, had, after a contest of four hours and a half, given a decisive repulse to the gunboats, with the inconsiderable loss of five killed and seven wounded. The accuracy of our fire had astonished the enemy and carried dismay through his fleet. Eighteen shots went through the sides of the Galena, according to the enemy's own account; and this river monster lost thirty of her crew in killed and wounded. Seventeen men were killed on another of the boats by the explosion of a gun. The boats had been unable to advance in the face of the accurate and deadly fire of our artillerists, and the next day they had dropped down the stream, quite satisfied of the impracticability of the water approach to Richmond.

Regarding all the circumstances in which this action had taken place, there is no extravagance in saying, that the scale of the war was turned in our favour by even so small an affair as that of Drewry's Bluff. It exploded the fanciful theories of the enemy's invincibility on the water, and went far to assure the safety of the now closely threatened Capital of the Confederacy.

But there were other causes about this time which conspired to renew the popular confidence in our arms, and to swell with gratitude and hope the hearts which had so long throbbed with anxiety in our besieged capital. We shall see how, for some time, at least, the safety of Richmond was trusted, not so much to the fortunes of the forces that immediately protected it, as to the splendid diversion of the heroic Jackson in the Valley of Virginia. To this famous expedition public attention was now turned, in the North as well as in the South, and its almost marvellous results, with marked unanimity, were ascribed to the zeal, heroism and genius of its commander alone.

### JACKSON'S CAMPAIGN IN THE VALLEY.

On the change of our military lines in Virginia, and the rapid shifting of the scene of active hostilities from the Potomac, Gen. Jackson had been assigned with a small force to guard the Valley of Virginia, and the approaches in that direction, to the armies of the enemy which enveloped Richmond.

Our first success was obtained in the upper portion of the Valley. On the morning of the 8th of May, our forces had approached the position of Milroy, the Yankee commander at McDowell. The brigade of General Johnson had secured an advantageous position on a hill, and the enemy, fearful of being surrounded, decided at last, after some signs of hesitation, to deliver battle. The action was not joined until about two hours of sunset. The fact was, that we engaged the enemy with not more than one third of his own numbers, which were about twelve thousand. But the contest was easily decided by the brave troops of Johnson's brigade, composed of Virginia volunteers, with the 12th Georgia regiment. They had stood for nearly two hours receiving with composed courage the cross fire of the enemy's artillery; and then, as the sun was sinking, they made the charge decisive of the day, and drove the enemy in consternation and utter rout from the field.

Our loss in this action was considerable. Of three hundred and fifty killed and wounded, nearly two-thirds were Georgians. The troops of this State on other occasions than this had left monuments of their courage in the mountains of Virginia. The loss of the enemy at McDowell exceeded that of the Confederates, and was conjectured to be double our own.

It was probably at the suggestion of his own judgment, and at the instance of his own military instincts, that Gen. Jackson determined to act on the aggressive, and to essay the extraordinary task of driving the Yankees from the Valley. In pursuance of this determination, his resolution was quickly taken to make a dash at Fremont's advance, west of Staunton, and then to turn upon Banks with the adventurous purpose of driving him into Maryland.

Gen. Banks, one of the military pets of the more truculent party of the abolitionists, had entered Virginia with the airs of a conqueror. As early as the 24th of April he had telegraphed to his government the story of uninterrupted and triumphant progress; he announced that he had "advanced near Harrisonburg;" and, with a characteristic flourish, he added: "The rebel Jackson has abandoned the Valley of Virginia permanently, and is en route for Gordonsville by the way of the mountains."

The first intimation the obtuse Yankee General had of his mistake was the astounding news that reached him on the evening of May 23d, that the "rebel Jackson" had descended on the guard at Front Royal, Colonel Kenly, 1st Maryland regiment, commanding, burned the bridges, driven the Federal troops towards Strasburg with great loss, captured a section of artillery, and taken about fourteen hundred prisoners.

It was now Banks's turn to betake himself to flight, or, in the official circumlocution of that commander, " to enter the lists with the enemy in a race or a battle, as he should choose, for the possession of Winchester, the key of the Valley." But he was not destined to reach his promised haven of security without disaster.

On the day following the sudden apparition of Jackson at Front Royal, the untiring commander had by a rapid movement succeeded in piercing Banks' main column while retreating from Strasburg to Winchester; the rear, including a body of the celebrated Zouaves d'Afrique, retreating towards Strasburg.

The Yankee General reached Winchester only to find fresh causes of alarm. The people of that ancient town, already sure of their deliverance, received the Yankees with shouts of derision and defiant cheers for Jackson. Some Confederate officers came into the enemy's camp with entire unconcern, supposing that their own troops occupied the town as a matter of course, and when captured, gave the Yankees the delightful assurance that an attack would be made by the terrible Jackson at daybreak.

On the 25th of May, Gen. Jackson gave the crowning stroke to the rapid movements of the past two days by attacking Winchester and driving out the cowardly enemy almost without resistance. Gen. Banks speaks of his retreat with a shamelessness that is at once simple and refreshing. He says "pursuit by the enemy was prompt and vigorous; but our movements were rapid;" and he writes to the authorities at Washington of his crossing of the Potomac: "There never were more grateful hearts in the same number of men than when at midday on the 30th of May we stood on the opposite shore." He had escaped with the loss of all the material and paraphernalia that constitute an army. He had abandoned, at Winchester all his commissary and ordnance stores. He had resigned that town and Front Royal to the undisputed possession of the Confederates. He had left in their hands four thousand prisoners, and stores amounting to millions of dollars. And all these prizes had been obtained by the Confederates in the brief period of a few days, and with a loss not exceeding one hundred in killed and wounded.

When General Jackson fell back from Winchester, after routing Banks, he managed, with great address, boldness and energy, to carry off his prisoners and spoils, and to bring off his army between the converging columns of Fremont, who approached his rear from the west, with eight brigades, and Shields, who approached from the east, with four brigades. If these brigades averaged twenty-five hundred men, the force of Fremont was twenty thousand and that of Shields ten thousand men. At Harrisonburg, Jackson left the main turnpike road of the Valley and marched towards Port Republic, the distance between these two places being about twelve miles. Port Republic is situated at the junction of South river, flowing north, and North river, flowing east. Jackson could retire no further without crossing North river, which was swollen, and there was then no bridge over it except at Port Republic. The two rivers uniting at that village form the Shenandoah, which flows north, and which could not then be crossed by an army. On the east side of that stream was the army of Shields, and on the west side were the armies of Fremont and Jackson. The latter halted near North river without crossing it, and, while in that position, his rear was approached and attacked by Fremont's whole army, on the morning of Sunday, the 8th of June, and, at the same time, Shields' force approached on the east side of the Shenandoah near Port Republic.

That part of Jackson's army which engaged Fremont on Sunday was commanded by General Ewell, while the rest of the army under General Jackson held Shields in check with artillery firing across the Shenandoah near Port Republic. The battle of Sunday took place about five miles from that village in the direction of Harrisonburg.

It began early in the morning and lasted all day, with occasional intervals. . It was mainly an artillery fight, but now and then, here and there, the infantry became hotly engaged. The force under Fremont was much larger than that under

Ewell, but the latter was strongly posted on eminences which favored the effectiveness of artillery and sheltered the infantry, while the enemy could only approach through open fields. Ewell's command was handled with remarkable skill, while Fremont's generalship was indifferent. Ewell's artillery was served with admirable precision and effect, and his infantry, whenever engaged, displayed great steadiness and gallantry. The result was, that when night put an end to the contest, Fremont had been driven back between one and two miles, with a loss, in killed and wounded, not less than two thousand, and probably much larger, while our loss did not exceed three hundred, and probably not two hundred. The judicious selection of a position in which to receive the enemy favored this result, but it was largely due to the superiour fighting qualities of our men.

Soon after nightfall, General Jackson began to withdraw his men from this battle-field, and pass them over North river by the bridge at Port Republic, with a view to attack Shields the next morning. He left in front of Fremont a small force to amuse and detain him, and, after retiring before him to Port Republic, to burn the bridge behind them, and thus to prevent Fremont from rendering any aid to Shields. All this was accomplished.

On Monday morning, Jackson passed the greater part of his army across the South river (the smallest of the streams) by means of a bridge made of planks laid on wagons placed in the river. Early in the morning a sufficient number had crossed to commence the battle, and they were led to the field between one and two miles distant, on the east bank of the Shenandoah. The enemy's force was found drawn up awaiting the attack.

The enemy's line extended from the river about half a mile across a flat bottom, free from timber, and covered with wheat, grass, &c. His left rested on the point of a low ridge coming out from the woods which skirt the bottom. On a slight elevation there and in some small knolls in the bottom, he had his artillery commanding the road and the wide uncovered level plain, over which Jackson's army was obliged to advance. The level and exposed ground offered scarcely any suitable position for planting our artillery. The advantage of position belonged altogether to the enemy. The capital fault of his disposition for battle was that the battery on his extreme left was posted near the woods without any infantry in the woods to defend it. By availing himself of this circumstance, and by a brilliant manœuvre and charge, Jackson turned the fortune of the day at a critical moment.

For some two hours the battle raged with great fury. Our infantry, at first but few, advanced with marvelous intrepidity in the face of a withering fire of artillery and musketry. At one moment the enemy advanced a section of a battery several hundred yards so as to enfilade our left wing, which already suffered terribly from the fire in front. It seemed that nothing could withstand the fury of the enemy's fire of all arms. His artillery was very fine, and was served with great effect by regulars. But other troops coming at double quick from Port Republic, came on the field, and, at the same time, the Louisiana brigade, under Taylor, emerged from the woods on the enemy's left. They had been sent by a considerable circuit through the woods, which extend all along the battle-field between the cleared ground and the neighbouring mountain. By a slight error of direction they came out of the woods a little too soon, and found themselves almost in front of the battery, which instantly began to shower grape upon them. But, immediately rectifying their direction, they charged the battery with irresistible impetuosity, and carried it. The contest then was speedily ended. The enemy's whole line gave way and was presently retreating in disorder, pursued by our cavalry. The pursuit was kept up about ten or twelve miles, but the flight continued all that day and the next. About five hundred prisoners were taken that day, and others after that were brought in daily. The loss of the enemy in killed and wounded was heavy, and so was our own. Six splendid cannon were captured on the field, another was taken in the pursuit, and still another had been captured on Sunday. The force of the enemy engaged was about six or seven thousand, and ours a little larger. Shields was not present, but his troops were commanded by General Tyler.

After the rout of the enemy had commenced, the last of our troops crossed over the bridge at Port Republic and burnt it. Fremont, cautiously following, appeared some time afterwards, and drew up his army in line of battle on the heights along the west bank of the Shenandoah, from which he overlooked the field of battle. While he stood there in impotent idleness, Jackson's army, having finally disposed of Shields, moved off at leisure to Brown's Gap, and there encamped, to rest for a few days from the fatigues of a month's campaign more arduous and more successful than any month's operations of the war. The exhaustion of our men and the interposition of a river, no longer bridged, secured Fremont from a second battle or a hasty flight. The next day he commenced his retreat down the Valley.

This famous campaign must, indeed, take a rank in the history of the war, unrivalled by any other in the rapidity of its movements and in the brilliancy of the results accomplished, compared with the means at its command. Its heroic deeds revived the hopes of the South, and threw the splendour of sunlight over the long lines of the Confederate host. By a series of rapid movements, which occupied but a few weeks, General Jackson had, with inferiour numbers, defeated successively four Generals, with as many armies, swept the Valley of Virginia of hostile forces, made the Federal authorities tremble in their capital, and frustrated the combinations by which the enemy had purposed to aid General McClellan and environ Richmond by large converging armies.

Our loss of life in this campaign was inconsiderable in numbers; but on the black list of killed, there was one name conspicuous throughout the Confederacy, and especially dear to Virginians. Colonel Turner Ashby, whose name was linked with so much of the romance of the war, and whose gentle and enthusiastic courage and knightly bearing had called to mind the recollections of chivalry and adorned Virginia with a new chaplet of fame, had, on the 5th of June, fallen in a skirmish near Harrisburg.

"The last time I saw Ashby," writes a noble comrade in arms, Colonel Bradley T. Johnson of the Maryland Line, "he was riding at the head of the column with General Ewell—his black face in a blaze of enthusiasm. Every feature beamed with the joy of the soldier. He was gesticulating and pointing out the country and positions to General Ewell. I could imagine what he was saying by the motions of his right arm. I pointed him out to my Adjutant. 'Look at Ashby; see how he is enjoying himself.'"

A few hours later and the brave Virginian, so full of life, was a corpse. Our men had fallen upon a body of the enemy concealed in a piece of woods and under the cover of a fence. Ashby was on the right of the 58th Virginia. He implored the men to stop their fire, which was ineffectual, and to charge the enemy. They were too much excited to heed him, and turning towards the enemy he waved his hand—"Virginians, charge!" In a second his horse fell. He was on his feet in an instant. "Men," he cried, "cease firing—charge, for God's sake, charge!" The next instant he fell dead—not twenty yards from the concealed marksman who had killed him.

To the sketch we have briefly given of this campaign, it is just to add one word of reflection. It had been frequently and very unwarrantably asserted that the people of what was once the garden spot of the South, the Shenandoah Valley, were favourably inclined to the Union cause, and that many of them had shown a very decided spirit of disloyalty to the Confederate authority. The best refutation of this slander is to be found in the enemy's own accounts of his experiences in that region.

The fact is, that the people of this Valley had suffered to a most extraordinary degree the fiery trials and ravages of war.

Their country had been bandied about from the possession of the Confederates to that of the Yankees, and then back again, until it had been stripped of everything by needy friends on the one side, and unscrupulous invaders on the other. Some portions of the country were actually overrun by three armies in two weeks. In such circumstances there were, no doubt, expressions of discontent, which had been hastily misinterpreted as disloyal demonstrations; but, despite these, there is just reason to believe that a spirit of patriotism and integrity abided in the Valley of Virginia, and that it had been maintained under trials and chastisements much greater than those which had befallen other parts of the Confederacy.

## MEMOIR OF TURNER ASHBY.

The writer had proposed a record in another and more extensive form of the principal events of the life of Turner Ashby; but the disappointment of assistance to sources of information from persons who had represented themselves as the friends of the deceased, and from whom the writer had reason to expect willing and warm co-operation, has compelled him to defer the execution of his original and cherished purpose of giving to the public a worthy biography of one whose name is a source of immortal pride to the South, and an enduring ornament to the chivalry of Virginia. But the few incidents roughly thrown together here may have a certain interest. They give the key to the character of one of the most remarkable men of the war; they afford an example to be emulated by our soldiers; they represent a type of courage peculiarly Southern in its aspects; and they add an unfading leaf to the chaplet of glory which Virginia has gathered on the blood-stained fields of the war.

It is not improper here to state the weight and significance given to the present revolution by the secession of Virginia. It takes time for revolutions to acquire their meaning and proper significance. That which was commenced by the Cotton States of the South, attained its growth, developed its purpose, and became instantly and thoroughly in earnest at the period when the *second secessionary movement*, inaugurated by Virginia, confronted the powers at Washington with its sublime spectacles.

Virginia did not secede in either the circumstance or sense in which the Cotton States had separated themselves from the Union. She did not leave the Union with delusive prospects of peace to comfort or sustain her. She did not secede in the sense in which separation from the Union was the primary object of secession. Her act of secession was subordinate; she was called upon to oppose a practical and overt usurpation on the part of the

Government, at Washington in drawing its sword against the sovereignty of States and insisting on the right of coercion; to contest this her separation from the Union was necessary, and became a painful formality which could not be dispensed with.

A just and philosophical observation of events must find that in this second revolutionary movement of the Southern States, the revolution was put on a basis infinitely higher and firmer in all its moral and constitutional aspects: that at this period it developed itself, acquired its proper significance, and was broadly translated into a war of liberty. The movement of Virginia had more than anything else added to the moral influences of the revolution and perfected its justification in the eyes of the world. It was plain that she had not seceded on an issue of policy, but one of distinct and practical constitutional right, and that, too, in the face of a war which frowned upon her own borders, and which necessarily was to make her soil the principal theatre of its ravages and woes. Her attachment to the Union had been proved by the most untiring and noble efforts to save it; her Legislature originated the Peace Conference, which assembled at Washington in February, 1861; her representatives in Congress sought in that body every mode of honourable pacification; her Convention sent delegates to Washington to persuade Mr. Lincoln to a pacific policy; and in every form of public assembly, every expedient of negotiation was essayed to save the Union. When these efforts at pacification, which Virginia had made with an unselfishness without parallel, and with a nobility of spirit that scorned any misrepresentation of her office, proved abortive, she did not hesitate to draw her sword in front of the enemy, and to devote all she possessed and loved and hoped for to the fortunes of the war. It is not necessary to recount at length the services of this ancient Commonwealth in the war for Southern independence. She furnished nearly all of the arms, ammunition and accoutrements that won the early battles; she gave the Confederate service, from her own armories and stores, seventy-five thousand rifles and muskets, nearly three hundred pieces of artillery, and a magnificent armory, containing all the machinery necessary for manufacturing arms on a large scale; and on every occasion she replied to the call for troops, until she drained her arms-bearing population to the dregs.

It is a circumstance of most honourable remark, that such has been the conduct of Virginia in this war, that even from the base and vindictive enemy tributes have been forced to the devoted courage and heroic qualities of her sons. The following extraordinary tribute from the Washington *Republican*, the organ of abolition at the Yankee capital, is a compliment more expressive than anything a Virginian could say for his own State and its present generation of heroes:

"If there has been any decadence of the manly virtues in the Old Dominion, it is not because the present generation has proved itself either weak or cowardly or unequal to the greatest emergencies. No people, with so few numbers, ever put into the field, and kept there so long, troops more numerous, brave, or more efficient, or produced Generals of more merit, in all the kinds and grades of military talent. It is not a worn-out, effete race which has produced Lee, Johnston, Jackson, Ashby and Stuart. It is not a worn-out and effete race which, for two years, has defended its capital

"against the approach of an enemy close upon their borders, and outnum-
"bering them thirty to one. It is not a worn-out and effete race which has
"preserved substantial popular unity under all the straits and pressure and
"sacrifices of this unprecedented war. 'Let history,' as was said of another
"race, 'which records their unhappy fate as a people, do justice to their
"rude virtues as men.' They are fighting madly in a bad cause, but they
"are fighting bravely. They have few cowards and no traitors. The hard-
"ships of war are endured without a murmur by all classes, and the dangers
"of war without flinching, by the newest conscripts; while their gentry, the
"offshoot of their popular social system, have thrown themselves into the
"camp and field with all the dash and high spirit of the European *noblesse* of
"the middle ages, risking, without apparent concern, upon a desperate ad-
"venture, all that men value; and after a generation of peace and repose
"and security, which had not emasculated them, presenting to their enemies
"a trained and intrepid front, as of men born and bred to war."

What has been said here of Virginia and her characteristics in the present revolution, is the natural and just preface to what we have to say of the man who, more than any one else in this war, illustrated the chivalry of the Commonwealth and the virtues of her gentry. Turner Ashby was a thorough Virginian. He was an ardent lover of the old Union. He was brought up in that conservative and respectable school of politics which hesitated long to sacrifice a Union which had been, in part, constructed by the most illustrious of the sons of Virginia; which had conferred many honours upon her; and which was the subject of many hopes in the future. But when it became evident that the life of the Union was gone, and the sword was drawn for constitutional liberty, the spirit of Virginia was again illustrated by Ashby, who showed a devotion in the field even more admirable than the virtue of political principles.

Turner Ashby was the second son of the late Colonel Turner Ashby, of "Rose Bank," Fauquier county, and Dorothea F. Green, the daughter of the late James Green, Sr., of Rappahannock county. Colonel Ashby, at his death, left three sons and three daughters—the eldest of whom did not exceed twelve years of age at the time of his death—to the sole care of their devoted mother. To her excellent sense, generous disposition and noble character, the Confederacy is indebted for two as noble and gallant men as have won soldiers' graves during this war.

The father of Turner Ashby was the sixth son, that reached manhood, of Captain Jack Ashby, a man of mark in the day in which he lived, and of whom many anecdotes are still extant, illustrative of his remarkable character. One of these belongs to the colonial times, and is interesting:

"When the news of the disastrous defeat and death of General Braddock
"reached Fort Loudoun, (now Winchester, Virginia,) John Ashby was there,
"and his celebrity as a horseman induced the British Commandant of the
"post to secure his services as bearer of despatches to the Vice-Royal Gov-
"ernor at Williamsburg. Ashby at once proceeded on his mission, and in an
"incredibly short time presented himself before the commander at Fort Lou-
"doun. This official, of choleric disposition, upon the appearance of Ashby,
"broke out in severe reproach for his delay in proceeding on his mission, and

"was finally struck dumb with astonishment, at the presentation of the Governor's reply to the dispatch! The ride is said to have been accomplished in the shortest possible time, and the fact is certified in the records of Frederick county court."

Upon the breaking out of the Revolution of 1776, Captain Jack Ashby raised a company in his neighbourhood in the upper part of Fauquier. It was attached to the third Virginia regiment, under command of General Marshall. He was in the battles of Brandywine, Germantown, and several other of the most desperately contested fields of the Revolution. From exposure and hardships endured upon the frontiers of Canada, he contracted disease, from which he was never entirely relieved to the day of his death. He continued in the service during the whole period of the Revolution, and after the proclamation of peace, quietly settled upon his beautiful farm not far from Markham Station, upon the Manassas Gap railroad. Four of his sons, John, Samuel, Nimrod and Thomson, served in the war of 1812.

The father of our hero died, as we have stated, leaving a family of children of tender age. Young Turner was put to school, where it does not appear that he showed any peculiar trait in his studies; but he was remarkable among his young associates for his sedate manners, his grave regard for truth, and his appreciation of points of honour.

Turner Ashby never had the advantages of a college education, but he had a good, healthy mind; he was an attentive student of human nature, and a convenient listener where information was to be gained; and he possessed those ordinary stores of knowledge which may be acquired by a moderate use of books and an attentive intercourse with men. He was engaged for some time in merchandise at Markham's Depot. The old homestead of his father still stands near there, and not far from the homestead of the Marshalls. The tastes of Ashby were too domestic for politics. He was at one time Whig candidate for the Virginia Legislature from Fauquier, but was defeated by a small majority. This was his only public appearance in any political strife, and but little else is known of him as a politician beyond his ardent admiration of and personal attachment to Robert E. Scott.

Ashby's attachment to domestic life was enlivened by an extreme fondness for manly pastimes. He was a horseman from very childhood, and had the greatest passion for equestrian exercises. His delight in physical excitements was singularly pure and virtuous; he shunned the dissipations fashionable among young men; and while so sober and steady in his habits as sometimes to be a joke among his companions, yet he was the foremost in all innocent sports, the first to get up tournaments and fox chases, and almost always the successful competitor in all manly games. His favorite horse was trained for tournaments and fox-hunting, and it is said to have been a common pastime of Ashby to take him into the meadow and jump him over hay cocks and stone fences. Some of his feats of horsemanship are memorable, and are constantly related in his neighbourhood. While at the Fauquier Springs, which he frequently visited, and where he got up tournaments after the fashion of the ancient chivalry, he once displayed his horsemanship by riding into the ball-room, up and down steep flights of steps, to the mingled terrour and admiration of the guests. No cavalier was more graceful. The reserve of his manner was thrown aside in such sports, and his black eyes and dark face were lighted up with the zeal of competition or the excitement of danger.

The gravity so perceptible at times in Ashby's manner was not the sign either of a melancholy or blank mind. He was too practical for reveries; he was rather a man of deep feelings. While he scorned the vulgar and shallow ambition that seeks for notoriety, he probably had that ideal and aspiration which *silent* men often have, and which, if called "ambition" at all, is to be characterized as the noble and spiritual ambition that wins the honours of history, while others contend for the baubles of the populace.

"He was," writes a lady of his neighbourhood, "a person of very deep "feelings, which would not have been apparent to strangers, from his natu-"ral reserve of manner; but there was no act of friendship or kindness he "would have shrunk to perform, if called on. While he was not a professor "of religion, there was always a peculiar regard for the precepts of the Bible "which showed itself in his irreproachable walk in life. Often have I known "him to open the Sabbath school at the request of his lady friends, in a little "church near his home, by reading a prayer and chapter in the Bible. Turner "Ashby seldom left his native neighbourhood, so strong were his local attach-"ments, and would not have done so, save at his country's call."

That call was sounded sooner than Ashby expected. At the first prelude to the bloody drama of the war—the John Brown raid—he had been conspicuous, and his company of horse, then called "The Mountain Rangers," did service on that occasion. He appeared to have felt and known the consequences which were to ensue from this frightful crusade. Thenceforward his physical and intellectual powers were directed to the coming struggle. On the occasion of the irruption of John Brown and his felon band at Harper's Ferry, he remarked to Mr. Boteler, the member of Congress from that district, that a crisis was approaching, and that the South would be continually subject to such inroads and insults, unless some prevention was quickly effected. He continued, however, a strong Union man until the election of Lincoln; he was anxious that harmony should be effected between the States, and the legacies of the past should be preserved in a constitutional and fraternal Union; but this hope was instantly dispelled by the result of the election; and as soon as it was announced, he went quietly and energetically to work, drilling his men, promoting their efficiency, and preparing for that great trial of arms which he saw rapidly approaching.

The next time that Mr. Boteler met Ashby at Harper's Ferry, was on the night of the 17th of April, 1861. Mr. Boteler took him aside, and said to him, "What flag are we going to fight under—the Palmetto or what?" Ashby lifted his hat, and within it was laid a Virginia flag. He had had it painted at midnight, before he left Richmond. "Here," said he, "is the flag I intend to fight under." That night the flag was run up by the light of the burning buildings fired by the Yankees, and the next morning the glorious emblem of the Old Dominion was seen floating from the Federal flagstaff—the first ensign of liberty raised by Virginia in this war.

It was not long after the arrival of Captain Ashby at Harper's Ferry with his cavalry, that he was placed in command at Point of Rocks by General

Johnston, supported by Captain R. Welby Carter's company of cavalry and Captain John Q. Winfield's infantry corps of "Brock's Gap Riflemen."

About the same time Colonel Angus W. McDonald, senior, of Winchester, Virginia, was commissioned to raise a Legion of mounted men for border service, the Lieutenant Colonelcy of which was at once tendered to Captain Ashby. Without final acceptance of this position, he, with his command, entered the Legion, the organization of which was soon accomplished.

The original Captains were Ashby, Winfield, S. W. Myers, Mason, Shands, Jordan, Miller, Harper and Sheetz.

This force was assembled at Romney, Hampshire county, very soon after the evacuation of Harper's Ferry by General Johnston.

The difficulty which existed as to Captain Ashby's acceptance of the Lieutenant-Colonelcy of the Legion, consisted in the fact that he felt under especial obligations to his company, who were unwilling to dispense with his personal command. The arrival of his brother Richard Ashby, from Texas, who joined the company as independent volunteer, appeared to open the way of relieving this difficulty, as the company was prepared to accept in him a Captain, in order to secure the promotion of their beloved leader.

But a melancholy providence was to occur at this time, which was to colour the life of Turner Ashby, and affect it more deeply than anything he had yet experienced. The county of Hampshire had already been invaded by the enemy, and Colonel, now Major General, A. P. Hill had already visited the county with several regiments of infantry, in order to repel the invader. This county was also chosen for the labour of the Mounted Legion.

It was shortly after the organization of the command, and its active duty entered upon, that Captain Ashby led a detachment to Green Spring Station, on the Baltimore and Ohio railroad, for the purpose of observation. He had with him eleven men, and his brother Richard led another small band of six. The latter was proceeding along the railroad westward, in the direction of Cumberland—some ten miles away—when he was ambuscaded at the mouth of a ravine just beside the railroad there, running just between the river bank and the steep mountain side. The enemy's force consisted of about eighteen men, commanded by Corporal Hays, of the Indiana Zouave regiment, which was stationed at Cumberland. His men, at length compelled to fall back before superior numbers, hastened down the railroad to rejoin Richard Ashby. Covering their retreat himself, he hastened to the rescue of one of his men severely wounded in the face by a sabre stroke, and in a hand to hand fight with Corporal Hays, severely wounded him in the head with his sabre. Following immediately his retreating companions, the horse which he rode proved false, and fell into a cattle-stop of the railroad with his unfortunate rider. He was overtaken, beaten, bruised, wounded and left for dead. He was removed many hours afterwards, and lived for several days, enjoying every kind attention, but his wounds proved mortal. He was buried in the beautiful Indian Mound Cemetery at Romney on the 4th of July, 1861.

During the engagement of his brother, Turner Ashby started up the railroad to his rescue; but in passing along the river's brink, his force was fired upon from Kelly's Island, on the north branch of the Potomac, about twelve miles east of Cumberland. The island lies some sixty feet from the Virginia bank, which is precipitous, and directly laid with the railroad track. On the other side of the island, which was reached through water to the saddle girth, there is a gently rising beach some thirty yards to the interiour, which is thickly wooded, and contains a dense undergrowth. Here in ambush lay, as was afterwards reported, about forty of the Indiana troops, and nearly sixty of Merley's branch riflemen—Maryland Union men of the vicinity—woodmen skilled with the rifle, and many of them desperate characters. After receiving the enemy's fire, Turner Ashby and his eleven at once charged, and after a sharp engagement, routed and dispersed their forces. It has been declared that not less than forty shots were fired at Ashby on that occasion, but not he nor his horse were harmed, and at least five of the enemy were probably slain by his hand.

From the date of his brother's death, a change passed over the life of Turner Ashby. He always wore a sad smile after that unhappy day, and his life became more solemn and earnest to the end of his own evanescent and splendid career. "Ashby," said a lady friend, speaking of him after this period, "is now a *devoted man.*" His behaviour at his brother's grave, as it is described by one of the mourners at the same spot, was most touching. He stood over the grave, took his brother's sword, broke it and threw it into the opening; clasped his hands and looked upward as if in resignation; and then pressing his lips, as if in the bitterness of grief, while a tear rolled down his cheek, he turned without a word, mounted his horse and rode away. Thenceforth his name was a terrour to the enemy.

Shortly after the death of his brother, his company consented to yield him up in order that he might accept the Lieutenant-Colonelcy of the Legion, and elected First Lieutenant William Turner (his cousin) captain in his stead. The Legion, numbering at that time nearly nine hundred effective men tolerably equipped and mounted, continued on duty in Hampshire until the 16th of July, 1861, when it started for Manassas, but did not arrive until after the battle. The command was immediately afterwards ordered to Staunton to join General Lee's forces—subsequently to Hollingsworth, one mile south of Winchester. In the meantime, Colonel Ashby, with several companies, was sent on detached duty to Jefferson, into which county the enemy was making frequent incursions from Harper's Ferry and Maryland.

In Jefferson, Ashby had command of four companies of cavalry and about eight hundred militia. Yankee raids were kept from the doors of the inhabitants, and the enemy made but little appearance in this portion of Virginia, until Banks crossed the Potomac in February, 1862.

It was about this time that Ashby's cavalry acquired its great renown. The Lincoln soldiers dreaded nothing so much as they did these hated troopers. Go where they would, out of sight of their encampments, they were almost sure to meet some of Ashby's cavalry, who seemed to possess the power of ubiquity. And, in truth, they had good cause both to hate and to fear Ashby's cavalry; for many a Federal horseman dropped from his saddle, and many a Federal soldier on foot dropped in his tracks, at the crack of Confederate rifles in the hands of Ashby's fearless sharpshooters.

During the time of the encampment at Flowing Springs, Colonel Ashby rarely ever came into town, which was about a mile and a half distant. Nothing could entice him from his duties; no admiration, no dinner parties or ovations, could move him to leave his camp. He always slept with his men. No matter what hour of the night he was aroused, he was always wakeful, self-possessed and ready to do battle. He was idolized by his men, whom he treated as companions and indulged without reference to rules of military discipline. He had great contempt for the military arts, was probably incapable of drilling a regiment, and preserved among his men scarcely anything more than the rude discipline of camp hunters. But though not a stickler for military rules, he would have no coward or eye-soldier in his command. If a man was dissatisfied, he at once started him off home. He allowed his men many liberties. A gentleman asked him one day where his men were. "Well," said he, "the boys fought very well yesterday, and there are not more than thirty of them here to-day."

Ashby's influence over his men was principally due to the brilliant and amazing examples of personal courage which he always gave them in front of the battle. His men could never find him idle. In battle his eye kindled up most gloriously. He wore a grey coat and pants, with boots and sash; he always looked like work, was frequently covered with mud, and appeared to be never fatigued or dejected. He would come and go like a dream. He would be heard of at one time in one part of the country, and then, when least expected, would come dashing by on the famous white horse, which was his pride.

When the fight occurred at Boteler's Mill, the militia were for the first time under fire. The enemy had encamped on the other side of the Potomac, opposite the mill. Our troops quietly crept upon them, and planted two pieces of cannon within range, and let drive at them with terrible effect, whereupon they fled. They afterwards returned in force, and ranged themselves on the other side with long range guns. Ashby, to encourage the militia, who were raw, advanced to the bank of the river, and rode his white horse up and down within point blank range of the enemy's fire. When the balls were hurtling thickest, he would rein in his horse and stand perfectly still, the very picture of daring and chivalry.

At Bolivar heights, when the enemy were firing upon our men and had shot down the gunners at the cannon, he sprang from his horse and seized the rammer himself. He was conspicuous in action at every point. His friends used to implore him not to ride his white horse—for he had also a black one—but he was deaf to every caution that respected the safety of his person.

The key to Ashby's character was his passion for danger. He craved the excitement of battle, and was never happier than when riding his noble steed in the thickest of the storm of battle. There are some minds which find a sweet intoxication in danger, and Macaulay has named a remarkable instance in William III., the silent and ascetic King of England, who was transformed into gaiety by the excitement of personal peril. "Danger," says the historian, "acted upon him like wine;" it made him full of animation and speech. Ashby's delight in danger was a royal one. It came from no brutal hardihood or animal spirits; and the Virginia cavalier is this far superiour to other famous partisans in this war, that he united with the adventures of courage the courtesies of a gentleman and Christian, and the refinements of a pure and gentle soul. He was never rude; he was insensible to the humours of the vulgar; and he never even threw into the face of his enemy a coarse taunt, or a specimen of that wit common in the army.

Turner Ashby was doubtless as perfect a specimen of modern chivalry as the South even has ever produced. His brilliant daring, his extreme courtesy to woman, his devotion to the *horse*, his open-hearted manner and his scorn of mean actions, are qualities as admirable now as in the days of Froissart's Chronicles. After the battle of Winchester, the Yankee women and families of officers sometimes came to Ashby to get passes. They were surprised to find with what readiness permits were granted. They would say, "Colonel Ashby, you may search our baggage. We assure you we are carrying away nothing which we are not at liberty to do." His reply was, "I have no right to look into ladies' baggage, or to examine their trunks. Southern gentlemen do no such thing." They said, "Colonel, you may search our persons, and see if we carry away anything contraband." The reply was, "Virginia gentlemen do not search the persons of ladies."

Few young men of Ashby's age could have resisted the intoxication of of praise heaped upon him from every quarter. The fact was, no aged and stern devotee to duty was ever more insensible, in the performance of his task, to the currents of popular favour than the young Paladin of the South. The following copy of a letter, written at the height of his reputation to an elderly gentlemen of Stafford county, illustrates the modesty which adorned the life of Turner Ashby, and the sense of duty which insured its most brilliant successes:

"MY DEAR SIR: I have just received your exceedingly kind and most flat-
"tering letter. Let me assure you that it gives me no little pleasure to know
"that my course, while doing my duty to my country, meets your approval,
"whose age and experience make it more to be estimated. That I have not
"sought self-aggrandizement, or regarded anything save what I believed to
"be my duty to my country in this war, I hope it is needless to assure you.
"When my course meets with the approval of the old patriots, I feel doubly
"satisfied that I have not mistaken what I believe to be my duty. What you
"are pleased to say of my brother (who fell as I, too, expect to fall, if my
"country needs it) is but too true. Had he been spared longer, he would
"doubtless have been of great value to our country. His fall, however, has
"not been without its lesson to the enemy, teaching them that Virginians
"know how to die as well as fight for their liberty. He died without a re-
"gret, feeling that his life was due to his country's cause. Please present
"me most kindly to all my friends in Stafford, and accept my highest respects
"for yourself.

"Your obedient servant,

"TURNER ASHBY."

We have already referred in the pages of this history to Ashby's share in
the several glorious campaigns of Jackson in the Valley; to his participation
in the battle of Kernstown; to his famous adventure with the Yankee pickets
at the bridge, and to some other of his daring exploits on the front and flanks
of the enemy. It was on the occasion of the battle of Kernstown that his
energy was exercised to an extraordinary degree in protecting the retreat and
annoying the skirts of the enemy. In thirty-eight out of forty-two days after
that battle he was fighting the enemy, keeping him in check, or cutting off his
communications. The terrible fatigues he incurred never seemed to depress
him, or to tax his endurance. An acquaintance testifies that it was not an
infrequent feat for him to ride daily over a line of pickets sixty or seventy
miles in extent.

At a later period of the Valley campaign, when Banks returned from
Strasburg and our troops were chasing him, Ashby would follow and charge
the Yankees as the Rockbridge Artillery poured in their fire. At one time he
was riding abreast of three hundred infantry, who were passing along the
turnpike. All at once he wheeled his horse, and leaping the fence with drawn
sword, cut his way right through them, then wheeling, he did the same thing
a second time. Riding up to the standard bearer, he seized it from him and
dashed him to the earth. The terrified wretches never raised a weapon
against him. Seventy-five of them, whom he cut off, laid down their arms,
and sat down at his order in the corner of the fence, where they remained
until his men came up to take care of them. The flag was that of a Vermont
regiment. A few days after, Mr. Boteler asked Ashby of the exploit. He
drew the flag from his bosom and gave it to him. It was presented by Mr.
Boteler to the Library of the State, at Richmond, where it may now be seen—
a testimony to one of the most brilliant deeds of Virginia's youthful hero.

A week after this adventure, Ashby was dead. But a few days before the
termination of his brilliant career, he received the promotion which had been
long due him from the Government. Just before leaving Richmond after the
adjournment of the first session of the permanent Congress, Mr. Boteler, who
was a member of that body and Ashby's constant friend, went to the President, told him that he was going home, and asked that one act of justice
should be done to the people of the Valley, which they had long expected.
He wished to be able to carry back to his people the assurance that Ashby
should be commissioned a Brigadier General. The order for the commission
was at once made out. When the announcement was made to Ashby, he exhibited no emotion, except that his face was lighted up by one of those sad
smiles which had occasionally brightened it since the death of his brother.

The manner of Ashby's death has already been mentioned in the preceding
pages of the brief historical narrative of the Valley campaign. The writer
is indebted for the particulars of that sad event to Colonel Bradley T. Johnson, the brave Maryland officer whose command was conspicuous in the affair
that cost Ashby his life, and earned an immortal honour in revenging his
death. He takes the liberty of extracting from a letter of this officer an account of the engagement:

"On the morning of Friday, the 6th of June," writes Colonel Johnson,

"we left Harrisonburg, not having seen the enemy for two days. To our
"surprise in the afternoon, his cavalry made a dash into our rear guard, and
"was whipped most effectually, their Colonel, Sir Percy Wyndham, being
"taken prisoner. My regiment was supporting a battery a short distance
"behind this cavalry fight. In half an hour we were ordered forward—that
"is, toward the enemy retracing the march just made. Our infantry con-
"sisted only of Brigadier General George H. Stewart's brigade, the 58th
"Virginia, 44th Virginia, two other Virginia regiments, and the Maryland
"Line—of the latter, only the 1st Maryland was taken back; the artillery
"and all the cavalry was left behind us. The 58th Virginia was first, my re-
"giment (the 1st Maryland) next, then came the 44th and the rest.
"A couple of miles east of Harrisonburg, we left the road and filed to the
"right, through the fields, soon changing direction again so as to move par-
"allel to the road. General Ewell soon sent for two of my companies as skir-
"mishers. Moving cautiously through the darkening shades of the tangled
"wood just as the evening twilight was brightening the trees in front of us
"in an opening, *spot, spot, spot*, began a dropping fire from the skirmish-
"ers, and instantly the 58th Virginia poured in a volley. Another volley
"was fired. The leaves began to fall, and the bullets hit the trees around.
"General Ewell came up in a gallop. 'Charge, Colonel, charge to the left!'
"And I charged, got to the edge of the wood, and found a heavy body of in-
"fantry and cavalry supporting a battery on a hill six hundred yards in front
"of me. But the Yankee balls came fast and thick on my flank. 'The
"58th are firing into us,' the leading Captain said. General Ewell and my-
"self, the only mounted officers, plunged after them, and found it was not
"their fire. I got back. 'Up, men, and take that hill,' pointing to my right.
"They went in with a cheer. In less than five seconds the front rank of the
"second company went down. The colour sergeant, Doyle, fell. The cor-
"poral who caught them from him fell. The next who took them fell, when
"Corporal Shanks, a six-footer, seized them, raising them over his head at
"arm's length. Captain Robertson lay dead; Lieutenant Snowden shot to
"death; myself on the ground, my horse shot in three places. But still we
"went forward, and drove the Bucktails from the fence where they had been
"concealed. * * * *"

It was as the brave Marylanders were pressing on in this charge that
Ashby, who was on the right of the 58th Virginia exhorting them, fell by an
intelligent bullet of the enemy. His death was quickly avenged. As our
troops reached the fence from which the shot had been fired, the line of Yankees melted away like mist before a hurricane.

"The account I have given you," writes Colonel Johnson, "of the manner
"of Ashby's death, is collated from the statements of many eye-witnesses of
"my skirmishing companies, who were all around him when he fell. I did
"not see it, though not thirty yards from him, but was busy with my own
"men; and I am specific in stating the source of his death, as there is a loose
"impression that he was killed by a shot from the 58th Virginia. I am per-
"suaded this is not so, from the statements of two very cool officers, Captain
"Nicholas and Lieutenant Booth, who were talking to him the minute before
"he fell. * * * * *

"Ashby was my first revolutionary acquaintance in Virginia. I was with
him when the first blow was struck for the cause we both had so much at
heart, and was with him in his last fight, always knowing him to be beyond
all modern men in chivalry, as he was equal to any one in courage. He
combined the virtues of Sir Philip Sidney with the dash of Murat. I contribute my mite to his fame, which will live in the Valley of Virginia, outside of books, as long as its hills and mountains shall endure."

No word escaped from Ashby's lips as he fell. It was not necessary. No dying legend, spoken in death's embrace, could have added to that noble life. Itself was a beautiful poem; a sounding oration; a sufficient legacy to the virtue of his countrymen.

## CHAPTER II.

The Situation of Richmond...Its Strategic Importance...What the Yankees Had Done to Secure Richmond...THE BATTLE OF SEVEN PINES...Miscarriage of Gen. Johnston's Plans...THE BATTLES OF THE CHICKAHOMINY...Storming of the Enemy's Entrenchments...McClellan Driven from his Northern Line of Defences...The Situation on the Other Side of the Chickahominy...Magruder's Comment...The Affair of Savage Station....The Battle of Frazier's Farm...A Terrible Crisis...Battle of Malvern Hill...The Enemy in Communication with his Gunboats....The Failure to Cut him off....Glory and Fruits of Our Victory.... Misrepresentations of the Yankees...Safety of Richmond...The War in Other Parts of the Confederacy...The Engagement of Secessionville...The Campaign of the West...The Evacuation of Corinth...More Yankee Falsehoods...Capture of Memphis...The Prize of the Mississippi...Statistics of its Navigation...Siege of Vicksburg...Heroism of "the Queen City"...Morgan's Raid into Kentucky...The Tennessee and Virginia Frontier...Prospects in the West...Plan of Campaign there.

Richmond is the heart of the State of Virginia. It is hundreds of miles from the sea, yet with water communication to Old Point, to Washington,. and to New York. It is the strategic point of. the greatest importance in the whole Confederacy. If Richmond had fallen before McClellan's forces, the North expected that there would follow all of North Carolina except the mountains, part of South Carolina, and all of Tennessee that was left to us.

On the Richmond lines, two of the greatest and most splendid armies that had ever been arrayed on a single field confronted each other; every accession that could be procured from the most distant quarters to their numbers, and everything that could be drawn from the resources of the respective countries of each, had been made to contribute to the strength and splendour of the opposing hosts.

Since the commencement of the war, the North had taxed its resources for the capture of Richmond; nothing was omitted for the accomplishment of this event; the way had to be opened to the capital by tedious and elaborate operations on the frontier of Virginia; this accomplished, the city of Richmond was surrounded by an army whose numbers was all that could be desired; composed of picked forces; having every advantage that science and art could bestow in fortifications and every appliance of war; assisted by gun-boat flotillas in two rivers, and endowed with everything that could assure success.

The Northern journals were unreserved in the statement that the commands of Fremont, Banks and McDowell had been consolidated into one army, under Major-General Pope, with a view of bringing all the Federal forces in Virginia to co-operate with McClellan on the Richmond lines. A portion of this army must have reached McClellan, probably at an early stage of the engagements in the vicinity of Richmond. Indeed, it was stated at a subsequent period by Mr. Chandler, a member of the Federal Congress, that the records of the War Department at Washington showed that more than one hundred and fifty thousand men had been sent to the lines about Richmond. There is little doubt but that, in the memorable contest for the safety of the Confederate capital, we engaged an army whose superiority in numbers to us was largely increased by timely reinforcements, and with regard to the operations of which the Northern Government had omitted no conditions of success.

### THE BATTLE OF SEVEN PINES.

Having reached the Chickahominy, McClellan threw a portion of his army across the river, and, having thus established his left, proceeded to pivot upon it, and to extend his right by the right bank of the Pamunkey, so as to get to the North of Richmond.

Before the 30th of May, General Johnston had ascertained that Keyes' corps was encamped on this side of the Chickahominy, near the Williamsburg road, and the same day a strong body of the enemy was reported in front of D. H. Hill. The following disposition of forces was made for the attack the next day, the troops being ordered to move at daybreak: General Hill, supported by the division of General Longstreet, (who had the direction of operations on the right,) was to advance by the Williamsburg road to attack the enemy in front; General Huger, with his division, was to move down the Charles City road, in order to attack in flank the troops who might be engaged with Hill and Longstreet, unless he found in his front force enough to occupy his division; General Smith was to march to the junction of the New Bridge road and the Nine Mile road, to be in readiness either to fall on Keyes' right flank, or to cover Longstreet's left.

The next day hour after hour passed, while Gen. Longstreet in vain waited for Huger's division. At two o'clock in the afternoon he resolved to make the attack without these troops, and moved upon the enemy with his own and D. H. Hill's division, the latter in advance.

Hill's brave troops, admirably commanded and most gallantly led, forced their way through the abattis which formed the enemy's external defences, and stormed their entrenchments by a determined and irresistible rush. Such was the manner in which the enemy's first line was carried. The operation was repeated with the same gallantry and success as our troops pursued their victorious career through the enemy's successive camps and entrenchments. At each new position they encountered fresh troops belonging to it, and reinforcements brought on from the rear. Thus they had to repel repeated efforts to retake works which they had carried. But their advance was never successfully resisted. Their onward movement was only stayed by the coming of night. By nightfall they had forced their way to the "Seven Pines," having driven the enemy back more than two miles, through their own camps, and from a series of entrenchments, and repelled every attempt to recapture them with great slaughter.

The attack on the enemy's right was not so fortunate. The strength of his position enabled him to hold it until dark, and the intervention of night alone saved him from rout. On this part of the field Gen. Johnston was severely wounded by the fragment of a shell.

In his official report of the operations of the day, General Johnston says: "Had Major-General Huger's division been in position and ready for action when those of Smith, Longstreet and Hill moved, I am satisfied that Keyes' corps would have been destroyed instead of being merely defeated." The slow and impotent movements of Gen. Huger were excused by himself on account of the necessity of building a bridge to cross the swollen stream in his front, and other accidental causes of delay.

But nothwithstanding the serious diminution of the fortunes of the day by Huger's mishaps, they were yet conspicuous. We had taken ten pieces of artillery and six thousand muskets, besides other spoils. Our total loss was more than four thousand. That of the enemy is stated in their own newspapers to have exceeded ten thousand—an estimate which is no doubt short of the truth.

On the morning of the first of June, the enemy made a weak demonstration of attack on our lines. The 9th and 14th Virginia regiments were ordered to feel for the enemy, and while thus engaged, suddenly came upon a body of fifteen thousand Yankees entrenched in the woods. Under the murderous fire poured into their ranks, our troops were forced to fall back, but were rallied by the self-devoted gallantry of their officers. Colonel Godwin, the dashing and intrepid commander of the 9th, received a Minie ball in the leg, and a moment later had his hip crushed by the fall of his horse, which was shot under him. He was thirty paces in advance of his regiment when the attack was made, encouraging his men. At last, reinforcements coming up, the attack of the enemy was vigourously repulsed. This was the last demonstration of the enemy, who proceeded to strengthen those lines of entrenchments from which he had not yet been driven.

THE SECOND YEAR OF THE WAR. 61

THE BATTLES OF THE CHICKAHOMINY.

Upon taking command of the Confederate army in the field, after General Johnston had been wounded in the battle of Seven Pines, Gen. Lee did not hesitate to adopt the spirit of that commander, which had already been displayed in attacking the enemy, and which indicated the determination on his part that the operations before Richmond should not degenerate into a seige.

The course of the Chickahominy around Richmond affords an idea of the enemy's position at the commencement of the action. This stream meanders through the Tide-water district of Virginia—its course approaching that of the arc of a circle in the neighborhood of Richmond—until it reaches the lower end of Charles City county, where it abruptly turns to the south and empties into the James. A portion of the enemy's forces had crossed to the south side of the Chickahominy, and were fortified on the Williamsburg road. On the north bank of the stream the enemy was strongly posted for many miles; the heights on that side of the stream having been fortified with great energy and skill from Meadow Bridge, on a line nearly due north from the city to a point below Bottom's Bridge, which is due east. This line of the enemy extended for about twenty miles.

Reviewing the situation of the two armies at the commencement of the action, the advantage was entirely our own. McClellan had divided his army on the two sides of the Chickahominy, and operating apparently with the design of half circumvallating Richmond, had spread out his forces to an extent that impaired the faculty of concentration, and had made a weak and dangerous extension of his lines.

On Thursday, the 26th of June, at three o'clock, Major-General Jackson—fresh from the exploits of his magnificent campaign in the Valley—took up his line of march from Ashland, and proceeded down the country between the Chickahominy and Pamunkey rivers. The enemy collected on the north bank of the Chickahominy, at the point where it is crossed by the Brooke turnpike, were driven off, and Brigadier-General Branch, crossing the stream, directed his movements for a junction with the column of General A. P. Hill, which had crossed at Meadow Bridge. General Jackson having borne away from the Chickahominy, so as to gain ground towards the Pamunkey, marched to the left of Mechanicsville, while General Hill, keeping well to the Chickahominy, approached that village and engaged the enemy there.

With about fourteen thousand men (General Branch did not arrive till nightfall), General Hill engaged the forces of the enemy until night put an end to the contest. While he did not succeed, in that limited time, in routing the enemy, his forces stubbornly maintained the possession of Mechanicsville and the ground taken by them on the other side of the Chickahominy. Driven from the immediate locality of Mechanicsville, the enemy retreated during the night down the river to Powhite swamp, and night closed the operations of Thursday.

STORMING OF THE ENEMY'S ENTRENCHMENTS.

The road having been cleared at Mechanicsville, Gen. Longstreet's *corps d'armee*, consisting of his veteran division of the Old Guard of the Army of the Potomac, and Gen. D. H. Hill's division, debouched from the woods on the south side of the Chickahominy, and crossed that river. Friday morning the general advance upon the enemy began; Gen. A. P. Hill in the centre, and bearing towards Cold Harbour, while Gen. Longstreet and Gen. D. H. Hill came down the Chickahominy to New Bridge. Gen. Jackson still maintained his position in advance, far to the left, and gradually converging to the Chickahominy again.

The position of the enemy was now a singular one. One portion of his army was on the south side of the Chickahominy, fronting Richmond, and confronted by Gen. Magruder. The other portion, on the north side, had fallen back to a new line of defences, where McClellan proposed to make a decisive battle.

As soon as Jackson's arrival at Cold Harbour was announced, Gen. Lee and Gen. Longstreet, accompanied by their respective staffs, rode by Gaines' Mill and halted at New Cold Harbour, where they joined Gen. A. P. Hill. Soon the welcome sound of Jackson's guns announced that he was at work.

The action was now to become general for the first time on the Richmond lines; and a collision of numbers was about to take place equal to any that had yet occurred in the history of the war.

From four o'clock until eight the battle raged with a display of the utmost daring and intrepidity on the part of the Confederate army. The enemy's lines were finally broken and his strong positions all carried, and night covered the retreat of McClellan's broken and routed columns to the south side of the Chickahominy.

The assault of the enemy's works near Gaines' Mill is a memorable part of the engagement of Friday, and the display of fortitude, as well as quick and dashing gallantry of our troops on that occasion, takes its place by the side of the most glorious exploits of the war. Gen. A. P. Hill had made the first assault upon the lines of the enemy's entrenchments near Gaines' Mill. A fierce struggle had ensued between his division and the garrison of the line of defence. Repeated charges were made by Hill's troops, but the formidable character of the works, and murderous volleys from the artillery covering them, kept our troops in check. Twenty-six pieces of artillery were thundering at them, and a perfect hail-storm of lead fell thick and fast around them. In front stood Federal camps, stretching to the northeast for miles. Drawn up in line of battle were more than three full divisions, commanded by McCall, Porter and Sedgwick. Banners darkened the air; artillery vomited forth incessant volleys of grape, canister and shell; and the wing of death waved everywhere in the sulphurous atmosphere of the battle.

It was past four o'clock when Pickett's brigade from Longstreet's division came to Hill's support. Pickett's regiments fought with the most determined valour. At last, Whiting's division, composed of the "Old Third" and Texan brigades, advanced at a double-quick, charged the batteries, and drove the enemy from his strong line of defence. The 4th Texas regiment was led by a gallant Virginian, Colonel Bradfute Warwick. As the regiment was marching on with an irresistible impetuosity to the charge, he seized a battle-flag which had been abandoned by one of our regiments, and, bearing it aloft, he passed both of the enemy's breast-works in a most gallant style, and as he was about to plant the colours on a battery that the regiment captured, his right breast was pierced by a Minie ball, and he fell mortally wounded.

The works carried by our noble troops would have been invincible to the bayonet, had they been garrisoned by men less dastardly than the Yankees. All had been done on our side with the bullet and the bayonet. For four hours had our inferiour force, unaided by a single piece of artillery, withstood over thirty thousand, assisted by twenty-six pieces of artillery.

To keep the track of the battle, which had swept around Richmond, we must have reference to some of the principal points of locality in the enemy's lines. It will be recollected that it was on Thursday evening when the attack was commenced upon the enemy near Meadow Bridge. This locality is about six miles distant from the city, on a line almost due north. This position was the enemy's extreme right. His lines extended from here across the Chickahominy, near the Powhite Creek, two or three miles above the crossing of the York River railroad. From Meadow Bridge to this railroad, the distance along the Chickahominy on the north side is about ten miles. The different stages between the points indicated, along which the enemy were driven, are Mechanicsville, about a mile north of the Chickahominy; further on, Beaver Dam

Creek, emptying into the Chickahominy; then the New Bridge road, on which Cold Harbour is located;- and then Powhite Creek, where the enemy had made his last stand, and been repulsed from the field.

The York River railroad runs in an easterly direction, intersecting the Chickahominy about ten miles from the city. South of the railroad is the Williamsburg road, connecting with the Nine Mile road at Seven Pines. The former road connects with the New Bridge road, which turns off and crosses the Chickahominy. From Seven Pines, where the Nine Mile road joins the upper one, the road is known as the old Williamsburg road, and crosses the Chickahominy at Bottom's Bridge.

With the bearing of these localities in his mind, the reader will readily understand how it was that the enemy was driven from his original strongholds on the north side of the Chickahominy, and how, at the time of Friday's battle, he had been compelled to surrender the possession of the Fredericksburg and Central railroads, and had been pressed to a position where he was cut off from the principal avenues of supply and escape. The disposition of our forces was such as to cut off all communication between McClellan's army and the White House, on the Pamunkey river; he had been driven completely from his northern line of defences; and it was supposed that he would be unable to extricate himself from his position without a victory or capitulation.

On Sunday morning, it appears that our pickets, on the Nine Mile road, having engaged some small detachments of the enemy and driven them beyond their fortifications, found them deserted. In a short while, it became known to our generals that McClellan, having massed his entire force on this side of the Chickahominy, was retreating towards James river.

The entrenchments, which the enemy had deserted, were found to be formidable and elaborate. That immediately across the railroad, at the six mile post, which had been supposed to be light earthwork, designed to sweep the railroad, turned out to be an immense embrasured fortification, extending for hundreds of yards on either side of the track. Within this work were found great quantities of fixed ammunition, which had apparently been prepared for removal and then deserted. All the cannon, as at other entrenchments, had been carried off. A dense cloud of smoke was seen issuing from the woods two miles in advance of the battery and half a mile to the right of the railroad. The smoke was found to proceed from a perfect mountain of the enemy's commissary stores, consisting of sugar, coffee and bacon, prepared meats, vegetables, &c., which he had fired. The fields and woods around this spot were covered with every description of clothing and camp equipage. No indication was wanting that the enemy had left this encampment in haste and disorder.

The enemy had been imperfectly watched at a conjuncture the most critical in the contest, and through an omission of our guard—the facts of which are yet the subject of some controversy—McClellan had succeeded in massing his entire force, and taking up a line of retreat, by which he hoped to reach the cover of his gunboats on the James. But the most unfortunate circumstance to us was, that since the enemy had escaped from us in his fortified camp, his retreat was favoured by a country, the characteristics of which are unbroken forests and wide swamps, where it was impossible to pursue him with rapidity, and extremely difficult to reconnoitre his position so as to bring him to decisive battle.

In an official report of the situation of forces on the Richmond side of the Chickahominy, General Magruder describes it as one of the gravest peril. He states that the larger portion of the enemy was on that side of the Chickahominy; that the bridges had all been destroyed, and but one rebuilt—the New Bridge—which was commanded fully by the enemy's guns; and that there were but twenty-five thousand men between McClellan's army of one hundred thousand and Richmond. Referring to a situation so extremely critical, he says: "Had McClellan massed his whole force in column, and advanced it against any point of our line of battle, as was done at Austerlitz under similar circumstances, by the greatest captain of any age, though the head of his column would have suffered greatly, its momentum would have insured him success, and the occupation of our works about Richmond, and, consequently, of the city, might have been his reward." Taking this view of the situation, General Magruder states that his relief was great when it was discovered the next day that the enemy had left our front and was continuing to retreat.

The facts, however, are contrary to the theory of General Magruder and to the self-congratulations which he derives from it. Our troops on the two sides of the river were only separated until we succeeded in occupying the position near what is known as New Bridge, which occurred before 12 o'clock M., on Friday, June 27, and before the attack on the enemy at Gaines' Mill. From the time we reached the position referred to, our communications between the two wings of our army may be regarded as re-established. The bridge referred to and another about three-quarters of a mile above were ordered to be repaired before noon on Friday, and the new bridge was sufficiently rebuilt to be passed by artillery on Friday night, and the one above it was used for the passage of wagons, ambulances and troops early on Saturday morning. Besides this, all other bridges above New Bridge and all the fords above that point were open to us.

### THE AFFAIR AT SAVAGE STATION.

During Sunday, a portion of the enemy was encountered upon the York river railroad, near a place called Savage Station, the troops engaged on our side being the division of General McLaws, consisting of Generals Kershaw and Semmes' brigades, supported by General Griffith's brigade from Magruder's division. The Federals were found to be strongly entrenched, and as soon as our skirmishers came in view, they were opened upon with a furious cannonade from a park of field pieces. Kemper's battery now went to the front, and for three hours the battle raged hotly, when the discomfited Yankees again resumed their retreat. Early in the day, on reaching the redoubts, General Griffith, of Mississippi, one of the heroes of Leesburg, was killed by the fragment of a shell. He was the only general officer killed on our side during the whole of the bloody week.

In this encounter with the enemy, the gallant 10th Georgia regiment suffered severely, engaging the enemy hand-to-hand, and leaving upon the field memorable evidences of their courage. The enemy, to use an expression of his prisoners, was "mowed down" by the close fire of our adventurous troops; and the failure of the attempt of McClellan to break through our lines at this point, left him to continue a hopeless retreat.

## THE BATTLE OF FRAYSER'S FARM.

By daybreak on Monday morning, the pursuit of the enemy was actively resumed. D. H. Hill, Whiting and Ewell, under command of Jackson, crossed the Chickahominy by the Grapevine Bridge, and followed the enemy on their track by the Williamsburg road and Savage's Station. Longstreet, A. P. Hill, Huger and Magruder pursued the enemy by the Charles City road, with the intention of cutting them off.

The divisions of Generals Hill and Longstreet were, during the whole of the day, moving in the hunt for the enemy. The disposition which was made of our forces brought Gen. Longstreet on the enemy's front, immediately supported by General Hill's division, consisting of six brigades. The forces commanded by General Longstreet were his old division, consisting of six brigades.

The position of the enemy was about five miles northeast of Darbytown, on the New Market road. The immediate scene of the battle was a plain of sedge pines, in the cover of which the enemy's forces were skilfully disposed—the locality being known as Frayser's farm. In advancing upon the enemy, batteries of sixteen heavy guns were opened upon the advance columns of General Hill. Our troops, pressing heroically forward, had no sooner got within musket range, than the enemy, forming several lines of battle, poured upon them from his heavy masses a devouring fire of musketry. The conflict became terrible, the air being filled with missiles of death, every moment having its peculiar sound of terrour, and every spot its sight of ghastly destruction and horrour. It is impossible that in any of the series of engagements which had taken place within the past few days, and had tracked the lines of Richmond with fire and destruction, there could have been more desperate fighting on the part of our troops. Never was a more glorious victory plucked from more desperate and threatening circumstances. While exposed to the double fire of the enemy's batteries and his musketry, we were unable to contend with him with artillery. But although thus unmatched, our brave troops pressed on with unquailing vigour and a resistless courage, driving the enemy before them. This was accomplished without artillery, there being but one battery in Gen. Hill's command on the spot, and that belonged to Longstreet's division, and could not be got into position. Thus the fight continued with an ardour and devotion that few battle-fields have ever illustrated. Step by step the enemy were driven back, his guns taken, and the ground he abandoned strewn with his dead. By half-past eight o'clock we had taken all his cannon, and, continuing to advance, had driven him a mile and a half from his ground of battle.

Our forces were still advancing upon the retreating lines of the enemy. It was now about half-past nine o'clock, and very dark. Suddenly, as if it had burst from the heavens, a sheet of fire enveloped the front of our advance. The enemy had made another stand to receive us, and from the black masses of his forces, it was evident that he had been heavily reinforced, and that another whole *corps d'armee* had been brought up to contest the fortunes of the night. Line after line of battle was formed. It was evident that his heaviest columns were now being thrown against our small command, and it might have been supposed that he would only be satisfied with its annihilation. The loss here on our side was terrible.

The situation being evidently hopeless for any further pursuit of the fugitive enemy, who had now brought up such overwhelming forces, our troops retired slowly.

At this moment, seeing their adversary retire, the most vociferous cheers arose along the whole Yankee line. They were taken up in the distance by the masses which for miles and miles beyond were supporting McClellan's front. It was a moment when the heart of the stoutest commander might have been appalled. The situation of our forces was now as desperate as it well could be, and required a courage and presence of mind to retrieve it, which the circumstances which surrounded them were not well calculated to inspire. They had fought for five or six hours without reinforcements. All our reserves had been brought up in the action. Wilcox's brigade, which had been almost annihilated, was re forming in the rear.

Riding rapidly to the position of this brigade, General Hill brought them by great exertions, up to the front, to check the advance of the now confident, cheering enemy. Catching the spirit of their commander, the brave, but jaded men, moved up to the front, replying to the enemy's cheers with shouts and yells. At this demonstration, which the enemy, no doubt, supposed signified heavy reinforcements, he stopped his advance. It was now about half-past ten o'clock in the night. The enemy had been arrested; and the fight—one of the most remarkable, long-contested and gallant ones that had yet occurred on our lines—was concluded with the achievement of a field under the most trying circumstances, which the enemy, with the most overpowering numbers brought up to reinforce him, had not succeeded in reclaiming.

General Magruder's division did not come up until eleven o'clock at night, after the fight had been concluded. By orders from Gen. Lee, Magruder moved upon and occupied the battleground; General Hill's command being in such a condition of prostration from their long and toilsome fight, and suffering in killed and wounded, that it was proper they should be relieved by the occupation of the battle-ground by a fresh *corps d'armee.*

### THE BATTLE OF MALVERN HILL.

Early on Tuesday morning, the enemy, from the position to which he had been driven the night before, continued his retreat in a southeasterly direction towards his gunboats in James river.

General Magruder was directed to proceed by the Quaker road, and to form on the right of Jackson. On account of a misunderstanding as to which was the Quaker road, the wrong route was taken by General Magruder; and the direction of his movement was subsequently changed, so as to place his troops on the right of Huger, who, in the meantime, had formed on the right of Jackson.

The enemy had now placed himself in communication with his gunboats in the river. He was strongly posted on the crest of a hill, commanding an undulating field, which fell to our right into a plain or meadow. His batteries of artillery were numerous, and were collected into two large bodies, strongly supported by infantry, and commanded perfectly the meadow on our right and the field in our front, except the open ravines formed by the undulations of the ground.

An order was dispatched by General Magruder to bring up from all the batteries thirty rifle pieces, if possible, with which he hoped to shatter the enemy's infantry. While delay was thus occasioned, he was ordered to make the attack. Returning rapidly to the position occupied by the main body of his troops, he gave Brigadier General Jones the necessary orders for the advance of his division. While this was being done, a heavy and crushing fire was opened from the enemy's guns, of great range and metal.

General Armistead having repulsed, driven back and followed up a heavy body of the enemy's skirmishers, an order was received from General Lee by Magruder, directing him "to advance rapidly, press forward his whole line, and follow up Armistead's successes, as the enemy were reported to be getting off." In the meantime Mahone's and Ransom's brigades of Huger's division having been ordered up, General Magruder gave the order that Wright's brigade, supported by Mahone's, should advance and attack the enemy's batteries on the right, and that Jones' division, expected momentarily, should advance on the front, and Ransom's brigade should attack on the left. The plan of attack was to hurl about fifteen thousand men against the enemy's batteries and supporting infantry—to follow up any successes they might obtain; and if unable to drive the enemy from his strong position, to continue the fight in front by pouring in fresh troops; and in case they were repulsed, to hold strongly the line of battle where we stood.

At about 5 o'clock P. M., the order was given to our men to charge across the field and drive the enemy from their position. Gallantly they sprang to the encounter, rushing into the field at a full run. Instantly, from the line of the enemy's breastworks, a murderous storm of grape and canister was hurled into their ranks, with the most terrible effect. Officers and men went down by hundreds; but yet, undaunted and unwavering, our line dashed on, until two-thirds of the distance across the field was accomplished. Here the carnage from the withering fire of the enemy's combined artillery and musketry was dreadful. Our line wavered a moment, and fell back to the cover of the woods. Twice again the effort to carry the position was renewed, but each time with the same result.

The hill was bathed with flames. Towards sunset the earth quivered with the terrific concussion of artillery and huge explosions. Shells raced athwart the horizon, exploding into deadly iron hail. The forms of smoke-masked men; the gleam of muskets on the plains, where soldiers were disengaged; the artistic order of battle; the wild career of wilder horsemen plunging to and fro across the field, formed a scene of exciting grandeur. In the forest, where eyes did not penetrate, there was nothing but the exhilarating and exhausting spasm of battle.

As the night fell, the battle slackened. We had not carried the enemy's position, but we occupied the field, and during the night posted our pickets within one hundred yards of his guns. The brigades of Mahone and Wright slept on the battle-field in the advanced positions they had won, and Armistead's brigade and a portion of Ransom's also occupied the battle-field.

The battle of Tuesday, properly known as that of Malvern Hill, was perhaps the most sanguinary of the series of bloody conflicts which had taken place on the lines about Richmond. Although not a defeat, it broke the chain of our victories. It was made memorable by its melancholy monument of carnage, which was probably greater than General Magruder's estimate, which states that our loss fell short of three thousand. But it had given the enemy no advantage, except in the unfruitful sacrifice of the lives of our troops; and the line of his retreat was again taken up, his forces toiling towards the river through mud, swamp and forest.

The skill and spirit with which McClellan had managed to retreat was, indeed, remarkable, and afforded no mean proofs of his generalship. At every stage of his retreat he had confronted our forces with a strong rear guard, and had encountered us with well organized lines of battle, and regular dispositions of infantry, cavalry and artillery. His heavy rifled cannon had been used against us constantly on his retreat. A portion of his forces had now effected communication with the river at points below City Point. The plan of cutting off his communication with the river, which was to have been executed by a movement of Holmes' division between him and the river, was frustrated by the severe fire of the gun-boats, and since then the situation of the enemy appeared to be that of a division or dispersion of his forces, one portion resting on the river, and the other, to some extent, involved by our lines.

It had been stated to the public of Richmond, with great precision of detail, that on the evening of Saturday, the 28th of June, we had brought the enemy to bay on the south side of the Chickahominy, and that it only remained to finish him in a single battle. Such, in fact, appeared to have been the situation then. The next morning, however, it was perceived that our supposed resources of generalship had given us too much confidence; that the enemy had managed to extricate himself from the critical position, and, having massed his forces, had succeeded, under cover of the night, in opening a way to the James river.*

Upon this untoward event, the operations of our army on the Richmond side of the Chickahominy were to follow the fugitive enemy through a country where he had admirable opportunities of concealment, and through the swamps and forests of which he had retreated with the most remarkable judgment, dexterity, and spirit of fortitude.

The glory and fruits of our victory may have been seriously diminished by the grave mishap or fault by which the enemy was permitted to leave his camp on the south side of the Chickahominy, in an open country, and to plunge into the dense cover of wood and swamp, where the best portion of a whole week was consumed in hunting him, and finding out his new position only in time to attack him under the uncertainty and disadvantage of the darkness of night.

But the successes achieved in the series of engagements

---

\* With reference to McClellan's escape from White Oak Swamp to the river, letters of Yankee officers, published in the Northern journals, stated that when McClellan on Saturday evening sent his scouts down the road to Turkey Island Bridge, he was astonished and delighted to find that our forces had not occupied that road, and immediately started his wagon and artillery trains, which were quietly passing down that road all night to the James river, whilst our forces were quietly sleeping within four miles of the very road they should have occupied, and should have captured every one of the enemy's one thousand wagons and four hundred cannon. It is further stated in these letters, that if we had blocked up that only passage of escape, their entire army must have surrendered or been starved out in twenty-four hours. These are the Yankees' own accounts of how much they were indebted to blunders on our part for the success of McClellan's retreat—a kind of admission not popular with a vain and self adulatory enemy.

which had already occurred were not to be lightly esteemed, or to be depreciated, because of errours which, if they had not occurred, would have made our victory more glorious and more complete. The siege of Richmond had been raised; an army of one hundred and fifty thousand men had been pushed from their strongholds and fortifications, and put to flight; we had enjoyed the *eclat* of an almost daily succession of victories; we had gathered an immense spoil in stores, provisions and artillery; and we had demoralized and dispersed, if we had not succeeded in annihilating, an army which had every resource that could be summoned to its assistance, every possible addition of numbers within the reach of the Yankee government, and every material condition of success to ensure for it the great prize of the capital of the Confederacy, which was now, as far as human judgment could determine, irretrievably lost to them, and secure in the protection of a victorious army.

The Northern papers claimed that the movements of McClellan from the Chickahominy river were purely strategic, and that he had obtained a position, where he would establish a new base of operations against Richmond. Up to the first decisive stage in the series of engagements—Cold Harbour—there were certainly plain strategic designs in his backward movement. His retirement from Mechanicsville was probably voluntary, and intended to concentrate his troops lower down, where he might fight with the advantages of numbers and his own selection of position. Continuing his retreat, he fixed the decisive field at Cold Harbour. Again having been pushed from his strongholds north of the Chickahominy, the enemy made a strong attempt to retrieve his disasters by renewing a concentration of his troops at Frayser's farm.

From the time of these two principal battles, all pretensions of the enemy's retreat to strategy must cease. His retreat was now unmistakeable; it was no longer a falling back to concentrate troops for action; it is, in fact, impossible to disguise that it was the retreat of an enemy who was discomfited and whipped, although not routed. He had abandoned the railroads; he had given up the strongholds which he had provided to secure him in case of a check; he had destroyed from eight to ten millions dollars' worth of stores; he had deserted his hospitals, his sick and wounded, and he had left in our hands thousands of prisoners and innumerable stragglers.

Regarding all that had been accomplished in these battles; the displays of the valour and devotion of our troops; the expenditure of blood; and the helpless and fugitive condition to which the enemy had at last been reduced, there was cause for the keenest regrets that an enemy in this condition was permitted to secure his retreat. It is undoubtedly true, that in' failing to cut off McClellan's retreat to the river, we failed to accomplish the most important condition for the completion of our victory. But although the result of the conflict had fallen below public expectation, it was sufficiently fortunate to excite popular joy, and grave enough to engage the most serious speculation as to the future.

The mouth of the Yankee Government was shut from any more promises of a speedy termination of the war; the powers of Europe saw that the Southern Confederacy was not yet crushed, or likely to be crushed, by its insolent foe; and the people of the South had again challenged the confidence of the world in the elasticity of their fortunes and the invincible destiny of their independence.

The fortune of events in other parts of the Confederacy, taking place about the time of the relief of Richmond, or closely following it, although less striking and dramatic, was not unpropitious. These events, a rapid survey of which takes us from the seacoast to the Mississippi frontier, added to the exultations which the victories of the Chickahominy had occasioned, and, although qualified by some disasters, enlarged and enlightened the prospects of the future.

A few days before the great battles had been joined around Richmond, a brilliant success over the Yankees had been obtained in an engagement on James Island in the neighborhood of Charleston. The battle of Secessionville, as it was called, occurred on the 16th of June. About four o'clock in the morning of that day, the enemy, taking advantage of the negligence of our pickets, drove them in, or captured them, some eight hundred yards in front of the battery at Secessionville, and, advancing rapidly upon this work in line of battle, arrived within a few hundred yards of it before we could open upon him. The men, however, were at their guns, which were at once well and rapidly served, while the infantry was moved promptly into position under the orders of Col. J. G. Lamar, the heroic commander of the post. It was not long after getting the infantry into position that the enemy were driven back in confusion. They were soon, however, reinforced, and made another desperate charge, when they were again driven back; a third time they came, but only to meet with the most determined repulse. They then made a flank movement on our right, on the west of Secessionville, where they were gallantly met by the Charleston battalion, which was soon reinforced by the Louisiana battalion. Three times had the heroic band of Confederates repulsed (often at the point of the bayonet) a force thrice their strength, under the fire of three gunboats and four land batteries. About ten o'clock the enemy retreated in great confusion, leaving their dead and wounded on the field, a number lying in our trenches. The loss of the enemy was at least four hundred in killed, wounded and prisoners. Their dead in front of the Secessionville works numbered one hundred and sixty-eight. Our loss was forty killed and about twice that number wounded.

In the situation in the West some important changes had transpired in the early months of the summer.

The evacuation of Corinth was determined upon by General Beauregard, after having twice offered the enemy battle outside of his entrenched lines, and was accomplished on the 30th of May. The transparent object of the Yankee commander was to cut off our resources by destroying the Mobile and Ohio and Memphis and Charleston Railroads. This was substantially foiled by the evacuation and withdrawal of our forces along the line of the former road. Remaining in rear of the Tuscumbia and its affluents, some six miles from Corinth, long enough to collect stragglers, General Beauregard resumed his march, concentrating his main forces at Baldwin. On the 7th of June he left Baldwin, it offering no advantages of a defensive character, and assembled the main body of his forces at Tupelo.

On the morning of the evacuation of Corinth, our effective force did not exceed forty-seven thousand men of all arms; that of the enemy, obtained from the best sources of information, could not have been less than ninety thousand men of all arms. The story of the evacuation was flourished by the Yankees as a great success on their side, and coupled with an audacious falsehood reported by Gen. Pope to Gen. Halleck, then in command of the enemy's forces in the West, to the effect that he had taken ten thousand prisoners and fifteen thousand stand of arms. The facts are, that the retreat was conducted with great order and precision; and that, despite the boasts of the North to the contrary, we lost no more prisoners than the enemy did himself, and abandoned to him in stores not more than would amount to one day's expense of our army.

The capture of Memphis was another step towards the realization of the enemy's great object of opening the navigation of the Mississippi, which was persistently demanded by the Northwestern States as the price of their contributions to the war and their support of the administration at Washington.*

* This city had been formally surrendered to the Yankees after

---

\* The Board of Trade, of St. Louis, published a paper on this subject, which assumed the ground that the object of the Confederacy was to hold the entire and exclusive control of the Mississippi. It went into detail to show how great the loss of the present obstruction of that highway was to the "loyal" Western States. It was the natural outlet to the produce of the Upper Valley. During the year 1860 the shipments from Cairo and points above the Mississippi and its tributaries, by way of the lower Mississippi, amounted to a million tons, of which 400,000 went from St. Louis. It averred that the difference in cost of freight by the river and the railroad was ten dollars a ton; also, that this, with the return freight, would amount to a total of $15,000,000 tax on the Western people by reason of the closing of the river.

a naval engagement in front of it on the 6th of June, in which our loss was eighty killed and wounded and seventy-five taken prisoners, and four gunboats sunk.

The occupation of Memphis by the enemy was a serious disaster to the South, although it did not open the Mississippi; for it gave him extraordinary facilities for almost daily reinforcements of men and supplies, and for the preparation of expeditions to penetrate to the heart of the Confederacy.

But the enemy received a check on the Mississippi where he had least expected it. On the 24th of June, his combined fleet retired, and abandoned the siege of Vicksburg, without accomplishing anything, after a siege of six weeks. No injury was sustained by any of the batteries at Vicksburg. The number of shells thrown into the city and at the batteries amounted to 25,000. The casualties in the city were one woman and one negro man killed, and among the soldiers on guard and at the batteries there were twenty-two killed and wounded. The lower bombarding fleet, under command of Coms. Farragut and Porter, consisted of 18 gun and mortar boats, 5 sloops of war and 70 transports; the upper fleet consisted of 11 gunboats and rams, and 13 transports, under command of Com. Davis.

The people of the South found in the defence of Vicksburg a splendid lesson of magnanimity and disinterested patriotism. For several weeks this city had resisted successfully the attack of the enemy's gunboats, mortar fleets and heavy siege guns. She was threatened by powerful fleets above and below, and yet, with unexampled spirit, the Queen City of the Bluffs sustained the iron storm that was rained upon her for weeks with continued fury.

New Orleans, Baton Rouge, Natchez and Memphis were in the hands of the Yankees, and their possession by the enemy might have furnished to Vicksburg, in its exposed and desperate situation, the usual excuses of timidity and selfishness for its surrender. But the brave city resisted these vile and unmanly excuses, and gave to the world one of the proudest and most brilliant illustrations of the earnestness and devotion of the people of the South that had yet adorned the war.

The fact that but little hopes could be entertained of the eventual success of the defence of Vicksburg against the powerful concentration of the enemy's navy, heightened the nobility of the resistance she made. The resistance of the enemy in circumstances which afford but a feeble and uncertain prospect of victory requires a great spirit; but it is more invaluable to us than a hundred easy victories; it teaches the enemy that we are invincible and overcomes him with despair; it exhibits to the world the inspirations and moral grandeur of our cause; and it educates our people in chivalry and warlike virtues by the force of illustrious examples of self-devotion.

But the people of the South had the satisfaction of witnessing an unexpected issue of victory in the siege of Vicksburg, and had occasion to learn another lesson that the history of all wars indicates, that the practical test of resistance affords the only sure determination, whether a place is defensible or not. With a feeling of inexpressible pride did Vicksburg behold two immense fleets, each of which had been heretofore invincible, brought to bay, and, unable to cope with her, kept at a respectful distance, and compelled to essay the extraordinary task of digging a new channel for the Mississippi.

In the month of July occurred the remarkable expedition of the celebrated John Morgan into Kentucky. The expedition of this cavalier was one of the most brilliant, rapid and successful raids recorded in history. Composed of a force less than one thousand, consisting of Morgan's own regiment, with some partisan rangers from Georgia, and a Texas squadron, to which was attached two companies of Tennessee cavalry, it penetrated as far as Cynthianna. It was Morgan's intention to make a stand at Richmond, Kentucky, to await reinforcements, as he was persuaded that nearly the whole people of that State were ready to rise and join him; but finding that the enemy was endeavoring to envelope him with large bodies of cavalry, he was compelled to fall back. On reaching Somerset, he took possession of the telegraph, and very coolly countermanded all the previous orders that had been given by Gen. Boyle at Louisville to pursue him.

He had left Knoxville on the fourth day of July with nine hundred men, and returned to Lexington on the 28th with nearly twelve hundred. In twenty-four days he had penetrated two hundred and fifty miles into a country in full possession of the Yankees; captured seventeen towns; met, fought and captured a Yankee force superiour to his own in numbers; captured three thousand stand of arms at Lebanon; and, from first to last, destroyed during his raid military stores, railroad bridges and other property to the value of eight or ten millions of dollars. He accomplished all this, besides putting the people of Cincinnati into a condition, described by one of their newspapers, as "bordering on frenzy," and returned to Tennessee with a loss in all his engagements of not more than ninety men in killed, wounded and missing.

While some activity was shown in extreme portions of the West, we shall see that our military operations from Greenbrier county, Virginia, all the way down to Chattanooga, Tennessee, were conducted with but little vigour. On the boundaries of East Tennessee, Southwestern Virginia and Kentucky, we had a force in the aggregate of thirty thousand men confronted by probably not half their number of Yankee troops; yet the Southwestern counties of Virginia and the Valley of the Clinch, in Tennessee, were entered and mercilessly plundered by the enemy in the face of our troops.

But we shall have occasion to notice the campaign in the West on a broader arena. We shall see how movements in this direction pressed back the discouraged and retreating foe. We shall see how these movements of the Confederates were intended to repossess the country previously occupied by them and to go forward to the redemption of the State of Kentucky, and the attack of one or more of the leading cities of the West; how, in the prosecution of this plan, North Alabama and Mississippi were speedily cleared of the footsteps of the foe; how all of Tennessee, save the strongholds of Memphis and Nashville, and the narrow districts commanded by them, were retrieved, and by converging armies, nearly the whole of Kentucky was occupied and held—and how, at last, all these achievements were reversed in a night's time, and the most valuable and critical points abandoned by our troops, or rather by the will of the unfortunate general who led them.

But our narrative does not yet open on the chequered page of the West. That important part of our history is prefaced by the brilliant story of the summer campaign of the upper Potomac, and is relieved by dazzling lights of glory on the old battle-grounds of Virginia.

## CHAPTER III.

Effect of McClellan's Defeat in the North...Call for more Troops...Why the North was not Easily Dispirited...The War as a Money Job...*Note:* General Washington's Opinion of New England...The Yankee Finances...Exasperation of Hostilities...The Yankee Idea of a "Vigourous Prosecution of the War"... Ascendancy of the Radicals...War Measures at Washington...Anti-Slavery Aspects of the War...Brutality of the Yankees...The Insensibility of Europe... Yankee Chaplains in Virginia...Seizures of Private Property...Pope's Orders in Virginia...Steinwehr's Order Respecting Hostages...The Character and Services of General John Pope...The "Army of Virginia"...Irruption of the Northern Spoilsmen...The Yankee Trade in Counterfeit Confederate Notes... Pope's "Chasing the Rebel Hordes"...Movement Against Pope by "Stonewall" Jackson...BATTLE OF CEDAR MOUNTAIN...McClellan Recalled from the Peninsula...The Third Grand Army of the North...Jackson's Surprise of the Enemy at Manassas...A Rapid and Masterly Movement...Change of the Situation...Attack by the Enemy upon Bristow Station and at Manassas Junction...Marshalling of the Hosts...Longstreet's Passage of Thoroughfare Gap... The Plans of General Lee...Spirit of our Troops...Their Painful Marches... THE SECOND BATTLE OF MANASSAS...A Terrible Bayonet Charge—Rout of the Enemy...A Hideous Battle-Field...General Lee and the Summer Campaign of Virginia...Jackson's Share in it...Extent of the Great Victory of Manassas... Excitement in Washington...The Yankee Army Falls Back Upon Alexandria and Washington...Review of the Situation...Rapid Change in our Military Fortunes...What the South had Accomplished...Comparison of Material Strength Between North and South...Humiliating Result to the Warlike Reputation of the North.

The effect of the defeat of McClellan before Richmond was received at the North with ill-concealed mortification and anxiety. Beneath the bluster of the newspapers, and the affectations of public confidence, disappointment, embarrassment and alarm were perceptible. The people of the North had been so assured of the capture of Richmond, that it was difficult to re-animate them on the heels of McClellan's retreat. The prospects held out to them so long, of ending the war in "sixty days," "crushing out the rebellion," and eating victorious dinners in Richmond, had been bitterly disappointed and were not to be easily renewed. The government at Washington showed its appreciation of the disaster its arms had sustained by making a call for three hundred thousand additional troops; and the people of the North were urged by every variety of appeal, including large bounties of money, to respond to the stirring call of President Lincoln.*

There is no doubt but that the North was seriously discouraged by the events that had taken place before Richmond. But it was a remarkable circumstance, uniformly illustrated in the war, that the North, though easily intoxicated by triumph, was not in the same proportion depressed by defeat. There is an obvious explanation for this peculiarity of temper. As long as the North was conducting the war upon the soil of the South, a defeat there involved more money expenditure and more calls for troops; it involved scarcely anything else; it had no other horrors, it did not imperil their homes; it might easily be repaired by time. Indeed, there was some sense in the exhortation of some of the Northern orators, to the effect that defeat made their people stronger than ever, because, while it required them to put forth their energies anew, it enabled them

---

* The Army *Register*, published at Washington, in its statement of the organization of the *regular* army, enumerates as its force six regiments of cavalry, five of artillery, ten of infantry, (old army), and nine of infantry, (new army.)

The strength of this branch of the service in men, may be thus stated:

| | |
|---|---|
| Total commissioned officers, | 2,388 |
| Total enlisted, | 40,626 |
| Aggregate, | 43,014 |

The figures which are collected below to show the organization of the *volunteer* army of the North, refer to the date of the *Register*, August 1, 1862.

It appears that at this date there were in the volunteer army of the North seventy regiments of cavalry, seventy of artillery, and eight hundred and sixty regiments of infantry.

These startling official figures give the following result:

| | |
|---|---|
| Total commissioned officers, | 39,922 |
| Total rank and file, | 1,052,480 |
| Aggregate, | 1,092,401 |

to take advantage of experience, to multiply their means of success, and to essay new plans of campaign. No one can doubt but that the celebrated Manassas defeat really strengthened the North; and doubtless the South would have realized the same consequence of the second repulse of the enemy's movements on Richmond, if it had been attended by the same conditions on our part of inaction and repose.

It is curious to observe how completely the ordinary aspects of war were changed and its horrours diminished, with reference to the North, by the false policy of the South, in keeping the theatre of active hostilities within her own borders. Defeat did not dispirit the North, because it was not brought to her doors. Where it did not immediately imperil the safety of the country and homes of the Yankees, where it gave time for the recovery and re-organization of the attacking party, and where it required for the prosecution of the war nothing but more money jobs in Congress and a new raking up of the scum of the cities, the effects of defeat upon the North might well be calculated to be the exasperation of its passions, the inflammation of its cupidity, and the multiplication of its exertions to break and overcome the misapplied power of our armies.

Indeed, the realization of the war in the North was, in many respects, nothing more than that of an immense money job. The large money expenditure at Washington supplied a vast fund of corruption; it enriched the commercial centres of the North, and by artificial stimulation preserved such cities as New York from decay; it interested vast numbers of politicians, contractors and dissolute public men in continuing the war and enlarging the scale of its operations; and, indeed, the disposition to make money out of the war accounts for much of that zeal in the North, which was mistaken for political ardour or the temper of patriotic devotion.*

---

* The following is an extract from an unpublished letter from Gen. Washington to Richard Henry Lee, and, as an exposition of the character of the Northern people from a pen sacred to posterity, is deeply interesting. There can be no doubt of the authenticity of the letter. It has been preserved in

But while politicians plundered the government at Washington and contractors grew rich in a single day and a fictitious

---

the Lee family, who, though applied to by Bancroft, Irving and others for a copy for publication, have hitherto refused it, on the ground that it would be improper to give to the world a private letter from the Father of his Country reflecting upon any portion of it while the Union endured. But now, that "these people" have trampled the Constitution under foot, destroyed the government of our fathers, and invaded and desolated Washington's own county in Virginia, there can be no impropriety in showing his private opinion of the Massachusetts Yankees:

[Copy.]

CAMP AT CAMBRIDGE, Aug. 29, 1775.

*Dear Sir:* * * *

As we have now nearly completed our lines of defence, we have nothing more, in my opinion, to fear from the enemy, provided we can keep our men to their duty, and make them watchful and vigilant; but it is among the most difficult tasks I ever undertook in my life, to induce these people to believe that there is or can be danger, till the bayonet is pushed at their breasts; not that it proceeds from any uncommon prowess, but rather from an unaccountable kind of stupidity in the lower class of these people, which, believe me, prevails but too generally among the officers of the Massachusetts part of the army, who are nearly of the same kidney with the private, and adds not a little to my difficulties, as there is no such thing as getting officers of this stamp to exert themselves in carrying orders into execution. To curry favour with the men (by whom they were chosen and on whose smiles possibly they may think they may again rely) seems to be one of the principal objects of their attention. I submit it, therefore, to your consideration, whether there is, or is not, a propriety in that resolution of the Congress which leaves the ultimate appointment of all officers below the rank of general to the governments where the regiments originated, now the army is become Continental? To me, it appears improper in two points of view—first, it is giving that power and weight to an individual Colony which ought of right to belong to the whole. Then it damps the spirit and ardour of volunteers from all but the four New England Governments, as none but their people have the least chance of getting into office. Would it not be better, therefore, to have the warrants, which the Commander-in-Chief is authorized to give *pro tempore*, approved or disapproved by the Continental Congress, or a committee of their body, which I should suppose in any long recess must always sit? In this case, every gentleman will stand an equal chance of being promoted, according to his merit: in the other, all offices will be confined to the inhabitants of the four New England Governments, which, in my opinion, is impolitic to a degree. I have made a pretty good slam among such kind of officers as the Massachusetts Government abounds in since I came to this camp, having broken one colonel and two captains for cowardly behaviour in the action on Bunker's Hill, two captains for drawing more provisions and pay than they

prosperity. dazzled the eyes of the observer in the cities of the North, the public finances of the Yankee government had long ago become desperate. It is interesting at this point to make a brief summary of the financial condition of the North by a comparison of its public debt with the assets of the government.

The debt of the present United States, audited and floating, calculated from data up to June 30, 1862, was at least $1,300,000,000. The daily expenses, as admitted by the Chairman of the Committee of Ways and Means, was between three and four millions of dollars; the debt, in one year from this time, could not be less than two thousand five hundred millions of dollars.

Under the census of 1860, all the property of every kind in all the States was estimated at less than $12,500,000,000. Since the war commenced, the depreciation has been at least one-fourth—$3,175,000,000. From $9,375,000,000 deduct the property in the seceded States, at least one-third—$3,125,000,000;—leaving, in the present United States, $6,250,000,000.

It will thus be seen, that the present debt of the North was one-fifth of all the property of every kind it possesses; and in

had men in their company, and one for being absent from his post when the enemy appeared there and burnt a house just by it. Besides these, I have at this time one colonel, one major, one captain and two subalterns under arrest for trial. In short, I spare none, and yet fear it will not all do, as these people seem to be too inattentive to everything but their *interest*.

\* \* \* \* \* \* \* \* \*

There have been so many great and capital errours and abuses to rectify—so many examples to make, and so little inclination in the officers of inferiour rank to contribute their aid to accomplish this work, that my life has been nothing else (since I came here) but one continual round of vexation and fatigue. In short, no pecuniary recompense could induce me to undergo what I have; especially, as I expect, by showing so little countenance to irregularities and public abuses as to render myself very obnoxious to a great part of these people. But as I have already greatly exceeded the bounds of a letter, I will not trouble you with matters relative to my own feelings.

Your affectionate friend and obedient servant,

(Signed) GEO. WASHINGTON.

*Richard Henry Lee, Esq.*

one year more it would probably be more than one-third. No people on earth had ever been plunged in so large a debt in so short a time. No government in existence had so large a debt in proportion to the amount of property held by its people.

In continuing the narrative of the campaign in Virginia, we shall have to observe the remarkable exasperation with which the North re-entered upon this campaign and to notice many deeds of blackness which illustrated the temper in which she determined to prosecute the desperate fortunes of the war. The military authorities of the North seemed to suppose that better success would attend a savage war, in which no quarter was to be given and no age or sex spared, than had hitherto been secured to such hostilities as are alone recognized to be lawful by civilized men in modern times. It is not necessary to comment at length upon this fallacy. Brutality in war was mistaken for vigour. War is not emasculated by the observances of civilization; its vigour and success consist in the resources of generalship, the courage of troops, the moral ardours of its cause. To attempt to make up for deficiency in these great and noble elements of strength by mere brutal severities—such as pillage, assassination, &c.—is absurd; it reduces the idea of war to the standard of the brigand; it offends the moral sentiment of the world, and it excites its enemy to the last stretch of determined and desperate exertion.

There had long been a party in the North who mistook brutality in war for vigour, and clamoured for a policy which was to increase the horrours of hostilities by arming the slaves, and making the invaded country of the South the prey of white brigands and "loyal" negroes. This party was now in the ascendancy. It had already obtained important concessions from the Washington government. Nine-tenths of the legislation of the Yankee Congress had been occupied in some form or other with the question of slavery. Universal emancipation in the South, and the utter overthrow of all property, was now the declared policy of the desperate and demented leaders of the war. The Confiscation Bill, enacted at the close of the session of Congress, confiscated all the slaves belonging to those who were loyal to the South, constituting nine-tenths at least of the slaves in the Confederate States. In the Border States occupied by the North, slavery was plainly doomed under a plan of emancipation proposed by Mr. Lincoln with the flimsy and ridiculous pretence of compensation to slaveholders.*

These concessions to the radical party in the North excited new demands. The rule which was urged upon the government, and which the government hastened to accept, was to spare no means, however brutal, to contest the fortunes of the war, and to adopt every invention of torture for its enemy. The slaves were to be armed and carried in battalions against their masters. The invaded country of the South was to be pillaged, wasted and burnt; the Northern troops, like hungry locusts, were to destroy everything green; the people in the invaded districts were to be laid under contributions, compelled to do the work of slaves, kept in constant terrour of their lives, and fire, famine and slaughter were to be the portion of the conquered.

Before the eyes of Europe the mask of civilization had been taken from the Yankee war; it degenerated into unbridled

---

\* According to the census of 1860—

| | | | | | |
|---|---|---|---|---|---|
| Kentucky had | . | . | . | . | 225,490 slaves. |
| Maryland, | . | .˙ | . | .˙ | 87,188 " |
| Virginia, | . | . | . | . | 490,887 " |
| Delaware, | . | . | . | . | 1,798 " |
| Missouri, | . | . | . | .˙ | 114,965 " |
| Tennessee, | . | . | . | . | 275,784 " |
| | | Making in the whole, | | 1,196,112 " | |

At the proposed rate of valuation, these would amount to $358,833,600
Add for deportation and colonization $100 each, 119,244,568

And we have the enormous sum of $478,078,133-

It is scarcely to be supposed that a proposition could be made in good faith, or that in any event the proposition could be otherwise than worthless, to add this vast amount to the public debt of the North at a moment when the treasury was reeling under the enormous expenditures of the war.

butchery and robbery. But the nations of Europe, which boasted themselves as humane and civilized, had yet no interference to offer in a war which shocked the senses and appealed to the common offices of humanity. It is to be observed, that during the entire continuance of the war up to this time, the British government had acted with reference to it in a spirit of selfish and inhuman calculation; and there is, indeed, but little doubt that an early recognition of the Confederacy by France was thwarted by the interference of that cold and sinister government, that ever pursues its ends by indirection and perfects its hypocrisy under the specious cloak of extreme conscientiousness. No greater delusion could have possessed the people of the South than that the *government* of England was friendly to them. That government, which prided itself on its cold and ingenious selfishness, seemed to have discovered a much larger source of profit in the continuation of the American war than it could possibly derive from a pacification of the contest. It was willing to see its operatives starving and to endure the distress of a "cotton famine," that it might have the ultimate satisfaction, which it anticipated, of seeing both parties in the American war brought to the point of exhaustion, and its own greatness enlarged on the ruins of a hated commercial rival. The calculation was far-reaching; it was characteristic of a government that secretly laughed at all sentiment, made an exact science of selfishness, and scorned the weakness that would sacrifice for any present good the larger fruits of the future.

This malevolent and venomous spirit of anti-slavery in the war pervaded the whole of Northern society. It was not only the utterance of such mobs as, in New York city, adopted as their war cry against the South, "*kill all the inhabitants;*" it found expression in the political measures, military orders and laws of the government; it invaded polite society, and was taught not only as an element of patriotism, but as a virtue of religion. The characteristic religion of New England, composed of about equal quantities of blasphemy and balderdash, went hand in hand with the war. Some of these pious demonstrations were curious, and bring to remembrance the fanaticism and rhapsodies of the old Puritans.*

The Yankee army chaplains in Virginia alternately disgusted and amused the country with the ferocious rant with which they sought to inspire the crusade against the South. One of these pious missionaries in Winchester, after the regular Sunday service, announced to the assembled Yankee troops an imaginary victory in front of Richmond, and then called for "three cheers and a tiger and Yankee Doodle." In a sermon preached near the enemy's camp of occupation, the chaplain proclaimed the mission of freeing the negroes. He told them they were free, and that, as the property amassed by their masters was the fruit of the labours of the blacks, these had the best title to it and should help themselves. At another place near the scene of the execution of John Brown for violation of law, sedition and murder, a sermon was preached by an army chaplain on some text enjoining "the mission of proclaiming liberty;" and the hymn given out and sung was—

"John Brown's body hangs dangling in the air,
Sing glory, glory, hallelujah!"

---

* No one affected the peculiarity of the Puritans more than Gov. Andrews, of Massachusetts. The following pious rant is quoted from one of his speeches at Worcester; in blasphemy and bombast it equals any of the fulminations of the "Pilgrim Fathers"—

"I know that the angel of the Lord, one foot on the earth and one on the sea, will proclaim in unanswerable language, that four millions of bondmen shall ere long be slaves no longer. We live in a war, not a riot; as we thought last year, with a half million in the field against an atrocious and rebellious foe. Our government now recognizes it as a war, and the President of the United States, fulminating his war orders, has blown a blast before which the enemy must fly. Rebellion must fall, and they who have stood upon the necks of so many bondsmen shall be swept away and four million souls rise to immortality.

"Ah, foul tyrants! do you hear him where he comes?
Ah, black traitors! do you know him as he comes?
In the thunder of the cannon and the roll of the drums,
As we go marching on.

"Men may die and moulder in the dust—
Men may die and arise again from the dust,
Shoulder to shoulder, in the ranks of the just,
When God is marching on.

These, however, were but indications displayed of a spirit in the North, which, with reference to the practical conduct of the war, were serious enough.

By a general order of the Washington Government, the military commanders of that government, within the States of Virginia, South Carolina, Georgia, Florida, Alabama, Mississippi, Louisiana, Texas and Arkansas, were directed to seize and use any property, real or personal, belonging to the inhabitants of this Confederacy which might be necessary or convenient for their several commands, and no provision was made for any compensation to the owners of private property thus seized and appropriated by the military commanders of the enemy.

But it was reserved for the enemy's army in Northern Virginia to exceed all that had hitherto been known of the savage cruelty of the Yankees, and to convert the hostilities hitherto waged against armed forces into a campaign of robbery and murder against unarmed citizens and peaceful tillers of the soil.

On the 23d of July, 1862, General Pope, commanding the forces of the enemy in Northern Virginia, published an order requiring that "all commanders of any army corps, divisions, brigades, and detached commands, will proceed immediately to arrest all disloyal male citizens within their lines, or within their reach, in rear of their respective commands. Such as are willing to take the oath of allegiance to the United States, and will furnish sufficient security for its observance,' shall be permitted to remain at their homes and pursue in good faith their accustomed avocations. Those who refuse shall be conducted South, beyond the extreme pickets of this army, and be notified that, if found again anywhere within our lines, or at any point in rear, they shall be considered spies and subjected to the extreme rigour of military law. If any person, having taken the oath of allegiance as above specified, be found to have violated it, he shall be shot, and his property seized and applied to the public use."

By another order of Brigadier-General Steinwehr, in Pope's command, it was proposed to hold under arrest the most prominent citizens in the districts occupied by the enemy, as hostages, to suffer death in case of any of the Yankee soldiers being shot by "bushwhackers," by which term was meant the citizens of the South who had taken up arms to defend their homes and families.

The Washington Government had found a convenient instrument for the work of villainy and brutality with which it proposed to resume the active campaign in Virginia.

With a view to renewed operations against Richmond, large forces of Yankee troops were massed at Warrenton, Little Washington and Fredericksburg. Of these forces, entitled the "Army of Virginia," the command was given to Major-General John Pope, who boasted that he had come from the West where "he had only seen the *backs* of the enemy."

This notorious Yankee commander was a man nearly forty years of age, a native of Kentucky, but a citizen of Illinois. He was born of respectable parents. He was graduated at West Point in 1842, and served in the Mexican War, where he was breveted Captain.

In 1849 he conducted the Minnesota exploring expedition, and afterwards acted as topographical engineer in New Mexico, until 1853, when he was assigned to the command of one of the expeditions to survey the route of the Pacific railroad. He distinguished himself on the overland route to the Pacific by "sinking" artesian wells and government money to the amount of a million of dollars. One well was finally abandoned incomplete, and afterwards a perennial spring was found by other parties in the immediate vicinity. In a letter to Jefferson Davis, then Secretary of War, urging this route to the Pacific, and the boring these wells, Pope made himself the *especial champion of the South.*

In the breaking out of the war, Pope was made a Brigadier-General of Volunteers. He held a command in Missouri for some time before he became particularly noted. When Gen.

Halleck took charge of the disorganized department, Pope was placed in command of the District of Central Missouri. He was afterwards sent to Southeastern Missouri. The cruel disposition of the man, of which his rude manners, and a vulgar bearded face, with coarse skin, gave indications, found an abundant field for gratification in this unhappy State. His proceedings in Missouri will challenge a comparison with the most infernal record ever bequeathed by the licensed murderer to the abhorrence of mankind. And yet, it was his first step in blood—the first opportunity he had ever had to feast his eyes upon slaughter and regale his ears with the cries of human agony.

Having been promoted to the rank of Major-General, Pope was next appointed to act at the head of a corps to co-operate with Halleck in the reduction of Corinth. After the evacuation of Corinth by Gen. Beauregard, Pope was sent by Halleck to annoy the rear of the Confederate army, but Beauregard turned upon, and repulsed his pursuit. The report of Pope to Halleck, that he had captured 10,000 of Beauregard's army, and 15,000 stand of arms, when he had not taken a man or a musket, stands alone in the history of lying. It left him without a rival in that respectable art.

Such was the man who took command of the enemy's forces in Northern Virginia. His bluster was as excessive as his accomplishments in falsehood. He was described in a Southern newspaper as "a Yankee compound of Bobadil and Munchausen." His proclamation, that he had seen nothing of his enemies "but their backs," revived an ugly story in his private life, and gave occasion to the witty interrogatory, if the gentleman who cowhided him for offering an indignity to a lady was standing with his back to him when he inflicted the chastisement. The fact was that Pope had won his baton of marshal by bragging to the Yankee fill. He was another instance, besides that of Butler, how easily a military reputation might be made in the North by bluster, lying, and acts of coarse cruelty to the defenceless. On what monstrous principles he commenced his career in Virginia, and what orders he issued, are still fresh in the public memory.

"I desire you to dismiss from your minds certain phrases, (said Pope to his army,) which I am sorry to find much in vogue among you. I hear constantly of taking strong positions and holding them; of lines of retreat and bases of supplies. Let us discard such ideas. The strongest position a soldier should desire to occupy is the one from which he can most easily advance upon the enemy. Let us study the probable line of retreat of our opponents, and leave our own to take care of itself. Let us look before and not behind. Disaster and shame lurk in the rear."

On establishing his headquarters at Little Washington, the county seat of Rappahannock, Pope became a source of mingled curiosity and dread to the feeble villagers. They were in a condition of alarm and anguish from the publication of his order, to banish from their homes all males who should refuse to take the Yankee oath of allegiance. Dr. Bisphaw of the village was deputed to wait upon the Yankee tyrant, and ask that the barbarous order be relaxed.

He painted, at the same time, the agony of the women and children, and stated that the effect would be to place six new regiments in the rebel service. "We can't take the oath of allegiance," said the Doctor, "and we won't—man, woman or child—but we will give a parole to attend to our own business, afford no communication with the South, and quietly stay upon our premises."

"I shall enforce the order to the letter," said General Pope. "I did not make it without deliberation, and if you don't take the oath you shall go out of my lines."

In the short period in which Pope's army was uninterrupted in its career of robbery and villainy in Northern Virginia, every district of country invaded by him or entered by his marauders was ravaged as by a horde of barbarians. This portion of Virginia will long bear the record and tradition of the irruption of the Northern spoilsmen. The new usage which had been instituted in regard to protection of Confederate property, and the purpose of the Washington government to subsist its troops upon the invaded country, converted the "Army of Virginia" into licensed brigands and let loose upon the country a torrent of unbridled and unscrupulous robbers. The Yankee troops appropriated remorselessly whatever came within their reach. They rushed in crowds upon the smoke-houses of the farmers. On the march through a section of country, every spring-house was broken open; butter, milk, eggs and cream were engulphed; calves and sheep, and, in fact, anything and everything serviceable for meat, or drink, or apparel, were not safe a moment after the approach of the Yankee plunderers. Wherever they camped at night, it would be found the next morning that scarcely an article, for which the fertility of a soldier could suggest the slightest use, remained to the owner. Pans, kettles, dishcloths, pork, poultry, provisions and everything desirable had disappeared. The place was stript, and without any process of commissary or quartermaster.

Whenever the Yankee soldiers advanced into a new section the floodgates were immediately opened and *fac simile* Confederate notes (this spurious currency being manufactured in Philadelphia and sold by public advertisement for a few cents to Yankee soldiers) were poured out upon the land.* They

---

* The Northern trade in this counterfeit money was open and undisguised; enticing advertisements of its profit were freely made in the Northern journals, and circulars were distributed through the Federal army proposing to supply the troops with "rebel" currency almost at the price of the paper on which the counterfeit was executed. We copy below one of these circulars found on the person of a Yankee prisoner; the curiosity being a court paper in the possession of Mr. Commissioner Watson, of Richmond:

"$20 *Confederate Bond!!* I have this day issued a Fac-simile $20 Confederate Bond — making, in all, fifteen different Fac-simile Rebel Bonds, Notes, Shinplasters and Postage Stamps issued by me the past three months.

Trade supplied at 50 cents per 100, or $4 per 1000. All orders by mail or express promptly executed.

☞ All orders to be sent by mail must be accompanied with 18 cents in postage stamps, in addition to the above price to prepay the postage on each 100 ordered. Address, S. C. UPHAM.

403 Chesnut Street, Philadelphia.

N. B. I shall have a $100 Rebel Note out this week."

were passed indiscriminately upon the unsuspecting inhabitants, poor as well as rich, old and young, male and female. In frequent instances, this outrage was perpetrated in return for kind nursing by poor, aged women.

These spurious notes passed readily, and seemed to be taken gladly for whatever was held for sale. Bank notes and shinplasters were given for change. Horses and other valuable property were often purchased with this bogus currency. A party of Yankee soldiers entered a country store, fortified with exhaustless quantities of Philadelphia Confederate notes, and commenced trade. Forty pounds of sugar was first ordered, and the storekeeper, pleased with the sudden increase of business, called in his wife to assist in putting up the order in small parcels. Seventy-five cents a pound was the cost. That was a small matter. Matches were purchased. Twenty-five cents per box was the charge. Tobacco also found a ready market. Each man provided himself with a straw hat; but the crowning act of all was the abstraction from the till of money already paid to the dealer for his goods, and the purchase of more goods with the same spurious medium.

Such acts of villainy and the daily robberies committed by Pope's soldiers were very amusing to the Northern people, and gave them a stock of capital jokes. "I not long ago saw," wrote a correspondent of a Yankee newspaper, "a dozen soldiers rushing headlong through a field, each anxious to get the first choice of three horses shading themselves quietly under a tree. The animals made their best time into the farthest corner of the field with the men close upon them, and the foremost men caught their prizes and bridled them as if they had a perfect immunity in such sort of things. A scene followed. A young lady came out and besought the soldiers not to take her favourite pony. The soldiers were remorseless and unyielding, and the pony is now in the army."

It is not within the design of these pages to pursue the stories of outrage, villainy and barbarism of the enemy's armies in Virginia; but with what we have said intended only the spirit of that army and the character of its leader, we shall hasten to describe the series of events which, at last, confronted it with an army of avengers on the historic Plains of Manassas, and culminated there in a victory, which liberated Virginia from its invaders, broke the "line of the Potomac" from Leesburg to Harper's Ferry, and opened an avenue for the first time into the territory of the North.

### THE BATTLE OF CEDAR MOUNTAIN.

The Northern newspapers declared that Pope was right when he said that he was accustomed to see the backs of his enemy, and were busy in assuring their readers that his only occupation was to chase "the rebel hordes." It was said that he had penetrated as far as Madison Court-house without seeing any enemy. The Southern troops, it was prophesied, would keep on their retreat beyond the Virginia Central railroad. Pope's army was now as far in the interiour, by overland marches, as any of the Yankee troops had ever been. The position of his advance was described as about ten miles east of Port Republic, with an eye on the Shenandoah Valley; and it was boasted that the second Napoleon of the Yankees had already complete possession of the country north of the Rapidan river, and only awaited his leisure to march upon Richmond.

These exultations were destined to a sharp and early disappointment. The Confederate authorities in Richmond knew that it was necessary to strike somewhere before the three hundred thousand recruits called for by the Washington government should be brought to the field to overwhelm them. It was necessary to retain in the strong works around Richmond a sufficient force to repulse any attack of McClellan's army; but at the same time the necessity was clear to hold Pope's forces in check and to make an active movement against him. The execution of this latter purpose was entrusted to

Jackson, the brave, eccentric and beloved commander,* who had achieved so many victories against so many extraordinary odds and obstacles; all the movements of the campaign being directed by the self-possessed, controlling and earnest mind of General Lee.

The insolent enemy received his first lesson at the hands of the heroic Jackson on the wooded sides and cleared slopes of the mountainous country in Culpeper. In consequence of the advance of the Confederates beyond the Rapidan, Major-General Pope had sent forward two army corps, commanded by General Banks, to hold them in check.

On the evening of the 8th of August, a portion of General Jackson's division, consisting of the 1st, 2d and 3d brigades, under the command of Gen. Charles S. Winder, crossed the Rapidan river, a few miles above the railroad, and, having advanced a mile into Culpeper county, encamped for the night. The next morning, the enemy being reported as advancing, our forces, Ewell's division being in advance, moved forward on the main road from Orange Court-house to Culpeper Courthouse, about three miles, and took position—our left flank resting on the Southwest Mountain and our artillery occupying several commanding positions. At 12 M., our forces commenced cannonading, which was freely responded to by the

---

* There have been a great many pen and ink portraits of the famous "Stonewall" Jackson; the singular features and eccentric manners of this popular hero affording a fruitful subject of description and anecdote. A gentleman, who was known to be a rare and quick judge of character, was asked by the writer for a description of Jackson, whom he had met but for a few moments on the battle-field. "He is a fighting man," was the reply; "rough mouth, iron jaw, and nostrils big as a horse's." This description has doubtless much force in it, although blunt and homely in its expression. The impression given by Jackson is that of a man perhaps forty years old, six feet high, medium size, and somewhat angular in person. He has yellowish-grey eyes, a Roman nose, sharp; a thin, forward chin, angular brow, a closed mouth, and light brown hair. The expression of his face is to some extent unhappy, but not sullen or unsocial. He is impulsive, silent and emphatic. His dress is official, but very plain, his cap-front resting nearly on his nose. His tall horse diminished the effect of his size, so that when mounted he appears less in person than he really is.

enemy, who did not seem ready for the engagement, which they had affected to challenge. Indeed, some strategy seemed necessary to bring them to fight. About 3 P. M., Gen. Early's brigade (Ewell's division) made a circuit through the woods, attacking the enemy on their right flank, the 13th Virginia regiment being in the advance as skirmishers. At 4 o'clock the firing began, and soon the fight became general. As Gen. Jackson's division, then commanded by Gen. Winder, were rapidly proceeding to the scene of action, the enemy, guided by the dust made by the artillery, shelled the road with great precision. It was by this shell that the brave Winder was killed. His left arm shattered and his side also wounded, he survived but an hour. At a still later period, a portion of Gen. A. P. Hill's division were engaged. The battle was mainly fought in a large field near Mrs. Crittenden's house, a portion being open, and the side occupied by the Yankees being covered with luxuriant corn. Through this corn, when our forces were considerably scattered, two Yankee cavalry regiments made a desperate charge, evidently expecting utterly to disorganize our lines. The result was precisely the reverse. Our men rallied, ceased to fire on the infantry, and, concentrating their attention on the cavalry, poured into their ranks a fire which emptied many a saddle, and caused the foe to wheel and retire, which, however, they effected without breaking their columns. For some time the tide of victory ebbed and flowed, but about dark the foe finally broke and retreated in confusion to the woods, leaving their dead and many of their wounded, with a large quantity of arms and ammunition upon the field. Daylight faded and the moon in her full glory appeared, just as the terrours of the raging battle gave way to the sickening scenes of a field where a victory had been won.

The battle of Cedar Mountain, as it was entitled, may be characterized as one of the most rapid and severe engagements of the war. In every particular it was a sanguinary and desperate struggle, and resulted in a complete and decisive victory for our arms. Our forces engaged amounted to about eight thousand, whilst those of the enemy could not have been less than fifteen thousand. Our loss was near six hundred killed, wounded and missing; that of the enemy little, if any, less than two thousand. We captured nearly five hundred prisoners, over fifteen hundred stand of arms, two splendid Napoleon guns, twelve wagon loads of ammunition, several wagon loads of new and excellent clothing, and drove the enemy two miles beyond the field of battle, which we held for two days and nights.

The battle was remarkable for an extraordinary and terrific "artillery duel." In fact, the fire was conducted with artillery alone for more than three hours. The opposing batteries unlimbered so close to each other that, during the greater part of the firing, they used grape and canister. Those working our battery could distinctly hear the hum of voices of the infantry support of the Federal battery. The Louisiana Guard artillery and the Purcell battery were ordered to take position and open on the enemy from the crest of a hill. Here they found themselves opposed by five batteries of the enemy within short range. The battle raged fiercely, the enemy firing with great precision. The accuracy of our fire was proved by the fact, that the enemy, though their guns were more than twice as numerous, were compelled to shift the position of their batteries five different times. Once during the fight, the enemy's sharpshooters, under cover of a piece of woods, crept up within a short distance of our batteries and opened on them, but were instantly scattered by a discharge of canister from one of the howitzers.

The battle of Cedar Mountain was the natural preface to that larger and severer contest of arms which was to baptize, for a second time, the field of Manassas with the blood of Southern patriots, and illuminate it with the splendid scenes of a decisive victory. It convinced the North of the necessity of a larger scale of exertion and a concentration of its forces in Virginia to effect its twice-foiled advance upon the capital of the Confederacy. It was decided by the Washington government to recall McClellan's army from the Peninsula, to unite his columns with those of Pope, to include also the forces at Fredericksburg, and, banding these in a third Grand Army more splendid than its predecessors, to make one concentrated endeavour to retrieve its unfortunate summer campaign in Virginia, and plant its banners in the city of Richmond.

Not many days elapsed before the evacuation of Berkeley and Westover, on the James river, was signalled to the authorities of Richmond by the large fleet of transports collected on the James and the Rappahannock. It became necessary to meet the rapid movements of the enemy by new dispositions of our forces; not a day was to be lost; and by the 17th of August, General Lee had assembled in front of Pope a force sufficient to contest his further advance, and to balk his threatened passage of the Rapidan.

After the battle of Cedar Mountain, the forces under Stonewall Jackson withdrew from the vicinity of the Rapidan, and were for some days unheard of, except that a strong force was in the vicinity of Madison Court-house, some twelve miles to the westward, in the direction of Luray and the Shenandoah valley; but it was supposed by the enemy that this was only a wing of the army under Ewell, intended to act as reserves to Jackson's army, and to cover his retreat back to Gordonsville. Not so, however. These forces of Ewell, as afterwards discovered by the Yankees to their great surprise, were the main body of Jackson's army, *en route* for the Shenandoah valley.

It was probably the design of Gen. Lee, with the bulk of the Confederate army, to take the front, left and right, and engage Gen. Pope at or near the Rapidan, while Jackson and Ewell were to cross the Shenandoah river and mountains, cut off his supplies by way of the railroad, and menace his rear. The adventure, on the part of Jackson, was difficult and desperate; it took the risk of any new movements of Pope, by which he (Jackson) himself might be cut off. It was obvious, indeed, that if Pope could reach Gordonsville, he would cut off

Jackson's supplies, but in this direction he was to be confronted by Gen. Lee with the forces withdrawn from Richmond. With the movement of Jackson the object was to keep Pope between the Rapidan and the Rappahannock rivers until Jackson had attained his position at Manassas, or perhaps at Rappahannock bridge; but Pope's retreat to the Rappahannock's north bank frustrated that design, and rendered it necessary for General Lee to follow up his advantage, and, by a system of feints, to take Pope's attention from his rear and divert it to his front.

On Monday, the 28th of August, at daybreak, Gen. Jackson's corps, consisting of General Ewell's division, General Hill's division, and General Jackson's old division, under command of General Taliaferro, and a force of cavalry under General Stuart, marched from Jeffersonton, in Culpeper county, and crossed the Rappahannock eight miles above that place, and marched by Orleans to Salem, in Fauquier. The next day they passed through Thoroughfare Gap, of Bull Run mountains, to Bristow and Manassas Stations, on the Orange and Alexandria railroad, effecting a complete surprise of the enemy, capturing a large number of prisoners, several trains of cars, and immense commissary and quartermaster stores, and several pieces of artillery. The distance marched in these two days was over fifty miles. On Wednesday, Manassas Station was occupied by Jackson's old division, whilst Ewell occupied Bristow, and Hill and Stuart dispersed the force sent from Alexandria to attack what the enemy supposed to be only a cavalry force.

The amount of property which fell into our hands at Manassas was immense—several trains heavily laden with stores, ten first class locomotives, fifty thousand pounds of bacon, one thousand barrels of beef, two thousand barrels of pork, several thousand barrels of flour, and a large quantity of oats and corn. A bakery, which was daily turning out fifteen thousand loaves of bread, was also destroyed. Next to Alexandria, Manassas was probably the largest depot established for the Northern army in Virginia.

The movement of Jackson, which we have briefly sketched, is the chief element of the situation in which the decisive engagements of Manassas were fought. In this connection it must be studied; it was the brilliant strategic preface to the most decisive victory yet achieved on the theatre of the war. The corps of Jackson, having headed off the Federal army under Pope, had now possession of Manassas Plains. It had accomplished its design, which was to force Pope back—deprive him completely of direct communication with Washington or Alexandria, and eventually induce his surrender or annihilation.

The principal and anxious topic in the North was, by what eccentric courses the famous Confederate commander had managed to get around the right wing of Pope's army, when it was supposed—and in fact the hasty exultation had already been caught up in the Yankee newspapers—that it was the "rebel" general who was cut off, and that he would probably make a desperate retreat into the mountains to escape the terrours of Pope. Indeed, it was some time before the full and critical meaning of the situation dawned upon the prejudiced mind of the Northern public. The idea was indulged that the capture of Manassas was only a successful raid by a body of rebel guerillas; and so it was dismissed by the newspapers with a levity, characteristic of their insolence and ignorance.

Weak and credulous as General Pope was, it is probable that the moment he heard that Jackson was in his rear, he was satisfied that it was no raid. The situation had been changed almost in a moment. Pope had evacuated Warrenton Junction and was moving along the railroad upon Manassas, anxious to secure his "line of retreat," and expecting, doubtless, with no little confidence, by rapid marches of a portion of his forces by the turnpike upon Gainesville, to intercept any reinforcements by the way of Thoroughfare Gap to Jackson, and to fall upon and crush him by the weight of numbers. A portion of the Confederate army now fronted to the South, and the Federal army towards Washington. The latter had been swollen by reinforcements, and the advance corps from Burnside was marching on rapidly from Fredericksburg to complete the amassment on the Federal side.

Although the situation of Gen. Pope was one unexpected by himself, and surrounded by many embarrassments, he yet had many circumstances of advantage in which to risk a great and decisive battle. The New York journals persisted in declaring that it was not the infallible Pope, but the "rebel" army that was "in a tight place." At any rate, Pope was not in the situation in which McClellan found himself when his right wing was turned by the Confederates in front of Richmond—that is, without supports or reinforcements. On the contrary, on his right, and on the way up from Fredericksburg, was the new army of the Potomac under Burnside; while advancing forward from Alexandria was the newly organized army of Virginia under McClellan. Such was the array of force that threatened the army we had withdrawn from Richmond, and in which the Northern populace indulged the prospect of a certain and splendid victory.

An encounter of arms of vital consequence was now to ensue on the already historic and famous Plains of Manassas— the beautiful stretch of hill and dale reaching as far as Centreville, varied by amphitheatres, an admirable battle ground; with the scenery of which the Southern troops associated the exciting thoughts of a former victory and a former shedding of the blood of their beloved and best on the memorable and consecrated spots that marked the field of battle.

THE ENGAGEMENT OF WEDNESDAY, THE 27TH OF AUGUST.

On Wednesday, the 27th, an attack was made by the enemy upon Bristow Station, and also at Manassas Junction.

On the morning of that day, at about eleven o'clock, Gen. Taylor's brigade, of Major-General Slocum's division of the army of the Potomac, consisting of the first, second, third and fourth New Jersey regiments, were ordered to proceed to

Manassas by rail from their camp near Fort Ellsworth, Alexandria.

The brigade arrived at Bull Run bridge about seven o'clock in the morning. The troops landed and crossed the bridge with as little delay as possible, and marched towards Manassas. After ascending the hill emerging from the valley of Bull Run, they encountered a line of skirmishers, of the Confederates, which fell back before them. The brigade marched on in the direction of Manassas, not seeing any of the enemy until within range of the circular series of fortifications around the Junction, when heavy artillery was opened upon them from all directions. General Taylor retired beyond the range of our guns to the rear of a sheltering crest of ground, from which he was driven by our infantry. Crossing at Blackburn's ford, he was pursued by our horse artillery, which fired into him, creating the utmost havoc. The brigade retreated in a disorganized mass of flying men towards Fairfax; it was pursued by our eager troops beyond Centreville, and the track of the flying and cowardly enemy was marked with his dead.

The flight of the enemy was attended by the most wild and terrible scenes, as he was pursued by our horse artillery, pouring canister into his ranks. The brigade was almost annihilated. General Taylor himself, his son on his staff, and his nephew, were wounded; also one-half of his officers.

At 3 o'clock, P. M., of the same day, the enemy attacked General Ewell, at Bristow, and that General, after a handsome little fight, in which he punished the enemy severely, retired across Muddy Run, as had previously been agreed upon, to Manassas Junction. This attack was made by the division of the enemy commanded by Gen. Hooker, which was dispatched to that point and detached from the advancing forces of Pope, who, of course, claimed the result of the affair as a signal Federal success.

## MOVEMENTS OF THURSDAY, THE 28TH OF AUGUST.

After sunset on Thursday General Jackson accomplished one of the most beautiful and masterly strategic movements of the war. He found himself many miles in advance of the rest of our army. The enemy might throw his immense columns between him and Longstreet—Alexandria and Washington was to his rear when he turned to attack the enemy. He determined to throw himself upon the enemy's flank, to preserve the same nearness to Alexandria, to place himself within support of the remainder of our army, and to occupy a position from which he could not be driven, even if support did not arrive in time. All this he accomplished that night, after destroying the stores, buildings, cars, &c., and burning the railroad bridges over Muddy Run and Bull Run. He marched at night with his entire force from Manassas Station to Manassas battle-field, crossing the Warrenton turnpike, and placing his troops in such position that he could confront the enemy should they attempt to advance by the Warrenton pike or by the Sudley road and ford, and have the advantage of communicating by the Aldie road with Longstreet, should he not have passed the Thoroughfare Gap, and at all events gain for himself a safe position for attack or defence. At seven o'clock, A. M., on Friday, General Stuart encountered the enemy's cavalry near Gainesville, on the Warrenton pike, and drove them back; and during the morning the 2d brigade of Gen. Taliaferro's division, under Colonel Bradley Johnson, again repulsed them. It was now ascertained that the enemy's column was advancing (or retreating) from Warrenton, along the line of the railroad and by way of the Warrenton turnpike, and that they intended to pass a part of their force over the Stone Bridge and Sudley ford. Gen. Jackson immediately ordered Gen. Taliaferro to advance with his division to attack their left flank; which was advancing towards Sudley Mill. Gen. Ewell's division marched considerably in the rear of the 1st division. After marching some three miles, it was discovered that the enemy had abandoned the idea of crossing at Sudley, and had left the Warrenton pike to the left, beyond Groveton, and were apparently cutting across to the railroad through the fields and woods. In a few minutes, however, he advanced across the turnpike to attack us, and Jackson's army was thrown forward to meet him.

From this sketch of the movements of the corps commanded by Gen. Jackson, it will be seen that though a portion of our forces, under Gens. Ewell and Jackson, were on Tuesday and a part of Wednesday, the 26th and 27th of August, on the Orange and Alexandria railroad, between Pope and Alexandria, on the approach of Pope from Warrenton they withdrew to the west and halted in the vicinity of the Warrenton turnpike, expecting to be rejoined by Longstreet, where they awaited the approach of the enemy and delivered him battle.

### THE BATTLE OF FRIDAY, THE 29TH OF AUGUST..

The conflict of Friday occurred near the village of Groveton, our right resting just above and near the village, and the left upon the old battle-field of Manassas. The division of General Anderson had not yet arrived, and the corps of Longstreet had not been fully placed in position. The enemy, probably aware of our movements, selected this opportunity to make an attack upon Jackson, hoping thereby to turn our left, destroy our combinations, and discomfert the plans which had already become apparent to the Federal commanders.

Gen. Longstreet's passage of the Thoroughfare Gap in the face of a force of two thousand of the enemy, is one of the most remarkable incidents of the late operations in Northern Virginia. The Gap is a wild, rude opening through the Bull Run Mountains, varying in width from one hundred to two hundred yards. A rapid stream of water murmurs over the rocks of the rugged defile, along which runs a stony winding road. On either side arise the mountains, those on the left presenting their flat, precipitous faces to the beholder, with here and there a shrub jutting out and relieving the monotonous grey of the rocky mass; and those on the right covered thickly with timber, impassable to any but the most active men. The strong position afforded by this pass, which might have been held against almost any force by a thousand determined troops and a battery of artillery, had been possessed by the enemy, who had planted his batteries at various points and lined the sides of the mountains with his skirmishers. As it was, the passage was effected by Longstreet's division with the loss of only three men wounded. This result was accomplished by a decisive piece of strategy, by which a small column of three brigades—Pryor's, Wilcox's and Featherstone's, and two batteries of rifle pieces—were thrown through Hopewell Gap some three miles to the left of Thoroughfare Gap, as we approached Manassas.

Under Jackson and Longstreet, the details of the plan of Gen. Lee had been so far carried out in every respect. For ten days or more the troops of both of these Generals in the advance were constantly under fire. The former had been engaged in no less than four serious fights. Many of the men were barefooted, in rags; provided with only a single blanket as a protection against the heavy dews and severe cold at night; frequently they would get nothing from daylight to daylight; rations at best consisted of bread and water, with a rare and economical intermingling of bacon; and the troops were in what at any other time they would have characterized as a suffering condition. Notwithstanding these adverse circumstances, not a murmur of complaint had been heard; marches of twenty, and in one instance of thirty, miles a day had been patiently endured, and the spirit of the army, so far from being broken, was elevated to a degree of enthusiasm which foreboded nothing but the victory it won.

On the morning of the 29th, the Washington Artillery of New Orleans and several other batteries were planted upon a high hill that commanded the extensive ground over which the enemy were advancing, and just in front of this, perhaps a little to the left, the fight began. The Federals threw forward a heavy column, supported by field batteries, and under cover of their fire made a bold stroke to divide our line. The blow fell upon a portion of Ewell's troops, who were concealed behind the embankment of a railroad, but no sooner had the enemy appeared within close range, than they received a terribly galling fire, which drove them panic-stricken from that portion of the field. As they ran, our artillery opened upon the flying mass with shell and round shot. Every ball could be seen taking effect. The enemy fell by scores, until finally the once beautiful line melted confusedly into the woods. Again they renewed the attack, and gradually the fight became general along nearly the entire column of Jackson.

As the afternoon progressed, however, Gen. Lee discovered that strong Yankee reinforcements were coming up, and he accordingly ordered the division of General Hood, belonging to Longstreet's corps, to make a demonstration on the enemy's left. This was done, perhaps an hour before dark, and the moment they became engaged the difference became perceptible at a glance. Jackson, thus strengthened, fought with renewed vigour, and the enemy not knowing the nature of the reinforcements, and diverted by our onset, which compelled him to change his lines, was proportionately weakened. The result was, that at dark Hood's division had driven the forces in front of them three-quarters of a mile from our starting point, and had it not been for the lateness of the hour, might have turned the defeat into an utter rout.

The conflict had been terrific. Our troops were advanced several times during the fight, but the enemy fought with desperation, and did not retire until nine o'clock at night, when they sullenly left the field to the Confederates. During the night orders came from head-quarters for our troops to fall back to their original positions, preparatory to our renewal of the action in the morning. It might have been this simple retrograde movement which led to the mendacious despatch sent by Pope to Washington, stating that he had whipped our army and driven us from the field,* but confessing that the Federal loss was eight thousand in killed and wounded.

THE BATTLE OF SATURDAY, THE 30TH OF AUGUST.

The grand day of the prolonged contest was yet to dawn. For two days each wing of our army under Generals Longstreet and Jackson had repulsed with vigour attacks made on them separately. General Pope had concentrated the greater portion of the army under his command for a desperate renewal of the attack on our lines. Friday night found those of our men who were not engaged in burying the dead and bringing away the wounded, sleeping upon their arms. All the troops of Longstreet's corps, with the exception of Gen. R. H. Anderson's, which was only three or four miles in the rear, had taken their places in the line of battle, and every one looked forward to the events of the coming day, the anticipations of which had sustained our soldiers under the terrible fatigue, discomforts and deprivations of the ten days' tedious march, by which reinforcements had at last reached the heroic and unyielding Jackson.

With the first streak of daylight visible through the light mist that ascended from the woods, our men were under arms. The pickets of the two armies were within a few hundred yards of each other. Every circumstance indicated that the battle would commence at an early hour in the morning. The waking of a portion of our batteries into life soon after daylight, and the frequent cannonading thereafter, the almost incessant skirmishing in front, with its exciting volleys of musketry, all conspired to produce this impression.

Our line of battle was an obtuse crescent in shape, and at

---

* It appears that Gen. R. H. Anderson's division, which came down the turnpike on their way to Sudley Church, where they had been ordered the day before, were stopped by our pickets and told that the enemy were in strong force immediately in front. The General countermarched his division, wagons and artillery, and fell back in rear of Longstreet for the night. It is probable that the enemy, seeing this, supposed it to be the falling back of our whole army.

least five miles long. Jackson's line, which formed one side, stretched from Sudley, on Bull Run, along the partly used track of the Manassas Independent line of railway, for a portion of the way, and thence towards a point on the Warrenton turnpike, about a mile and a half in rear or west of Groveton. His extreme right came within about six hundred yards of the turnpike.

Longstreet's command, which formed our right wing, extended from the point near the turnpike on which Jackson's right flank rested, and prolonged the line of battle far to the right, stretching beyond the line of the Manassas Gap railroad.

It is thus seen that a point on the Warrenton turnpike, a mile and a half west of Groveton, was the centre of our position, and the apex of our crescent, whose convexity was towards the west. It was here, in an interval between Jackson's right and Longstreet's left that our artillery was placed. Eight batteries were planted on a commanding elevation.

The enemy's line of battle conformed itself to ours, and took, therefore, a crescent form, of which the centre or more advanced portion was at Groveton, whence the wings declined obliquely to the right and left. Their batteries were in rear of their infantry, and occupied the hills which they had held in the fight of July, 1861, but pointed differently.

The disposition of the enemy's forces was, General Heintzelman on the extreme right and Gen. McDowell on the extreme left, while the army corps of Generals Fitz John Porter and Seigel, and Reno's division of General Burnside's army, were placed in the centre.

The elevation occupied by our artillery, under command of Colonel Stephen D. Lee, of South Carolina, was the most commanding ground that could have been selected for the purpose. It was about the centre of the entire army. To the front, the land breaks beautifully into hill and dale, forming a sort of amphitheatre. Around the field, and occasionally shooting into it in narrow bands, are heavy woods.

Early in the morning the immense masses of the enemy's infantry were seen in line of battle, and far in the distance immense clouds of dust filled the heavens. During this time our batteries were pitching their shot and shell into the Federal ranks, and returning the fire of their artillery on the brow of an opposite hill. Sometimes it was fierce, but generally it was a deliberate interchange of fire.

About 1 A. M. a regiment advanced rapidly on the enemy's left, determined to drive out our pickets from an orchard, where all the morning they had been keeping up a brisk fire. This effort succeeded, and our brave sharp-shooters retired through the orchard in good order. As soon as they got well out of the way, our batteries opened upon the enemy, and in ten minutes they were retreating, sheltering themselves in the ravines and behind a barn. At 2 o'clock the forces that had been moving almost the whole day towards our left, began to move in the opposite direction, and it appeared that they were retiring towards Manassas, two or three miles distant. Several attempts were now made to advance upon our left like those to drive in our pickets on our right, but a few shells served to scatter the skirmishers and drive them into the woods that skirted this beautiful valley on either hand. When it appeared more than probable that the enemy, foiled in his attempt to make us bring on the fight by these little advances on our right and left, was about to retire, and merely kept up the cannonading in order to conceal his retreat, suddenly, at 4 P. M., there belched forth from every brazen throat in our batteries a volley that seemed to shake the very earth.

It was at this instant that the battle was joined. As the sporting whirls of smoke drifted away the cause of the tumult was at once discerned. A dense column of infantry, several thousand strong, which had been massed behind and near a strip of woods, had moved out to attack Jackson, whose men were concealed behind an excavation on the railroad. As soon as they were discovered our batteries opened with tremendous power, but the Federals moved boldly forward, until they came within the range of our small arms where for fully fifteen minutes, they remained desperately engaged with our infantry. As the fight progressed, a second line emerged from the cover and went to the support of those in front, and finally a third line marched out into the open field below us and there halted, hesitated, and soon commenced firing over the heads of their comrades beyond.

Jackson's infantry raked these three columns terribly. Repeatedly did they break and run, and rally again under the energetic appeals of their officers, for it was a crack corps of the Federal army—that of Generals Sykes and Morrell; but it was not in human nature to stand unflinchingly before that hurricane of fire. As the fight progressed, Lee moved his batteries to the left, until reaching a position only four hundred yards distant from the enemy's lines, he opened again. The spectacle was now magnificent. As shell after shell burst in the wavering ranks, and round shot ploughed broad gaps among them, one could distinctly see through the rifts of smoke the Federal soldiers falling and flying on every side. With the explosion of every bomb, it seemed as if scores dropped dead, or writhed in agony upon the field. Some were crawling on their hands and knees; some were piled up together; and some were lying scattered around in every attitude that imagination can conceive.

Presently the Yankee columns began to break and men to fall out to the rear. The retreating numbers gradually increase, and the great mass, without line or form, now move back like a great multitude without guide or leader. From a slow, steady walk, the great mass, or many parts of it, move at a run. Jackson's men, yelling like devils, now charge upon the scattered crowd; but it is easily seen that they themselves had severely suffered, and were but a handful compared with the overwhelming forces of the enemy. The flags of two or three regiments do not appear to be more than fifty yards apart. The brilliant affair has not occupied more than half an hour, but in that brief time more than a thousand Yankees have been launched into eternity, or left mangled on the ground.

The whole scene of battle now changes. It will be seen in referring to the disposition of our forces, that Jackson's line, which formed our left, stretched from Bull Run towards a point on the Warrenton turnpike. In his severe action with the enemy, his left, advancing more rapidly than his right, had swept around by the Pittsylvania House, and was pressing the Federals back towards the turnpike. It was now the golden opportunity for Longstreet to attack the exposed left flank of the enemy in front of it.

Hood's Brigade charged next the turnpike. In its track it met Sickles' Excelsior Brigade, and almost annihilated it. The ground was piled with the slain. Pickett's Brigade was on the right of Hood's, next came Jenkins' Brigade, and next was Kemper's, which charged near the Conrad House. Evans' and Anderson's were the reserve, and subsequently came into action.

Not many minutes elapsed after the order to attack passed along our entire line before the volleys of platoons, and finally the rolling reports of long lines of musketry, indicated that the battle was in full progress. The whole army was now in motion. The woods were full of troops, and the order for the supports to forward at a quick step was received with enthusiastic cheers by the elated men. The din was almost deafening, the heavy notes of the artillery, at first deliberate, but gradually increasing in their rapidity, mingled with the sharp treble of the small arms, gave one an idea of some diabolical concert in which all the furies of hell were at work. Through the woods, over gently rolling hills, now and then through an open field we travel on towards the front. From an elevation we obtain a view of a considerable portion of the field. Hood and Kemper are now hard at it, and as they press forward, never yielding an inch, sometimes at a double quick, you hear those unmistakable yells, which tell of a Southern charge or a Southern success.

Reaching the vicinity of the Chinn House, the eye at once embraces the entire vista of battle—at least that portion of it which is going on in front of Longstreet. Some of our men are in the woods in the rear, and some in the open field where stretches the undulating surface far away towards Bull Run. The old battle ground is plainly discernible less than two miles distant, and to the right and left, as well as in front, the country is comparatively unobstructed by heavy woods. Just before you, only three or four hundred yards away, are the infantry of the enemy, and at various points in the rear are their reserves and batteries. Between the armies, the ground is already covered with the dead and wounded, for a distance lengthwise of nearly a mile.

Our own artillery are likewise upon commanding positions, and you hear the heavy rush of shot, the terrible dumps into the ground, and the crash of trees through which they tear with resistless force on every side.

Nothing can withstand the impetuosity of our troops. Every line of the enemy has been broken and dispersed, but rallies again upon some other position behind. Hood has already advanced his division nearly half a mile at a double-quick, the Texans, Georgians and Hampton Legion loading and firing as they run, yelling all the while like madmen. They have captured one or two batteries and various stands of colors, and are still pushing the enemy before them. Evans, at the head of his brigade, is following on the right, as their support, and pouring in his effective volleys. Jenkins has come in on the right of the Chinn House, and, like an avalanche, sweeps down upon the legions before him with resistless force. Still further to the right is Longstreet's old brigade, composed of Virginians—veterans of every battle-field—all of whom are fighting like furies. The First Virginia, which opened the fight at Bull Run on the 17th of July, 1861, with over six hundred men, now reduced to less than eighty members, is winning new laurels; but out of the little handful, more than a third have already bit the dust. Toombs and Anderson, with the Georgians, together with Kemper and Jenkins, are swooping around on the right, flanking the Federals, and driving them towards their centre and rear. Eschelman, with his company of the Washington Artillery; Major Garnett, with his battalion of Virginia batteries, and others of our big guns, are likewise working around upon the enemy's left, and pouring an enfilading fire into both their infantry and artillery.

While the grand chorus of battle is thundering along our front, Jackson has closed in upon the enemy on their right, and Longstreet has similarly circumscribed them on their left. In other words, the V shaped lines with which we commenced the engagement have opened at the angle, while the two opposite ends of the figure are coming together. Lee has advanced his battalion of artillery from the centre, and from hill-top to hill-top, wherever he can effect a lodgement, lets loose the racing masses of iron that chase each other through the Federal ranks. Pryor, Featherstone and Wilcox being on the extreme left of Longstreet's line, are co-operating with the army of Jackson.

It was at this point of the battle, when our infantry pouring down from the right and left, made one of the most terrible and sublime bayonet charges in the records of war. There was seen emerging from the dust a long, solid mass of men, coming down upon the worn and disheartened Federals, at a bayonet charge, on the double-quick. This line of bayonets, in the distance, presented a spectacle at once awful, sublime, terrible and overwhelming. "They came on," said a Northern account referring to the Confederates, "like demons emerging from the earth." With grim and terrible energy, our men came up within good range of the enemy's columns; they take his fire without a halt; a momentary confusion ensues as the leaden showers are poured into our ranks; but the next moment the bugles sound the order to our phalanxes, and instantly the huge mass of Confederates is hurled against the enemy's left wing. The divisions of Reno and Schenck—the choicest veterans of the Federal army are swept away. Setting up a yell of triumph, our men push over the piles of their own dead and the corpses of many a Federal, using the ▓▓▓▓et at close quarters with the enemy.

The rout of the enemy was complete. It had been a task of almost superhuman labour to drive the enemy from his strong points, defended as they were by the best artillery and infantry in the Federal army, but in less than four hours from the commencement of the battle our indomitable energy had accomplished every thing. The arrival of R. H. Anderson with his reserves soon after the engagement was fairly opened, proved a timely acquisition, and the handsome manner in which he brought his troops into position showed the cool and skillful General. Our Generals, Lee, Longstreet, Jackson, Hood, Kemper, Evans, Jones, Jenkins, and others, all shared the dangers to which they exposed their men. How well their Colonels and the subordinate officers performed their duty is best testified by the list of killed and wounded.

In determining the fortunes of the battle our cavalry had in more than one instance played a conspicuous part.

As the columns of the enemy began to give way, General Beverly Robinson was ordered by Gen. Longstreet to charge the flying masses with his brigade of cavalry. The brigade numbering a thousand men, composed of Munford's, Myers', Harman's and Flournoy's regiments, was immediately put in motion, but before reaching the infantry General Robinson discovered a brigade of the enemy fifteen hundred strong drawn up on the crest of a hill directly in his front. Leaving one of his regiments in reserve, he charged with the other three full at the enemy's ranks. As our men drew near, the whole of the Yankee line fired at them a volley from their carbines, most of the bullets, however, whistling harmlessly over their heads. In another instant the enemy received the terrific shock of our squadrons. There was a pause, a hand-to-hand fight for a moment, and the enemy broke and fled in total rout. All organization was destroyed, and every man trusted for his safety only in the heels of his horse.

Night closed upon the battle. When it was impossible to

use fire-arms the heavens were lit up by the still continued flashes of the artillery, and the meteor flight of shells scattering their iron spray. By this time the enemy had been forced across Bull Run, and their dead covered every acre from the starting point of the fight to the Stone Bridge. In its first stages the retreat of the enemy was a wild, frenzied rout; the great mass of the enemy moving at a full run, scattering over the fields and trampling upon the dead and living in the mad agony of their flight. The whole army was converted into a mob; regiments and companies were no longer distinguishable; and the panic stricken fugitives were slaughtered at every step of their retreat—our cavalry cutting them down, or our infantry driving their bayonets into their backs.

In crossing Bull Run many of the enemy were drowned, being literally dragged and crushed under the water, which was not more than waist deep, by the crowds of frenzied men pressing and trampling upon each other in the stream. On reaching Centreville the flight of the enemy was arrested by the appearance of about thirty thousand fresh Yankee troops—General Franklin's corps. The mass of fugitives was here rallied, to the extent of forming it again into columns, and with this appearance of organization, it was resolved by General Pope to continue his retreat to the entrenchments of Washington.

Thus ended the second great battle of Manassas. We had driven the enemy up hill and down, a distance of two and a half miles, strewing this great space with his dead, captured thirty pieces of artillery, and some six or eight thousand stand of arms. Seven thousand prisoners were paroled on the field of battle. For want of transportation valuable stores had to be destroyed as captured, while the enemy, at their various depots, are reported to have burned many millions of property in their retreat.

The appearance of the field of battle attested in the most terrible and hideous manner the carnage in the ranks of the enemy. Over the gullies, ravines and valleys, which divided the opposite hills the dead and wounded lay by thousands, as far as the eye could reach. The woods were full of them. In front of the Chinn House, which had been converted into a hospital, the havoc was terrible. The ground was strewn not only with men, but arms, ammunition, provisions, haversacks, canteens, and whatever else the affrighted Federals could throw away, to facilitate their flight. In front of the positions occupied by Jackson's men, the killed were more plentiful. In many instances as many as eighty or ninety dead marked the place where had fought a single Yankee regiment. Around the Henry and Robinson houses the dead were more scattered, as if they were picked off, or killed while running. The body of a dead Yankee was found lying at full length upon the grave of the aged Mrs. Henry, who was killed by the enemy's balls in the old battle that had raged upon this spot. Three others were upon the very spot where Bartow fell, and within a few feet of the death place of Gen. Bee was still another group. A little further on a wounded Federal had lain for the last two days and nights, where by extending his hand on either side he could touch the dead bodies of his companions. His head was pillowed on one of these. Confederate soldiers were also to be found in the midst of these putrifying masses of death; but these were comparatively rare. The scenes of the battle-field were rendered ghastly by an extraordinary circumstance. There was not a dead Yankee in all that broad field who had not been stripped of his shoes or stockings—and in numerous cases been left as naked as the hour he was born. Our bare-footed and ragged men had not hesitated to supply their necessities even from the garments and equipments of the dead.

The enemy admitted a loss down to Friday night of 17,000 men, Pope officially stating his loss on that day to have been 8,000. In one of the Baltimore papers it was said that the entire Yankee loss, including that of Saturday, was 32,000 men—killed, wounded and prisoners. This statement allows 15,000 for the loss on Saturday. That the loss of that particular day was vastly greater than the enemy admit, we take to be certain. They are not the persons to over-estimate their own losses, and, in the meantime, Gen. Lee tells us that over 7,000 of them were taken and paroled on the field. If they fought the battle with anything like the desperation they pretend, considering that it lasted five hours, they certainly had more than 8,000 killed and wounded. Four days after the battle there were still three thousand wounded Yankees uncared for within the lines of Gen. Lee. It is very certain, if they were not cared for, it was because the number of wounded was so great that their turn had not come. Our own wounded, not exceeding, it is said, 3,000, could very well be attended to in a day, and then the turn of the Yankees would come. Yet so numerous were they, that at the end of four days three thousand of them had not received surgical assistance. This indicates an enormous list of wounded, and confirms the report of one officer, who puts down their killed at 5,000, and their wounded at three times that figure, making 20,000 killed and wounded, and of others who say that their killed and wounded were to us in the proportion of five, six, and even seven to one. As many prisoners were taken, who were not included in the 7,000 paroled men mentioned by Gen. Lee, we do not think we make an over-estimate when we set down the whole Yankee loss at 30,000 in round numbers. Their loss on Friday, estimated by Pope himself at 8,000, added to their loss on Saturday, makes 38,000. Previous operations, including the battle of Cedar Run, the several expeditions of Stuart, and the various skirmishes in which we were almost uniformly victorious, we should think would fairly bring the total loss of the enemy to 50,000 men, since our forces first crossed the Rapidan. This is a result almost unequalled in the history of modern campaigns.

The results of Gen. Lee's strategy were indicative of the resources of military genius. Day after day the enemy were beaten, until his disasters culminated on the plains of Manassas. Day after day our officers and men manifested their superiority to the enemy. The summer campaign in Virginia. had been conducted by a single army. The same toil-worn troops who had relieved from siege the city of Richmond, had advanced to meet another invading army, reinforced not only by the defeated army of McClellan, but by the fresh corps of Generals Burnside and Hunter. The trials and marches of these troops are extraordinary in history. Transportation was inadequate; the streams which they had to cross were swollen to unusual height; it was only by forced marches and repeated combats they could turn the position of the enemy, and, at last succeeding in this, and forming a junction of their columns, in the face of greatly superior forces, they fought the decisive battle of the 30th of August, the crowning triumph of their toil and valour.

The route of the extraordinary marches of our troops presented, for long and weary miles, the touching pictures of the trials of war. Broken down soldiers (not all "stragglers") lined the road. At night time they might be found asleep in every conceivable attitude of discomfort—on fence rails and in fence corners—some half bent, others almost erect, in ditches and on steep hill-sides, some without blanket or overcoat. Daybreak found them drenched with dew, but strong in purpose; with half rations of bread and meat, ragged and barefooted, they go cheerfully forward. No nobler spectacle was ever presented in history. These beardless youths and gray-haired men, who thus spent their nights like the beasts of the field, were the best men of the land—of all classes, trades and professions. The spectacle was such as to inspire the prayer that ascended from the sanctuaries of the South—that God might reward the devotion of these men to principle and justice by crowning their labours and sacrifices with that blessing which always bringeth peace.

The victory which had crowned the campaign of our armies in Virginia, illuminates the names of all associated with it. But in the achievement of that victory, and in the history of that campaign, there is one name which, in a few months, had mounted to the zenith of fame; which in dramatic associations, in rapid incidents, and in swift and sudden renown, challenged comparison with the most extraordinary phenomena in the annals of military genius. This remark is not invidious in its spirit, nor is it forced into the context of this sketch. A personal allusion may be spared in the narrative, when that allusion is to the most remarkable man in the history of this war.

We refer to General Stonewall Jackson and that wonderful chapter of military achievements which commenced in the Valley of Virginia and concluded at Manassas. It was difficult to say what this man had not accomplished that had ever before been accomplished in history with equal means and in an equal period of time.

In the spring Gen. Jackson had been placed in command of the small army of observation which held the upper valley of the Shenandoah and the country about Staunton. It was intended that he should remain *quasi* inactive, to watch the enemy and to wait for him; but he soon commenced manœuvering on his own responsibility, and ventured upon a scale of operations that threw the higher military authorities at Richmond into a fever of anxiety and alarm.

In less than thirty days he dashed at the Yankee advance, and driving it back, wheeled his army, swept down the Valley and drove Banks across the Potomac. Returning to the upper Valley, he manœuvered around for three weeks—in the meantime dealing Fremont a heavy blow at Cross Keys and defeating Shields in the Luray valley—and, then suddenly swept down the Virginia Central. Railroad, via Gordonsville, on McClellan's right, before Richmond. The part he played in winding up the campaign on the Peninsula is well known. Almost before the smoke had lifted from the bloody field of the Chickahominy, we hear of him again on his old stamping ground above Gordonsville. Cedar Mountain was fought and won from Pope before he knew his campaign was opened. Jackson fell back; but only to flank him on the right. Pope retired from the Rapidan to the Rappahannock, but Jackson swung still further round to the North and outflanked him again. Yet again he gave up the Rappahannock and fell back south of Warrenton, and, for the third time, Jackson outflanked him through Thoroughfare Gap, and at last got in his rear. Pope now had to fight; and the victory which perched upon our banners was the most brilliant of the war.

It is curious to observe with what insolent confidence the North had anticipated a crowning triumph of its arms on the field of Manassas, even when the air around Washington was burdened with the signals of its defeat. The North did not tolerate the idea of defeat. On the very day of the battle, Washington was gay with exultation and triumph over an imagined victory. At thirty minutes past twelve o'clock, the Washington *Star* published a dispatch declaring, that it had learned from parties just from Fairfax county, that the firing had stopped; and added, "we trust the fact means a surrender of the rebels, and do not see how it can mean aught else." At a later hour of the afternoon, a dispatch was received at the War Department, from Major-General Pope, announcing a brilliant victory in a decisive battle with the Confederate forces on the old Bull Run battle-field. It was stated that he had defeated the Confederate army, and was driving it in discomfiture before him. This dispatch had a magical effect. The War Department, contrary to its usual custom, not only permitted, but officially authorized the publication of the dispatch.* Citizens of every grade, of both sexes and of all ages, were seen in groups around the corners and in the places of public resort speculating upon the particulars, and the consequences of the decisive victory reported. The triumph of the Federal arms was apparently shown to be more complete by reason of the announcement that General Stonewall Jackson, with sixteen thousand of his troops, had been cut off and captured.

It was at this point of exultation that another dispatch was received from General Pope, stating that the uncertain tide of battle had unfortunately turned against the Federal army, and that he had been compelled to abandon the battle-field during the evening. The revulsion was great; the untimely hallelujahs were interrupted, and the population of Washington, from its hasty and indecent exultations of the morning, was soon to be converted into a panic-stricken community, trembling for its own safety.

Indeed, the victory achieved by the Confederates was far more serious than the most lively alarm in Washington could at first imagine. The next morning after the battle, the last feeble resistance of the Federals at Centreville was broken. The finishing stroke was given by the Confederates under Gen. A. P. Hill, who, on the 1st of September, (Monday,) encountered a large body of the enemy at Germantown, a small village in Fairfax county, near the main road leading from Centreville to Fairfax Court House. The enemy, it appears, had succeeded in rallying a sufficient number of their routed troops at the point named, to make another show of opposition to the advance of the victorious Confederates on their territory. On Sunday, the pursuit of Pope's army was commenced and pressed with vigour on the Fairfax Court House road, and on Monday morning at daylight the enemy were discovered drawn up in line of battle across the road, their right extending to the village of Germantown. General Hill immediately ordered the attack, and after a brief but hotly contested fight, the enemy withdrew. During the night, the enemy fell back to Fairfax Court House and abandoned his position at Centreville. The next day, about noon, he evacuated Fairfax Court House, taking the road to Alexandria and Washington.

Thus were realized the full and glorious results of the second victory of Manassas; thus were completed the great objects of the brilliant summer campaign of 1862 in Virginia; and thus, for a second time, on the famous borders of the Potomac, the gates were thrown wide open to the invasion of the North, and to new fields of enterprise for the victorious armies of the South.

The rapid change in the fortunes of the Confederacy, and

the sharp contrast between its late forlorn situation and what were now the brilliant promises of the future, were animating and suggestive topics.

Little more than three months had elapsed since the columns of a hostile army were debouching on the plains near Richmond, when an evacuation of the city and a further retreat of the Confederate army were believed by nearly all official persons the most prudent and politic steps that the government could take under the circumstances. Little more than three months had elapsed since our armies were retreating weak and disorganized before the overwhelming force of the enemy, yielding to them the sea-coast, the mines, the manufacturing power, the grain fields, and even entire States of the Confederacy. Now we were advancing with increased numbers, improved organization, renewed courage, and the prestige of victory upon an enemy defeated and disheartened.

As the opposing armies of the war now stood, the South had causes for congratulation and pride such, perhaps, as no other people ever had in similar circumstances. The North had a population of twenty-three millions against eight millions serving the South, and of these eight millions nearly three millions were African slaves. The white population of New York and Pennsylvania was greater than that of the Confederate States. Manufacturing establishments of all descriptions rendered the North a self-sustaining people for all the requirements of peace or war, and, with these advantages, they retained those of an unrestricted commerce with foreign nations. The North had all the ports of the world open to its ships; it had furnaces, foundries and workshops; its manufacturing resources, compared with those of the South, were as five hundred to one; the great marts of Europe were open to it for supplies of arms and stores; there was nothing of material resource, nothing of the apparatus of conquest that was not within its reach.

The South, on the other hand, with only a few insignificant manufactories of arms and materials of war, textile fabrics, leather, &c., had been cut off by an encircling blockade for fifteen months from all those supplies upon which she had depended from the North and from Europe, in the way of arms, munitions of war, clothing, medicines, and many of the essentials of subsistence. The South was without the vestige of a navy, except a straggling ship or two, while that of the North in this war was equal to a land force of three or four hundred thousand men. The South was nearly exhausted of the commonest articles of food, while the Northern States had a superabundance of all the essentials and luxuries of life. The Northern troops, *en masse*, were better armed, equipped and subsisted than those of any other nation, while those of the South were armed with all sorts of weapons—good, bad and indifferent—clothed in rags and fed upon half rations.

The result of all this immense and boasted superiority on the part of the North, coupled with the most immense exertions, was that the South remained unconquered. The result was humiliating enough to the warlike reputation of the North. It had not been separated from its feeble adversary by seas or mountains, but only by a geographical line; nature had not interfered to protect the weak from the strong. Three "grand armies" had advanced against Richmond; and yet not only was the South more invincible in spirit than ever, but her armies of brave and ragged men were already advancing upon the Northern borders, and threatening, at least so far as to alarm their enemy, the invasion of Ohio and Pennsylvania and the occupation of the Northern capital.

## CHAPTER IV.

Rescue of Virginia from the Invader...Gen. Loring's Campaign in the Kanawha Valley...A Novel Theatre of the War...Gen. Lee's Passage of the Potomac...His Plans...Disposition of our Forces...McClellan again at the Head of the Yankee Army...THE BATTLE OF BOONSBORO'...THE CAPTURE OF HARPER'S FERRY—Its Fruits...THE BATTLE OF SHARPSBURG...Great Superiority of the Enemy's Numbers...Fury of the Battle...The Bridge of Antietam...A Drawn Battle...Spectacles of Carnage...The Unburied Dead...General Lee Retires into Virginia...McClellan's Pretence of Victory...The Affair of Shepherdstown...Charges against McClellan...His Disgrace...Review of the Maryland Campaign—Misrepresentations of Gen. Lee's Objects...His Retreat...Comment of the New York "Tribune"...The Cold Reception of the Confederates in Maryland...Excuses for the Timidity of the Marylanders... What was Accomplished by the Summer Campaign of 1862...The Outburst of Applause in Europe...Tribute from the London "Times"—Public Opinion in England...Distinction between the People and the Government—The Mask of England...OUR FOREIGN RELATIONS IN THE WAR...A Historical Parallel of Secession...Two Remarks on the "Neutrality" of Europe...The Yankee Blockade and the Treaty of Paris—The Confederate Privateers—Temper of the South...Fruits of the Blockade.

THE close of the summer found the long-harassed soil of Virginia cleared of the footsteps of the invader. The glorious victory of Manassas was followed by other propitious events in this State of lesser importance, but which went to complete the general result of her freedom from the thraldom of the Yankee.

In the early part of September the campaign of General Loring in the Valley of the Kanawha was consummated by a vigorous attack on the enemy at Fayette Court House, and the occupation of Charleston by our troops. On the 10th of that month we advanced upon the enemy's front at Fayette Court House, while a portion of our forces made a detour over the mountain as to attack him in the rear. The fighting continued from noon until night, our artillery attacking desperately in front; and the enemy took advantage of the darkness to effect his escape, not, however, without leaving his trains in our hands.

The Yankees made a stand at Cotton Hill, seven miles further on. A few hours' fighting dislodged them, and we pursued on to Kanawha Falls, where they again made a stand; but a few hours' contest made us again masters of the field, with more than a million dollars' worth of stores and some prisoners.

The advance of our troops to Charlestown was the signal to the enemy for an inhuman attempt to burn the town, the women being driven from their homes on fifteen minutes' notice. As our troops approached the town, dense clouds of black smoke were seen to hang over it, mingled with the lurid glare of burning buildings, while the shrieks of frightened women and children filled the air. The sight stung to madness our troops. Two regiments of Kanawha Valley men, beholding in plain view the homes of their childhood blazing, and catching the cries of distress of their mothers, wives and sisters, rushed, furious and headlong, to the rescue. Happily they were not too late to arrest the conflagration, and a few public buildings and some private residences were all that fell under the enemy's torch.

The campaign of the Kanawha was accomplished by us with a loss of not more than a hundred men. The results were apparently of great importance, as we had secured the great salines of Virginia,* driven the enemy from the Valley of the

---

* But few persons, even in the South, have adequate ideas of the resources and facilities for the production of salt in the Kanawha Valley, and of the value of that small strip of Confederate territory. In Kanawha county alone forty furnaces were in operation; some operated by gas and some by coal. Salt by the million of bushels had been sold here from year to year at twelve cents and twenty cents per bushel, filling the markets of the West and South. Ships for Liverpool had formerly taken out salt as ballast; and yet, at one time in the war, owing to the practical cutting off of the saline supplies in Virginia, this article, formerly of such cheap bulk, had been sold in Richmond at a dollar and a half *a pound*.

Kanawha, and put our forces in position to threaten his towns on the bank of the Ohio. But unhappily we shall have occasion hereafter to see that these results were ephemeral, and that this unfortunate part of Virginia was destined to other experiences of the rigour of the enemy.

For the present the progress of events takes us from the old battle-fields of the South and introduces us to a novel theatre of the war—that theatre being located for the first time on the soil and within the recognized dominions of the enemy.

On the fourth day of September Gen. Lee, leaving to his right Arlington Heights, to which had retreated the shattered army of Pope, crossed the Potomac into Maryland.

The immediate designs of this movement of the Confederate commander were to seize Harper's Ferry and to test the spirit of the Marylanders; but in order to be unmolested in his plans, he threatened Pennsylvania from Hagerstown, throwing Gov. Curtain almost into hysterics, and animating Baltimore with the hope that he would emancipate her from the iron tyranny of Gen. Wool.

After the advance of our army to Frederick, the Northern journals were filled with anxious reports of a movement of our troops in the direction of Pennsylvania. While the people of the North were agitated by these reports, the important movement undertaken for the present by Gen. Lee was in the direction of Virginia. It appears that for this purpose our forces in Maryland were divided into three corps, commanded by Generals Jackson, Longstreet and Hill. The forces under Jackson having re-crossed the Potomac at Williamsport and taken possession of Martinsburg, had then passed rapidly behind Harper's Ferry, that a capture might be effected of the garrison and stores known to be there. In the meantime, the corps of Longstreet and Hill were put in position to cover the operations of Jackson and to hold back McClellan's forces, which were advancing to the relief of Harper's Ferry.

Gen. McClellan had resumed the chief command of the Federal armies on the second day of September. On the fourteenth of that month, he fought his first battle in Maryland, called the battle of Boonsboro' or of South Mountain.

## THE BATTLE OF BOONSBORO'.

When Jackson had diverged to the left from the line of march pursued by the main body of the Confederates re-crossing the Potomac and moving rapidly upon Harper's Ferry, Gen. Longstreet had meanwhile continued his march to Hagerstown, and there awaited the result. To frustrate this design, and relieve Gen. Miles and the ten or twelve thousand men who occupied Harper's Ferry, the enemy moved their entire force upon the Gap in the mountains, to which we have alluded, and there sought to break through the barrier we were so jealously guarding, divide our lines, and defeat our armies in detail. Foreseeing this intention on the part of the Federals, Gen. Lee had posted the division of Gen. D. H. Hill in and around the Gap, on the opposite side and summit, with instructions to hold the position at every hazard, until he was notified of the success of the movement of Jackson and his co-operates. It was certainly no part of the original plan to fight a pitched battle here, except to secure this one desirable result.

The pass is known as Boonsboro' Gap, being a continuation over the broad back of the mountain of the national turnpike. The road is winding, narrow, rocky and rugged, with either a deep ravine on one side and the steep sides of the mountain on the other, or like a huge channel cut through a solid rock. Near the crest are two or three houses, which, to some extent, overlook the adjacent valleys, but elsewhere the face of the mountain is unbroken by a solitary vestige of the handiwork of man.

The battle commenced soon after daylight, by a vigorous cannonade, under cover of which, two or three hours later, first the skirmishers and then the main bodies became engaged. A regular line of battle on our part, either as regards numbers or regularity, was impossible, and the theatre of the fight was therefore limited. The fortunes of the day, which were desperate enough in the face of the most overwhelming numbers, were stubbornly contested by the Confederates. The brigade of Gen. Garland of Virginia, the first engaged, lost its brave commander. While endeavoring to rally his men, he fell, pierced in the breast by a musket ball, and died upon the field.

While our lines were giving way under the pressure of the enemy's numbers, the welcome sounds of reinforcements were borne on the air. The corps of Gen. Longstreet was at Hagerstown, fourteen miles distant, and at daylight commenced its march towards the scene of action. Hurrying forward with all speed, stopping neither to rest nor eat, the advance arrived at the pass about four o'clock, and were at once sent into the mountain. Brigade after brigade, as rapidly as it came up, followed, until by five o'clock nearly the entire command, with the exception of the brigade of General Toombs, which had been left at Hagerstown, was in position, and a portion of it already engaged. Evans was assigned to the extreme left, Drayton to the right, and Hood, with his "ragged Texans," occupied the centre.

The accession of fresh numbers at once changed the tone and temper of the combat. The ominous volleys of musketry rolled down the mountain in almost deafening succession. But advance we could not. The enemy in numbers were like a solid wall. Their bayonets gleamed from behind every rock and bush. Retreat, we would not, and thus we fought, doggedly giving and taking the fearful blows of battle, until long after nightfall.

The cessation of firing left the respective forces, with some exceptions, in nearly the same relative situation as at the commencement of the battle. The enemy gained nothing and we lost nothing. On the contrary, our object had been obtained. We had encountered a force of the enemy near five-fold our own, and after a bloody day, in which our killed and wounded were quite twenty-five hundred and those of the enemy probably more, we had held him in check until Gen. Jackson was heard from and the success of his enterprise rendered certain.

## THE CAPTURE OF HARPER'S FERRY.

While the action of Boonsboro' was in progress, and the enemy attempting to force his way through the main pass on the Frederick and Hagerstown road, the capture of Harper's Ferry was accomplished by the army corps of Gen. Jackson.

During the night of the 14th September, General Jackson planted his guns, and in the morning opened in all directions on the Federal forces drawn up in line of battle on Bolivar Heights. The white flag was raised at twenty minutes past seven. At the moment of surrender, Col. Miles, the Federal commander, was struck by a piece of shell, which carried away his left thigh. "My God, I am hit," he exclaimed, and fell into the arms of his aid-de-camp.

The extent of the conquest is determined by the fact that we took eleven thousand troops, an equal number of small arms, seventy-three pieces of artillery, and about two hundred wagons. The force of the enemy which surrendered consisted of twelve regiments of infantry, three companies of cavalry and six companies of artillery. The scene of the surrender was one of deep humiliation to the North. It was indeed a repetition of the revolutionary glories of Yorktown to see here the proud, gaily-dressed soldiers of the oppressor drawn up in line, stacking their arms, and surrendering to the ragged, barefoot, half-starved soldiers of liberty.

## THE BATTLE OF SHARPSBURG.

On the 17th of September Gen. Lee had retired to unite his forces, as far as possible, to confront the still advancing forces of McClellan, which, having obtained possession of Crampton's Gap on the direct road from Frederick City to Sharpsburg, were pressing our forces, and seemed determined on a decisive battle. Sharpsburg is about ten miles north of Harper's Ferry and about eight miles west of Boonsboro'.

This town lies in a deep valley. The country around it is broken. Ascending a hill just on the outer edge of the town, and looking towards the Blue Ridge, the eye ranges over the greater portion of the eventful field. To the right and left is a succession of hills which were occupied by the Confederates. In front is the beautiful valley of the Antietam, divided longitudinally by the river which empties into the Potomac on your right, and behind, forming a background to the picture, only two miles distant, are the steep, umbrageous sides of the Blue Ridge.

The morning of the 17th found Gen. Lee strongly posted, but with no more than forty-five thousand men when the battle commenced. The force of the enemy could not have been much short of one hundred and fifty thousand men; of whom one hundred thousand were trained soldiers, disciplined in camp and field since the commencement of the war.

The forces of the enemy were commanded by McClellan in person, and numbered the whole command of Gen. Burnside, recently augmented by the addition of several new regiments; the army corps lately under Gen. McDowell, now under command of Gen. Hooker; Gen. Sumner's corps; Gen. Franklin's corps; Gen. Banks' corps, commanded by Gen. Williams; and Sykes' division of Fitz John Porter's corps. Their line of battle was between four and five miles long, with their left stretching across the Sharpsburg road. Burnside was on the extreme left; Porter held a commanding eminence to the right of Burnside, though Warren's brigade of Porter's corps was subsequently posted in the woods on the left in support of Burnside's men; Sumner's corps was on an eminence next to the right or north from Porter, and General Hooker had the extreme right.

On the afternoon of Tuesday, the 16th, the enemy opened a light artillery fire on our lines. At three next morning every man was at his post, and awaited in solemn silence the day dawn. No sooner did the light break in the east than the picket firing began, and increased in fury until about sunrise, when artillery and infantry together grappled in the terrible fight.

Large masses of the Federals, who had crossed the Antietam above our position, assembled on our left. They advanced in three compact lines. The divisions of Generals McLaws, R. H. Anderson, A. P. Hill and Walker, who were expected to have joined Gen. Lee on the previous night, had not come up. Generals Jackson's and Ewell's divisions were thrown to the left of Generals Hill and Longstreet. The enemy advanced between the Antietam and the Sharpsburg and Hagerstown turnpike, and was met by Gen. D. H. Hill's and the left of Gen. Longstreet's divisions, where the conflict raged, extending to our entire left.

When the troops of D. H. Hill were engaged, the battle raged with uncommon fury. Backwards, forwards, surging and swaying like a ship in storm, the various columns are seen in motion. It is a hot place for the enemy. They are directly under our guns, and we mow them down like grass. The raw levies, sustained by the veterans behind, come up to the work well, and fight for a short time with an excitement incident to their novel experiences of a battle; but soon a portion of their line gives way in confusion. Their reserves come up, and endeavor to retrieve the fortunes of the day. Our centre, however, stands firm as adamant, and they fall back.

Prior to the arrival of the divisions of McLaws, Anderson and Walker, who had been advanced to support the left wing and centre, as soon as they had crossed the Potomac on the morning of the 17th, that portion of our line was forced back by superior numbers. As soon, however, as these forces could be brought into action, the enemy was driven back, our line was restored, and our position maintained during the rest of the day.

Time and again did the Federals perseveringly press close up to our ranks, so near indeed that their supporting batteries were obliged to cease firing, lest they should kill their own men, but just as often were they driven back by the combined elements of destruction which we brought to bear upon them. It was an hour when every man was wanted. And nobly did our brave soldiers do their duty. "It is beyond all wonder," writes a Federal officer, "how men such as the rebel troops are can fight as they do. That those ragged wretches, sick, hungry, and in all ways miserable, should prove such heroes in fight, is past explanation. Men never fought better. There was one regiment that stood up before the fire of two or three of our long range batteries and of two regiments of infantry, and though the air around them was vocal with the whistle of bullets and the scream of shells, there they stood and delivered their fire in perfect order." *

In the afternoon the enemy advanced on our right, where General Jones's division was posted, and he handsomely maintained his position. The bridge over the Antietam creek was guarded by General Toombs's brigade, which gallantly resisted the approach of the enemy; but their superior numbers enabling them to extend their left, they crossed below the bridge, and forced our line back in some confusion.

Our troops fought until they were nearly cut to pieces, and then retreated only because they had fired their last round. It was at this juncture that the immense Yankee force crossed the river, and made the dash against our line, which well nigh

---

\* There are some characteristic anecdotes of the close quarters in which the battle of Sharpsburg was fought and the desperate valour shown in such straits. At one passage of the battle, Colonel Geary of the famous Hampton Legion, one of the most celebrated corps of the army, found himself confronted by an overwhelming force of the enemy. An officer came forward and demanded his surrender. "Surrender! Hell!" exclaimed the intrepid South Carolinian, as with the spring of a tiger he seized the officer and clapped a pistol to his head, "if you don't surrender your own command to me this instant, you infernal scoundrel, I'll blow your brains out." The astonished and affrighted Yankee called out that he surrendered. But his men were not as cowardly as himself, and the flag of the regiment he commanded was only taken after the colour-bearer had been cut down by our swords.

proved a success. But it was at this moment also that welcome and long-expected reinforcements reached us. At four o'clock in the afternoon General A. P. Hill's division came up and joined the Confederate right. It was well that General Burnside's advance on the Federal left was so long delayed, and was eventually made with overwhelming numbers. The day closed with Gen. Burnside clinging closely to the bridge, beyond which he could not advance, with General Jackson on the same ground as the Confederates held in the morning, upon as level and drawn a battle as history exhibits. But it was fought for half the day with 45,000 men on the Confederate side, and for the remaining half with not more than an aggregate of 70,000 men, against a host which is admitted to have consisted of 130,000 men, and may have been more.

It is certain that if we had had fresh troops to hurl against Burnside at the bridge of Antietam, the day would have been ours. The anxious messages of this officer to McClellan for reinforcements were again and again repeated as the evening wore on, and the replies of that commander showed that he understood where was the critical point of the battle. As the sun was sinking in the west, he dispatched orders to General Burnside, urging him to hold his position, and as the messenger was riding away he called him back—"Tell him if he *cannot* hold his ground, then the bridge, to the last man!—always the bridge.! If the bridge is lost, all is lost."

The enemy held the bridge, but of other portions of the field we retained possession. Varying as may have been the successes of the day, they left us equal masters of the field with our antagonist. But our loss had been considerable; it was variously estimated from five to nine thousand; and we had to deplore the fall of Generals Branch and Starke, with other brave and valuable officers. The loss of the enemy was not less than our own.* They had fought well and been ably

---

* The New York *Tribune* said: "The dead lie in heaps, and the wounded are coming in by thousands. Around and in a large barn about half a mile from the spot where General Hooker engaged the enemy's left, there were

commanded. But they had the advantage not only of numbers, but of a position from which they could assume an offensive or defensive attitude at will, besides which their signal stations on the Blue Ridge commanded a view of our every movement.

The battle-field of Sharpsburg will long be remembered from the terrible and hideous circumstance that so many of the dead were left unburied upon it. Some of them laid with their faces to the ground, whither they had turned in the agony of death, and in which position they had died; others were heaped in piles of three and four together, with their arms interlocked, and their faces turned upwards towards the sky. Scores of them were laid out in rows, as though the death-shot had penetrated their breasts as they were advancing to the attack. Covered with mud and dust, with their faces and clothes smeared with blood and gore, there they rotted in the sun!

The close of this great battle left neither army in a condition to renew the conflict, although our own brave troops were desperately ready to do so. But the next morning McClellan had disappeared from our front, and, knowing the superiority of the enemy's numbers, and not willing to risk the combinations he was attempting, Gen. Lee crossed the Potomac without molestation, and took position at or near Shepherdstown.

The enemy claimed a victory, but the best evidence, if any were wanting, to prove that he was really defeated and his army crippled, is found in the fact that he did not renew the fight on the succeeding day, and on the next permitted Gen. Lee to re-cross the Potomac without an attempt to ob-

---

counted 1,250 wounded. In Sumner's corps alone, our loss in killed, wounded and missing amounts to five thousand two hundred and eight. The 15th Massachusetts regiment went into the battle with five hundred and fifty men, and came out with one hundred and fifty-six. The 19th Massachusetts, of four hundred and six, lost all but one hundred and forty-seven. The 5th New Hampshire, about three hundred strong, lost one hundred and ten enlisted men and fourteen officers. Massachusetts, out of eight regiments engaged, loses upwards of fifteen hundred, and Pennsylvania has suffered more than any other State."

struck him. The pretence of victory on this occasion cost McClellan his command. On the 20th of September he made a feint or a weak and hesitating attempt to cross the Potomac at Shepherdstown, when the column which had crossed was fallen upon by A. P. Hill and pushed into the river, which was filled with the dead and wounded attempting to escape.

The charges against McClellan consequent upon his pretended victory, were sustained by the official testimony of the Yankee commander-in-chief. The report of Gen. Halleck accused McClellan of disobedience of orders, in refusing to advance against the enemy after the battle of Sharpsburg, upon the plea that the army lacked shoes, tents, stores, and other necessaries, which General Halleck held to be entirely unfounded, asserting that all the wants of the army were duly cared for, and that any causes of delay that might have occurred were trivial and speedily remedied. He furthermore charged McClellan with willful neglect of a peremptory order of the 6th of October to cross the Potomac immediately, to give battle to the Confederates or to drive them South.

A fatal consequence to the Yankees of the campaign in Maryland was the sacrifice to popular clamour and official envy of him whom they had formerly made their military pet and "Napoleon," and who, although the extent of his pretensions was ridiculous, was really esteemed in the South as the ablest General in the North. The man who succeeded him in the command of the army of the Potomac was. Gen. Ambrose Burnside, of Rhode Island. He had served during the Mexican war as a second lieutenant; and at the time he was raised to his important command, the captain of the company with which he had served in Mexico, Edmund Barry, was a recruiting agent in Richmond for the "Maryland Line."

We have perhaps imperfectly sketched the movements of the Maryland campaign.* But we have sought to determine its

---

\* It would be difficult to find a more just summary of the campaign in Northern Virginia and on the Upper Potomac, or one the statements of which

historical features without any large enumeration of details. It was mixed with much of triumph to us; it added lustre to our arms; it inflicted no loss upon us for which we did not exact full retribution; it left the enemy nothing but barren re-

may be more safely appropriated by history than the following address of Gen. Lee to his army:

"HEADQUARTERS ARMY NORTHERN VIRGINIA,
October 2d, 1862.

*General Orders, No. 116.*

In reviewing the achievements of the army during the present campaign, the Commanding General cannot withhold the expression of his admiration of the indomitable courage it has displayed in battle, and its cheerful endurance of privation and hardship on the march.

Since your great victories around Richmond you have defeated the enemy at Cedar Mountain, expelled him from the Rappahannock, and, after a conflict of three days, utterly repulsed him on the Plains of Manassas, and forced him to take shelter within the fortifications around his capital.

Without halting for repose you crossed the Potomac, stormed the heights of Harper's Ferry, made prisoners of more than eleven thousand men, and captured upwards of seventy pieces of artillery, all their small arms and other munitions of war.

While one corps of the army was thus engaged, the other insured its success by arresting at Boonsboro' the combined armies of the enemy, advancing under their favourite General to the relief of their beleaguered comrades.

On the field of Sharpsburg, with less than one-third his numbers, you resisted, from daylight until dark, the whole army of the enemy, and repulsed every attack along his entire front, of more than four miles in extent.

The whole of the following day you stood prepared to resume the conflict on the same ground, and retired next morning, without molestation, across the Potomac.

Two attempts, subsequently made by the enemy, to follow you across the river, have resulted in his complete discomfiture, and being driven back with loss.

Achievements such as these demanded much valour and patriotism. History records few examples of greater fortitude and endurance than this army has exhibited; and I am commissioned by the President to thank you, in the name of the Confederate States, for the undying fame you have won for their arms.

Much as you have done, much more remains to be accomplished. The enemy again threatens us with invasion, and to your tried valour and patriotism the country looks with confidence for deliverance and safety. Your past exploits give assurance that this confidence is not misplaced.

R. E. LEE,
General Commanding."

sults; and it gave us a valuable lesson of the state of public opinion in Maryland.

There is one point to which the mind naturally refers for a just historical interpretation of the Maryland campaign. The busy attempts of newspapers to pervert the truth of history were renewed in an effort to misrepresent the designs of Gen. Lee in crossing the Potomac, as limited to a mere incursion, the object of which was to take Harper's Ferry, and that accomplished, to return into Virginia and await the movements of McClellan. It is not possible that our commanding General can be a party to this pitiful deceit, to cover up any failure of his, or that he has viewed with any thing but disgust the offer of falsehood and misrepresentation made to him by flatterers.

Let it be freely confessed, that the object of General Lee in crossing the Potomac was to hold and occupy Maryland; that his proclamation issued at Frederick, offering protection to the Marylanders,, is incontrovertible evidence of this fact; that he was forced to return to Virginia, not by stress of any single battle, but by the force of many circumstances, some of which history should blush to record; that, in these respects, the Maryland campaign was a failure. But it was a failure relieved by brilliant episodes, mixed with at least one extraordinary triumph of our arms, and to a great extent compensated by many solid results.

In the brief campaign in Maryland, our army had given the most brilliant illustrations of valour; it had given the enemy at Harper's Ferry a reverse without parallel in the history of the war; it had inflicted upon him a loss in men and material greater than our own; and, in retreating into Virginia, it left him neither spoils nor prisoners, as evidence of the successes he claimed. The indignant comment of the New York *Tribune* on Lee's retirement into Virginia is the enemy's own record of the barren results that were left them. "He leaves us," said this paper, "the *debris* of his late camps, two disabled pieces of artillery, a few hundred of his stragglers, perhaps two thousand of his wounded, and as many more of his unburied dead. Not a sound field-piece, caisson, ambulance or wagon, not a tent, a box of stores or a pound of ammunition. He takes with him the supplies gathered in Maryland, and the rich spoils of Harper's Ferry." The same paper declared, that the failure of Maryland to rise or to contribute recruits, (all the accessions to our force, obtained in this State, did not exceed eight hundred men,) was the defeat of Lee, and about the only defeat he did sustain; that the Confederate losses proceeded mainly from the failure of their own exaggerated expectations; that Lee's retreat over the Potomac was a master-piece; and that the manner in which he combined Hill and Jackson for the envelopment of Harper's Ferry, while he checked the Federal columns at Hagerstown Heights and Crampton Gap, was probably the best achievement of the war.

The failure of the people of Maryland to respond to the proclamation of Gen. Lee issued at Frederick, inviting them to his standard, and generously assuring protection to all classes of political opinion, admits of some excuse; but the explanations commonly made on this subject do not amount to their vindication. It is true that when Gen. Lee was in Frederick, he was forty-five miles from the city of Baltimore—a city surrounded by Federal bayonets, zealously guarded by an armed Federal police, and lying in the shadow of Fort McHenry and of two powerful fortifications located within the limits of the corporation. It is true that our army passed only through two of the remote counties of the State, namely: Frederick and Washington, which with Carroll and Alleghany, are well known to contain the most violent "Union" population in Maryland. It is true that the South could not have expected a welcome in these counties or a desperate mutiny for the Confederacy in Baltimore. But it was expected that Southern sympathizers in other parts of the State, who so glibly ran the blockade on adventures of trade, might as readily work their way to the Confederate army as to the Confederate markets; and it was not expected that the few recruits who timidly advanced to our lines would have been so easily dismayed by the rags of our soldiers and by the prospects of a service that promised equal measures of hardship and glory.

The army which rested again in Virginia had made a history that will flash down the tide of time a lustre of glory. It had done an amount of marching and fighting that appears almost incredible even to those minds familiar with the records of great military exertions. Leaving the banks of James River, it proceeded directly to the line of the Rappahannock, and moving out from that river, it fought its way to the Potomac, crossed that stream and moved on to Fredericktown and Hagerstown, had a heavy engagement at the mountain gaps below, fought the greatest pitched battle of the war at Sharpsburg; and then recrossed the Potomac back into Virginia. During all this time, covering the full space of a month, the troops rested but four days. Of the men who performed these wonders, one-fifth of them were barefoot, one-half of them in rags and the whole of them half famished.

The remarkable campaign which we have briefly sketched, extending from the banks of the James River to those of the Potomac, impressed the world with wonder and admiration, excited an outburst of applause among living nations, which anticipated the verdict of posterity, and set the whole of Europe ringing with praises of the heroism and fighting qualities of the Southern armies. The South was already obtaining some portion of the moral rewards of this war, in the estimation in which she was held by the great martial nations of the world. She had purchased the rank with a bloody price. She had extorted homage from the most intelligent and influential organs of public opinion in the Old World, from men well versed in the history of ancient and modern times, and from those great critics of cotemporary history, which are least accustomed to the language of extravagant compliment.

The following tribute from the London *Times*—the great organ of historic precedent and educated opinion in the Old World—was echoed by the other journals of Europe:

"The people of the Confederate States have made them-selves famous. If the renown of brilliant courage, stern devotion to a cause, and military achievements almost without a parallel, can compensate men for the toil and privations of the hour, then the countrymen of Lee and Jackson may be consoled amid their sufferings. From all parts of Europe, from their enemies as well as their friends, from those who condemn their acts as well as those who sympathize with them, comes the tribute of admiration. When the history of this war is written, the admiration will doubtless become deeper and stronger, for the veil which has covered the South will be drawn away and disclose a picture of patriotism, of unanimous self-sacrifice, of wise and firm administration, which we can now only see indistinctly. The details of extraordinary national effort which has led to the repulse and almost to the destruction of an invading force of more than half a million men, will then become known to the world, and, whatever may be the fate of the new nationality, or its subsequent claims to the respect of mankind, it will assuredly begin its career with a reputation for genius and valour which the most famous nations may envy."

It is at first appearance strange, that while such was the public opinion in England of our virtues and abilities, that that government should have continued so unjust and obstinate with respect to our claims for recognition. But the explanation is easy. The demonstrations of the conflict which awakened such generous admiration of us in the breasts of a majority of the English people were to the government the subjects only of jealous and interested views. We had trusted too much to manifestations of public opinion in England; we had lost sight of the distinction between the people and government of that country, and had forgotten that the latter had, since the beginning of this war, been cold and reserved, had never given us anything to hope from its sympathies or its principles, and had limited its action on the American question to the unfeeling and exacting measures of selfishness.

The bloody and unhappy revelation which the war has made of enormous military resources has naturally given to Europe, and especially to England, an extraordinary interest in its continuation. It is probable that she would not have hesitated to recognize the South, unless firmly pursuaded of our ability and resolution to carry on the war, and unless she had another object to gain besides that of a permanent division in the nationality and power of her old rival. That object was the exhaustion of both North and South. England proposed to effect the continuation of the war, as far as possible, to the mutual ruin of the two nations engaged in it, by standing aside and trusting that after vast expenditures of blood and waste of resources the separation of the Union would be quite as surely accomplished by the self-devotion of the South, as by the less profitable mode of foreign intervention.

In this unchristian and inhuman calculation, England had rightly estimated the resolution and spirit of the South. We were prepared to win our independence with the great prices of blood and suffering that she had named. But we understood what lurked behind the mask of British conscience, and we treasured the lesson for the future.

## OUR FOREIGN RELATIONS IN THE WAR.

It is not amiss in this connection to make a summary in reference to the relations between the Confederacy and the neutral powers of Europe during the progress of the war to the present period of our narrative.

The confederation of the Southern States in 1861 was the third political union that had been formed between the States of North America. The first act of secession dates as far back as 1789, when eleven of the States, becoming dissatisfied with the old articles of confederation made in 1778, seceded and formed a second union. When in 1861 eleven of the States again seceded and united themselves under the style of the Confederate States of North America, they exercised a right which required no justification, and which in a former instance had not been contested by any party at home, or made the subject of discussion with any third power.

On every attempt for the opening of formal diplomatic intercourse with the European powers, the commissioners of the Confederate States had met with the objection that these powers could not assume to judge between the conflicting representations of the two parties as to the true nature of their previous mutual relations; and that they were constrained by international usage and the considerations of propriety to recognize the self-evident fact of the existence of a war, and to maintain a strict neutrality during its progress.

Of this neutrality, two remarks are to be made:

First. It was founded upon the grave errour that the separate sovereignty and independence of the States had been merged into one common sovereignty; an errour easily induced by the delegation of power granted by these States to the Federal government to represent them in foreign intercourse, but one that should have been as easily dispelled by appeals to reason and historical fact.

Secondly. The practical operation of this falsely assumed and falsely named "neutrality" was an actual decision against the rights of the South, and had been but little short of active hostilities against her.

By the governments of England and France, the doctrines announced in the treaty of Paris were ignored, and the monstrous Yankee blockade, by some forty or fifty vessels, of a coast line nearly three thousand miles in extent, came to be acknowledged and respected. When this recognition of the blockade was made, it is very certain that the whole Yankee navy, if employed on that service and nothing else, could not furnish vessels enough to pass signals from point to point along the coast. At the time this paper blockade was declared and acknowledged, the Navy Register shows that the Federal Government had in commission but forty vessels all told. These were scattered over the world: some of them were in the

China seas, some in the Pacific, some in the Mediterranean, some in our own part of the world, and some in another. The actual force employed in the blockading service did not give one vessel for every fifty miles of coast. In addition to these considerations, it had been shown by unquestionable evidence, furnished in part by the officials of the European powers themselves, that the few Southern ports really guarded by naval forces of the Yankees had been invested so inefficiently that hundreds of entries had been effected into them since the declaration of the blockade.

During nearly two years of struggle had this boasted "neutrality" of the European powers operated as active hostility against us, for they had helped the enemy to prevent us, with a force which was altogether inadequate, from obtaining supplies of prime necessity.

Nor was this all. We had no commerce; but in that the enemy was rich. We had no navy; in that he was strong. Therefore, when England and her allies declared that neither the armed cruisers nor the prizes of either of the belligerents should have hospitality and protection in neutral ports, the prohibition, directed against both belligerents, was in reality effective against the Confederate States alone, for they alone could find a hostile commerce on the ocean.

Thus it was that, in the progress of the war, the neutral nations of Europe had pursued a policy which, nominally impartial, had been practically most favourable to our enemies and most detrimental to us.

The temper which this injustice produced in the South was fortunate. The South was conscious of powers of resistance of which the world was incredulous; and the first feverish expectations of recognition by the European powers were replaced by a proud self-reliance and a calm confidence, which were forming our national character, while contributing at the same time to the immediate successes of our arms.

The recognition by France and England of Lincoln's paper blockade, had by no means proved an unmitigated evil to us.

It had forced us into many branches of industry, into which, but for that blockade, we should have never entered. We had excellent powder mills of our own, and fine armories which turned out muskets, rifles, sabres, &c. The war found no more than half a dozen furnaces in blast in the whole Confederacy, and most of those had been destroyed by the enemy. But the government had given such encouragement to the iron men that new mines had been opened in other parts of the Confederacy, and furnaces enough were already up or in the course of erection, to supply the wants of the government. In the last spring we had planted not more than one-fourth of the usual breadth of land in cotton, and our surplus labour was directed to breadstuffs and provisions. All these were the fruits to us of a blockade which threatened England especially with a terrible reaction of her own injustice, and was laying up a store of retribution for Europe.

## CHAPTER V.

Movements in the West...The Splendid Programme of the Yankees...Kentucky the Critical Point...Gen. Kirby Smith's Advance into Kentucky...THE BATTLE OF RICHMOND...Reception of the Confederates in Lexington...Expectation of an Attack on Cincinnati...Gen. Bragg's Plans...Smith's Movement to Bragg's Lines...Escape of the Yankee Forces from Cumberland Gap...Affair of Munfordsville...Gen. Bragg between the Enemy and the Ohio...An Opportunity for a Decisive Blow...Buell's Escape to Louisville...The Inauguration of Governor at Frankfort...An Idle Ceremony...Probable Surprise of Gen. Bragg...THE BATTLE OF PERRYVILLE...Its Immediate Results in our Favour...Bragg's Failure to Concentrate his Forces...His Resolution of Retreat...Scenes of the Retreat from Kentucky...Errours of the Campaign...A Lame Excuse...Public Sentiment in Kentucky—The Demoralization of that State...The Lessons of Submission.

On the same day that victory perched on our banners on the plains of Manassas, an important success was achieved by our brave troops in another part of the Confederacy. A victory gained at Richmond in Kentucky gave a companion to Manassas, and opened in the West a prospect of the advance of our troops simultaneous with the dawn of new hopes and aspirations in the East.

A few paragraphs are sufficient for the rapid summary of events necessary to the contemplation of the situation in the West, in which the battle of Richmond was won.

The North had prepared a splendid programme of operations in the country west of the Alleghany. But few persons on the Southern seaboard had adequate ideas of the grandeur of the enemy's preparations or of the strength of the forces concentrating on the march in the Western country. These preparations exceeded in magnitude all military movements designed or attempted since the commencement of the war; for they contemplated not only the expulsion of our forces from Kentucky and Tennessee and the States west of the Mississippi, but the penetration through the Gulf States of the heart of the South. The army, now well on its way into Middle Tennessee, had Northern Alabama and Georgia for its ultimate destination; that of Grant was already advanced into Mississippi; that of McClernand, organizing at Columbus and Memphis, was intended to operate on the Mississippi; another army was already operating in Missouri and Arkansas; and a gunboat fleet had been placed on the waters of the Mississippi, which was said to be terrible in destructiveness and impregnable in strength. Such was the extent of the enemy's plans of campaign in the West.

The situation left the South but little choice than that of making an aggressive movement by which North Alabama and Middle and East Tennessee might be cleared of the forces of the enemy and they compelled to fall back to assist General Buell in Kentucky—this State being fixed as the critical point in the West and the field of the active campaign. The brief retirement of Gen. Beauregard from active command on account of ill health, which was made shortly after his evacuation of Corinth, left the way open to the promotion of Gen. Bragg, a favourite of the administration, who had a certain military reputation, but as an active commander in the field had the confidence neither of the army nor of the public. The first steps of the campaign were easily decided by this commander. It was to use the forces of Gen. Kirby Smith to threaten Cincinnati, and thus distract the attention and divide the forces of the enemy; while Gen. Bragg himself, co-operating with Smith, was to fulfill the great purpose of the campaign, which was the expulsion of the enemy from Kentucky and the capture of Louisville, thus subjecting the whole of that great grain-growing and meat-producing commonwealth, with all its rich stores, to our control.

Early in the month of August, Gen. McCown, under the orders of Gen. Smith, moved his division from London to Knoxville in East Tennessee. Thence our troops moved to the gaps in the Cumberland mountains, being joined by Clai-

THE SECOND YEAR OF THE WAR.           151

borne's division at the lower gap, when the whole force was ordered through with the trains and artillery. From this time our troops made forced marches until they reached Barboursville, which is on the main thoroughfare by which the Yankees received their supplies at the gap by way of Lexington. Halting there long enough only to get water, our wearied army was pushed on to the Cumberland Ford. Here a few days' rest was allowed to the troops, who had performed their hard march over stony roads, with their almost bare feet, and with green corn garnished with a small supply of poor beef for their food.

### THE BATTLE OF RICHMOND.

On the 29th of August our troops were in striking distance of the enemy at Richmond. Until our advance descended the Big Hill, it met with no opposition from the enemy. Here, on the morning of the 29th, the enemy was discovered to be in force in our front, and a bold reconnoissance of the cavalry under Colonel Scott, in the afternoon, indicated a determination to give us battle. Although Churchill's division did not get up until quite late in the afternoon, and then in an apparently exhausted state, Gen. Smith determined to march to Richmond the next day, even at the cost of a battle with the whole force of the enemy. The leading division, under Gen. Claiborne, was moved early the next morning, and, after advancing two or three miles, they found the enemy drawn up in line of battle in a fine position, near Mount Zion Church, six miles from Richmond. Without waiting for Churchill's division, Claiborne at once commenced the action, and by half-past seven o'clock in the morning, the fire of artillery was brisk on both sides. As our force was almost too small to storm the position in front, without a disastrous loss, General Churchill was sent with one of his brigades to turn the enemy's right. While this movement was being executed, a bold and well-conducted attempt, on the part of the enemy, to turn

Claiborne's right, was admirably foiled by the firmness of Col. Preston Smith's brigade, who repulsed the enemy with great slaughter. In the meantime Gen. Churchill had been completely successful in his movement upon the enemy's right flank, where, by a bold charge, his men completed a victory already partially gained by the gallantry of our troops on the left.

The Yankees having been repulsed and driven in confusion from this part of the field, might have retreated without risking another passage at arms, had they not misapprehended our movements.

Gen. Smith having ordered the cavalry to go around to the north of Richmond and attempt to cut off the retreat of the enemy, our artillery ceased firing, and the enemy, thinking our army was preparing for a retreat, had the foolhardiness to rally on their own retreat and attempt a charge upon the Texas and Arkansas troops under McCray, who, to the great astonishment of the enemy, instead of running away, met them on the half-way ground. This gallant brigade of Texans and Arkansians had to fight the battle alone. Although the odds opposed to them were fearful, yet, by reserving their own fire, under the deafening roar of the enemy's guns, and by a well-timed and dashing charge upon the advancing lines, they completely routed and put to flight the hosts of the enemy. They fled in the wildest confusion and disorder. Their knapsacks, swords, pistols, hats and canteens, scattered along the road, would have marked the route they travelled, even if their dead and dying had not too plainly showed the way.

In passing a deserted camp of the enemy, Gen. Smith found from some of the wounded that Gen. Nelson, the Yankee commander, with reinforcements, had arrived after the second battle. A march of two miles brought us within sight of the town, in front of which, and on a commanding ridge, with both flanks resting upon woods, Nelson had determined to make a final stand. Churchill, with a brigade, was sent off to the left, when a deafening roar of musketry soon announced the raging of a furious combat. In the meanwhile, Preston Smith, bringing up his division at a double-quick, formed in front of the enemy's centre and left. Almost without waiting the command of the officers, this division coolly advanced under the murderous fire of a force twice their number, and drove them from the field in the greatest confusion, and with immense slaughter. The exhausted condition of our men, together with the closing in of night, prevented the pursuit of the enemy more than a mile beyond Richmond.

The results of the day were gratifying enough. With less than half his force, Gen. Smith had attacked and carried a very strong position at Mount Zion Church, after a hard fight of two hours. Again, a still better position at White's farm, in half an hour; and finally, in the town of Richmond, just before sunset, our indomitable troops deliberately walked (they were too tired to run) up to a magnificent position, manned by ten thousand of the enemy, many of them perfectly fresh, and carried it in fifteen minutes. In the last engagement, we took prisoners from thirteen regiments. Our loss in killed and wounded was about four hundred; that of the enemy was about one thousand, and his prisoners five thousand. The immediate fruits of the victory were nine pieces of artillery and ten thousand small arms, and a large quantity of supplies. These latter were greatly increased by the capture of Richmond and Frankfort, the whole number of cannon taken being about twenty.

On the first day of September Gen. Smith took up the line of March for Lexington; and on the morning of the fourth day of that month, our forces, consisting of a Texas brigade and an Arkansas, brigade under the command of General Churchill, and General Claiborne's division and Gen. Heath's division, all under the command of Gen. Kirby Smith, marched through the city amidst the hearty and generous welcome of thousands of men, women and children.

The entrance of our troops into Lexington was the occasion of the most inspiriting and touching scenes. Streets, windows and gardens were filled with ladies and little girls with streamers of red and blue ribbons and flags with stars. Beautiful women seized the hard brown hands of our rough and ragged soldiers, and with tears and smiles thanked them again and again for coming into Kentucky and freeing them from the presence and insults of the hated and insolent Yankees. For hours the enthusiasm of the people was unbounded. At every corner of the streets, baskets of provisions and buckets of water were placed for the refreshment of our weary soldiers, and hundreds of our men were presented with shoes and hats and coats and tobacco from the grateful people. Private residences were turned for the time into public houses of entertainment, free to all who could be persuaded to go and eat. But if the reception of the infantry was enthusiastic, the tears, the smiles, and shouts and cheers of wild delight which greeted General John Morgan's cavalry as they came dashing through the streets amidst clouds of dust, was without a parallel. The wildest joy ruled the hours. The bells of the city pealed forth their joyous welcome, whilst the waving of thousands of white handkerchiefs and tiny Confederate flags attested the gladness and delight of every heart.

It would have been well if the enthusiasm which welcomed Gen. Smith in this town could have been confirmed as a true token of the public sentiment of Kentucky. But while this sentiment was developing itself, the exultation which greeted our troops at Lexington was reflected in other parts of the Confederacy; and from the results already achieved in the Western campaign, the Southern public was raised to the pinnacle of hopeful expectation. When it was known at the seat of government in Virginia that Gen. Smith, after crushing the force opposed to him at Richmond, had gone on and captured Lexington, Paris and Cynthiana, and established his lines almost in sight of Cincinnati, the public indulged the prospect of the speedy capture of this great city of the West, with its valuable stores and yards for building gunboats. What might have been the result of a sudden attack on this city (for one of our brigades was in striking distance of it) is left to conjecture. The order was to menace, not to attack; and the purposes of the campaign projected by Gen. Bragg required that Smith's command, after making its demonstration on the Ohio, should fall back into the interiour to co-operate with the splendid army he had already brought into Kentucky.

Gen. Bragg had entered the State by the eastern route from Knoxville and Chattanooga. The direct route by the way of Nashville would have brought him on Buell's front; but he chose to make the crossing of the Cumberland river several miles above Nashville, apparently with the design of making a flank movement on Buell. The immediate effect of this movement was to cause the Yankees to evacuate East Tennessee, and to relieve North Alabama from Federal occupation; but the enemy, learning that Cincinnati was not in immediate danger, had abundant time to remove the forces collected for the defence of that city, to be united with Buell's army in Kentucky.

The sudden disappearance of Smith from in front of Cincinnati, and the rapidity of his movement, intimated clearly enough that he was making a forced march to reach Bragg and strengthen him before a decisive trial of his strength with Buell. But the movement deprived us of a victory that might have been cheaply won; for it gave opportunity of escape to the Yankee Gen. Morgan, who had been completely hemmed in at Cumberland Gap, with an army of ten or twelve thousand men and abundance of arms and equipments.

The distance to the Ohio River is about two hundred and fifty miles, and includes the most mountainous portions of Kentucky. There are scarcely fifty miles of the entire route in which there are not defiles and passes where a small force could have kept the enemy at bay. The famous cavalry commander, John H. Morgan, had been sent with a portion of his command to harrass the retreating enemy; and this intrepid officer, with seven hundred and fifty men, arrested the Yankee army for five days, and might have captured them with the half of Marshall's infantry, who were within little more than a day's march. But reinforcements were not sent forward, and no alternative was left to Morgan but—after inflicting such damage as he could upon the enemy—to rejoin Smith's march, which had now taken the direction of Frankfort.

On the 17th of September, Gen. Bragg captured about five thousand of the enemy at Munfordsville, with the inconsiderable loss on our side of about fifty men in killed and wounded. He had thrown his lines between Buell's force at Bowling Green and Louisville, and it was confidently expected that he would engage him, drive him across the Ohio or the Mississippi, or at least disconcert his hopes of preparations and increase of forces at Louisville. Buell's entire force at this time was not computed at over thirty-five thousand, for which our army, in the best possible spirits and confidence, was an overmatch.

It is probable that at this juncture the struggle in Kentucky might have been decided by a fight on a fair field with an army our inferiour in all respects. Viewed in the light of subsequent events, it is difficult to determine what good object Gen. Bragg could have had in declining a contest with the enemy but a few miles distant. It is still more inexplicable that after the success of Munfordsville he should have stood idly by and suffered Buell and his wagon trains to pass between him and the Ohio River, almost in sight of his lines. He had passed Buell to enter Kentucky, and having accomplished it, his reasons for allowing his enemy to repass him and enter Louisville are inadmissible to any justification that can be offered by practical good sense. Whatever explanations have been made of them, it is certain that at this time the public has not abandoned its opinion, that General Bragg's failure to deliver battle at the important conjuncture which placed him between the enemy and the Ohio, was the fatal errour of the Kentucky campaign.

On the 4th of October, Gen. Bragg joined Smith's army at Frankfort, where was conducted the inauguration of the Provisional Governor of Kentucky, Mr. Hawes. This ceremony, however, was scarcely anything more than a pretentious farce. Scarcely was it completed, when the Yankees threatened the State capital, and the newly-installed Governor had to flee from their approach. The delusion, that Buell's army was quietly resting in Louisville, was dispelled by the news received at Frankfort on the inauguration day, to the effect that the Yankees were in large force within twelve miles of the place. But the apparent movement on Frankfort was a mere feint, while the enemy was concentrating to force our left wing near Perryville.

### THE BATTLE OF PERRYVILLE.

Having arrived at Harrodsburg from Frankfort, Gen. Bragg, finding the enemy pressing heavily in his rear near Perryville, determined to give him battle there, and ordered Gen. Polk to make the attack next day. But he had made an unfortunate disposition of his forces, for on the day before the division of Withers had been sent to Salvisa to reinforce General Kirby Smith and cut off Sill's division. Hardee's and Buckner's divisions were marched to Perryville, leaving Gen. Cheatham's at Harrodsburg, which, however, came up to Perryville on the night of the 7th of October, before the engagement. Withers' failed to intercept Gen. Sill's division, but captured the rear-guard, consisting of seven hundred and fifty men, with an ammunition train; and on the morning of the 9th, General Withers' and Gen. Kirby Smith's forces reached Harrodsburg, having been too late to participate in the decisive events of the preceding day.

The morning of the 8th October found not more than fifteen thousand Confederate troops confronting an enemy three times their numbers. The forces opposed to us at Perryville consisted of the right wing of the "Army of the Ohio," composed of Buell's veteran army, with Major-General Geo. W. Thomas as Commander-in-Chief of the field, and Gen. Alex. McCook commanding the first corps. We fought nine divisions of the

Abolition army, composed at least of five thousand each, making forty five thousand men.

Gen. Buckner's division, which was posted on our extreme right, with Anderson's division, formed the left wing of the army of the Mississippi, under Major-General Hardee. Cheatham's and Withers' divisions formed the right wing, under Major-Gen. Polk. Thus we had but three divisions in the field.

The action opened a little past noon. It was only skirmishing for a considerable time, Colonel Powell's brigade holding the extreme left of our lines, and gallantly driving the enemy back for about a mile against superior forces. It was about this time, towards 4 P. M., when General Smith's brigade, belonging to Cheatham's division, was ordered back to our assistance, that General Adams, with his brave Louisianians, was holding the enemy in check against fearful odds, when he was forced to fall back from his position. General Hardee, seeing the importance of holding the point, ordered General Adams to retake it, telling him he would be supported by reinforcements. It was while advancing again, and anxiously looking for the reinforcements, that General Adams, seeing some soldiers firing at what he supposed to be our own men, ordered them to cease firing. "I tell you, sir, they are Yankees," cried one of the officers. "I think not, and you had better go forward first and ascertain," replied Adams. "I'll go, sir, but I don't think it necessary, for I know they are Yankees," insisted the officer. "Well," ―― Adams, "I'll go myself," and dashing forward on his charger, he had not proceeded one hundred yards when a furious storm of Minie balls whizzed by his ears from the enemy. The General turned immediately, and riding up, shouted to our troops to pour in their fire. Towards six o'clock the firing became incessant on both sides. There stood Adams, with his little brigade, holding back a division of the enemy, left, as it were, alone to his fate, until, seeing no chance of being reinforced, he gradually fell back, in most excellent order, but not without considerable loss.

Towards night the engagement subsided. Fearfully outnumbered, our troops had not hesitated to engage at any odds, and despite the checks they had encountered at times, the enemy was driven two miles from his first line of battle. As darkness fell the conflict was over. A few shots from long range guns were exchanged. The full round moon rose in the east and lighted the dismal scene. In half an hour the picket fires of the opposing armies were visible five hundred yards distant, and our wearied men laid down on their arms.

The immediate results of the battle of Perryville were in our favour. We had captured fifteen pieces of artillery by the most daring charges, had inflicted the loss of four thousand men on the enemy, and held several hundred of his prisoners. Our own loss was estimated at twenty-five hundred, in killed, wounded and missing. The enemy had lost one of their best generals on the field—Jackson. Seeing his men wavering, he had advanced to the front line, and, waving his sword, cheered and urged them on. While thus displaying an extraordinary courage he was struck in the right breast by a piece of an exploded shell, and fell from his horse. It is said by those near him that he said only, "Oh God!" and died without a struggle.

But the success of Perryville was of no importance to us; it was merely a favourable incident and decided nothing. It is probable General Bragg had it in his power here, by concentrating his troops, to crush the enemy's force in Kentucky; but he allowed himself to be deceived as to the disposition of the enemy's forces, scattered his own, and engaged and defeated the head of the Yankee column with less than fifteen thousand men.* Had he fallen with his whole available force,

---

\* It is proper to state, that an apology for General Bragg, in this matter, was offered in the public prints, to the effect that before the battle of Perryville General Kirby Smith had communicated to General Bragg his positive belief that the real attack was threatened upon him, whilst the feint was upon Perryville, and urged reinforcements; and that this was the reason why General Withers' division was sent to General Kirby Smith and was not sent to Generals Polk and Hardee.

forty thousand men, on the enemy at Perryville, it is not improbable that he might have dispersed the Yankee army and given it such a blow that it would not have made a stand this side the Ohio river.

Unfortunately the battle of Perryville was another experience of Shiloh, without any decisive results. Had we have had five thousand more men, or had Withers been there, we might have completely routed the enemy, leaving us the way clear to Louisville. No troops in the world ever fought with more desperate courage than ours. Whole regiments of our men went into that fight barefooted, fought barefooted, and had marched barefooted from Chattanooga. The brunt of the battle was borne by General Cheatham's gallant Tennesseeans. No soldiers of the Confederacy ever fought with greater bravery.

Ascertaining that the enemy was heavily reinforced during the night, General Bragg withdrew his force early the next morning to Harrodsburg, where he was joined by Smith and Withers. On the 10th, all our forces fell back to Camp Breckinridge (Dick Robinson), the cavalry holding the enemy in check at Danville. It was supposed that General Bragg would have made a stand here, as the place was very defensible and gave him the opportunity of sweeping the country and driving off by private enterprise or cavalry force vast herds of cattle, so much needed by our army. The camp is in an acute angle formed by the junction of Kentucky and Dick's rivers, with high and impassable and perpendicular cliffs for long distances up these rivers, except at a few crossings; and the upper line of the angle has high and commanding hills, suited for artillery defences. It was said that it was impregnable to any other attack than that of famine.

But moved by various considerations, and excited by the superiority of Buell's numbers, it was determined by General Bragg that the whole army should make its exodus from Kentucky; and in order to secure the immense quantity of captured stores, goods, clothing, &c., much of which had also been purchased, with some five thousand head of cattle, horses, mules, &c., that the retreat should commence on the night of the 12th. On that day, Sunday, orders were received to cook four days' rations for the march. Major-General McCown, with General Hilliard's Legion, and a cavalry force and artillery, was ordered to defend Fishing Ford, across Dick's river, and commanding the road to Camp Breckinridge, in our rear, to the last extremity.

The distress of those people of Kentucky who were friendly to the South, on learning that they were to be abandoned by our troops, was the most affecting circumstance of the sad retreat. When our troops abandoned Lexington, the terrour, dismay and anguish of the inhabitants were extreme. The women ran through the streets crying and wringing their hands, while families hastily gathered their clothing, packed their trunks, and obtained wagons to depart, the greatest distress prevailing.

The retreat commenced on Sunday night, the 12th October, Major Adrain's cavalry conducting the advance train of Gen. Kirby Smith. That night piles of goods, clothes, &c., were burned that could not be carried off from the warehouse. Long before day on the morning of the 13th, the whole camp was astir. If any one doubted that we were actually retreating, the burning piles of abandoned stores, gun-carriages, &c., were sufficient to convince him of the deplorable fact.

At gray dawn the troops reached Bryantsville, about two miles from the camp, where the whole command of conducting the retreat was turned over to Gen. Polk. Already train after train of wagons had passed, and others were still forming and joining in the immense cavalcade. Ammunition trains and batteries of captured artillery had preceded. Then followed trains of goods, wares and merchandise, provision trains of army stores, trains of captured muskets, escorts of cavalry, artillery drawn by oxen. Then came private trains of refugee families, flying with their negroes for safety—ladies and children in carriages, stage coaches, express wagons, omnibuses,

11

buggies, ambulances, jersey wagons, and every conceivable vehicle imaginable, and following, came the wagons of the different brigades of General Smith's army, with infantry, cavalry and artillery in the rear. Intermixed with the throng were thousands of head of cattle, horses and mules.

The effect of our retreat along the road everywhere was sinking and depressing in the extreme. No miniature banners waved, no white 'kerchiefs greeted our troops with approving smiles from lovely women, and no wild cheer was heard responsive to the greetings which had attended their march to Kentucky. Trembling women stole to the doors to look upon the strange, mystified scene before them, and as the truth gradually forced itself upon them, their eyes filled with tears, and they shrank back, fearing even to make the slightest demonstration of friendliness—all was sullen, downcast and gloomy.

The enemy was in pursuit, and making a strong effort to flank us, so as to cut off our trains, and it was necessary to urge on the teams night and day for fear of capture. For some portion of the way the road lay along the bed of Dick's river, a miserable rocky branch, which our troops had to cross and recross for six miles in a dark and hazy night. Scenes of terrible confusion and delay occurred along this road. Wagons broke down, were overturned, and frequently stalled, and in the former case were often abandoned. The bawling of the teamsters to their mules, the cracking of their whips, and volleys of oaths in the most outlandish gibberish, which none but the mules could understand, were kept up all night. In the day time more cheerful scenes relieved the retreat. The foliage of the forest trees and brushwood enlivened the wayside with their rich hues of dark maroon splendor to brilliant crimson.

The retreat was admirably covered by Gen. Wheeler. From the battle-field at Perryville to Cumberland Gap this General conducted his movements in the same masterly manner that had characterized him in the previous part of the campaign.

He retarded the enemy by various means. When he reached the hilly country he obstructed the road by felled trees. By all such ingenious devices, he, with a small force, enabled the baggage trains and straggling infantry to escape capture. From Altamont to Cumberland Gap he encountered the enemy twenty-nine times, seriously damaged him, and saved much of our infantry from capture. At Rock Castle the enemy abandoned the pursuit; our whole train of stores being up, and not even a wagon lost, except those abandoned on account of breaking down.

We must leave here an account of the movements of Gen. Bragg until the time shall come for us to see how his retreat from Kentucky through Cumberland Gap transferred the most important scenes of the war in the West to the memorable lines of Nashville. Deplorable as was this retreat, it was not without some circumstances that palliated it, or relieved the grief of the public mind. It is certain that it was a disappointment to the enemy, who had expected to crush our forces in Kentucky, and were not prepared for the news of their liberation from the toils which they flattered themselves had been so industriously and elaborately woven around them.

It is probable, too, that under the circumstances, after our own army had blundered so badly in the first steps of the campaign, its retreat from Kentucky, without the burden of defeat and without material losses, was preferable to alternatives which otherwise would have probably befallen it. It had entered into Gen. Beauregard's plan of campaign in the West, before he had been superseded, to regain the control of the Tennessee and Cumberland rivers, and thus prepare for future operations. The construction of works on the Cumberland and Tennessee rivers so as to command them, was plainly an important concern; and, according to General Beauregard's idea, should have been preliminary to the active campaign in the West. With these works, it appears probable that an advance might have been made with safety into Kentucky; and even had we failed in the taking of Louisville and Cincinnati, which was a part of Gen. Beauregard's plan, and been compelled to fall back, it is thought not improbable that we could have made a successful stand on the Cumberland. But Gen. Bragg had failed to adopt these suggestions. Had he succeeded, after our victory at Perryville, in driving the enemy back to Louisville, unless he had been able to take that place, he would have been compelled to retreat so soon as the Tennessee and Cumberland rivers should have risen sufficiently to have admitted the entrance of the enemy's gunboats and transports. Taking this view, it may be said that as we did not have command of these rivers, it was fortunate that our army left Kentucky when it did, otherwise it might have found great difficulty after the winter rains commenced in getting away at all.

For the failure of Gen. Bragg's campaign in Kentucky, the excuse was offered that the people of that State had been unfriendly, that they had not joined his standard in considerable numbers, and that they had disappointed his own and the common expectation of the Southern public with respect to their political sentiments. It is scarcely necessary to remark how little applicable such an excuse is to positive blunders in the conduct of an army, and to those imperfections of judgment and faults of strategy which, whatever may be their remote connection, are the immediate occasions and responsible causes of disaster.

But it is to be admitted that the South was bitterly disappointed in the manifestations of public sentiment in Kentucky; that the exhibitions of sympathy in this State were meagre and sentimental, and amounted to but little practical aid of our cause. Indeed, no subject was at once more dispiriting and perplexing to the South than the cautious and unmanly reception given to our armies, both in Kentucky and Maryland. The references we have made to the sentiment of each of these States, leaves but little room to doubt the general conclusion, that the dread of Yankee vengeance, and love of property, were too powerful to make them take risks against these in favour of a cause for which their people had a mere preference, without any attachments to it higher than those of selfish calculation.

There must, indeed, be some explanation for the extraordinary quiet of the people of Maryland and Kentucky under the tyranny that ruled them, and for that submission, the painful signs of which we had unwillingly seen. This explanation was not to be found in the conduct of the United States. It is a remarkable fact that the Lincoln government had not taken any pains to change the opinions and prejudices of the people in these two States. It had made no attempt to conciliate them; it had performed no act calculated to awaken their affection; it had done nothing to convert their hearts to the support of an administration to which they were originally hostile.

It would be a foolish and brutal explanation to attribute the submission of these States to cowardice. The people of these States were brave; they were descended from noble ancestries, and they had the same blood and types of race that were common to the South. The sons of Kentucky and Maryland who had fought under the Confederate flag were as noble specimens of the Southern soldier as any to be found in our armies. But the people of these States, who had stayed at home and been schooled in the lessons of submission, appeared to have lost the spirit and stature of their ancestors, and dragged the names of Maryland and Kentucky in the dust.

The only just explanation that can be furnished of the abject attitude of these States is, that having taken the first steps of submission to a pitiless despotism, they had been easily corrupted into its subjects. The lessons of history furnish many exhibitions of how easily the spirit of a community is crushed by submission to tyranny; how the practice of non-resistance makes of men crawling creatures. The mistake is in making the first step of submission; when that is accomplished, demoralization becomes rapid, and the bravest community sinks into emasculation. Under the experience of non-resistance to the rule of a despot, men become timid, artful and miserly; they spend their lives in consulting the little ends of personal selfishness. This corruption in Kentucky, as well as in Maryland, had gone on with visible steps. Their history was a lesson which the South might well remember, of the fatal consequences of any submission to despotic will, for however specious its plea, all records of man's experience have shown that it undermines the virtues of a people, and degenerates at last into servile acquiescence in its fate.

## CHAPTER VI.

Our Lines in the Southwest...General Breckenridge's Attack on Baton Rouge...Destruction of the Ram Arkansas...Gen. Price's Reverse at Iuka... Desperate Fighting...THE BATTLE OF CORINTH...Van Dorn's Hasty Exultations...The Massacre of College Hill...Wild and Terrible Courage of the Confederates...Our Forces Beaten Back...Our Lines of Retreat Secured...The Military Prospects of the South Overshadowed...THE DEPARTMENT OF THE TRANS-MISSISSIPPI...Romance of the War in Missouri...Schofield's Order Calling Out the Militia...Atrocities of the Yankee Rule in Missouri...Robbery Without "Red Tape"...The Guerilla Campaign...The Affair of Kirksville... Execution of Col. McCullough...The Affair of Lone Jack...Timely Reinforcement of Lexington by the Yankees...The Palmyra Massacre...The Question of Retaliation with the South...THE MILITARY AND POLITICAL SITUATION... Survey of the Military Situation...Capture of Galveston by the Yankees...The Enemy's Naval Power...His Iron Clads.. Importance of Founderies in the South...Prospect in the Southwest...Prospect in Tennessee...Prospect in Virginia...Stuart's Raid into Pennsylvania...Souvenirs of Southern Chivalry... The "Soft-mannered Rebels"...Political Complexion of the War in the North...Lincoln's "Emancipation Proclamation"...History of Yankee Legislation in the War...Political Errour of the Emancipation Proclamation—Its Effect on the South...The Decay of European Sympathy with the Abolitionists...What the War Accomplished for Negro Slavery in the South...Yankee Falsehoods and Bravados in Europe...Delusion of Conquering the South by Starvation.. Caricatures in the New York Pictorials...The Noble Eloquence of Hunger and Rags...Manners in the South...Yankee Warfare...The Desolation of Virginia...The Lessons of Harsh Necessity...Improvement of the Civil Administration of the Confederacy...Ordnance, Manufacturing Resources, Quartermasters' Supplies, &c.

The crisis in Kentucky was probably hastened by certain disastrous events which had taken place on our lines in the Southwest. A large Confederate force had been left in North Mississippi when Gen. Bragg moved into Kentucky, and the speculation was not remote that, with the Memphis and Charleston railroad open from Chattanooga to a point near the position of our army in Mississippi, that portion of our forces in the West might render important assistance to, or, in some emergency, effect a co-operation with the armies that had been marched into Kentucky.

But the story of the Southwest was one of almost unbroken disaster, owing less, perhaps, to inadequate numbers than to the blind and romantic generalship which carried them into the jaws of destruction. There was one golden link in the chain of events here, and that was the heroic defence of Vicksburg. But while this famous town so nobly disputed the palm of the Mississippi, her example of victorious resistance was obscured, though not overshadowed, by other events in the Southwest.

On the 5th of August, an attack make by General Breckenridge with less than three thousand men on Baton Rouge, was severely repulsed by an enemy nearly twice his numbers, fighting behind fortifications which were almost impregnable, and assisted by a fleet of gunboats in the river. The unequal attack was made by our troops with devoted courage; they succeeded in driving the enemy to the arsenal and tower, and to the cover of his gunboats; but they were compelled to withdraw with diminished and exhausted numbers before a fire which it was impossible to penetrate.

This check (for it deserves no more important or decisive title) was in a measure occasioned, or, at least, was accompanied, by a disaster of real importance. This was the destruction of the great Confederate ram Arkansas, already famous for having run the gauntlet of the hostile fleet at Vicksburg, and the promises of whose future services had given to the South many brilliant but illusory hopes. The Arkansas left Vicksburg to co-operate in the attack upon Baton Rouge. After passing Bayou Sara her machinery became deranged or disabled. But two alternatives were left—to blow her up or suffer her to be captured by the Yankee gunboats. The former was resorted to, and this proud achievement of naval architecture floated a wreck on the Mississippi River.

The failure of another enterprise of attack on the enemy, made by Gen. Price at Iuka on the 20th of September, was much more disastrous than the affair of Baton Rouge. Overmatched by numbers, Gen. Price was, after some partial and temporary success, forced back, with a loss greater than that of the enemy. In this engagement our loss was probably eight hundred in killed and wounded. But never had troops fought with more terrible resolution or wilder energy than the soldiers of Price. The fighting was almost hand to hand; and as an instance of the close and deadly combat, it may be mentioned that an Ohio battery was taken by our men four different times, and as often retaken by greatly superiour numbers of the enemy. The desperation of our soldiers astonished those who, by the weight of numbers alone, were able to resist them. Several of our men endeavored to tear the colours from the hands of the Yankees by main force, and either perished in the attempt or were made prisoners. In one spot next morning, there were counted seventeen Confederate soldiers lying dead around one of their officers. Sixteen feet square would cover the whole space where they died.

But there was yet to ensue the great disaster which was to re-act on other theatres of the war and cast the long shadow of misfortune upon the country of the West.. It was destined to take place at Corinth, where Major-General Rosecranz, commanding the Yankee army of the Mississippi and Tennessee, was stationed with at least forty thousand men.

### THE BATTLE OF CORINTH.

The armies of Gens. Van Dorn and Price—under Gen. Van Dorn as the ranking officer—having formed a junction at Ripley, marched thence for the purpose of engaging the enemy in battle, though it was well known that the battle must be waged under the serious disadvantages of great disparity in numbers and strength of position.

On the 2d of October our forces marched from Pocahontas to Chewalla, points on the Memphis and Charleston railroad, thus moving from the west on Corinth, the stronghold of the enemy. That night the soldiers rested on their arms, in eager and confident expectation of meeting the foe in battle array on the ensuing morning.

On Friday, October 3d, the order of battle was formed—the right being held by Gen. Van Dorn's troops, composing only one division, under Gen. Lovell; while the left was occupied by Gen. Price's troops, composed of two divisions—the extreme left under Gen. Herbert, and the right under Gen. Maury, whose division, as thus placed, formed the centre of the whole force. Advancing in this order, at 7½ o'clock in the morning Gen. Lovell's division arrived within long range of the enemy, who had marched out some miles in front of the extreme outer lines of his fortifications. Immediately the artillery of Gen. Villipigue, whose brigade was in the advance, opened fire upon the enemy, who, in a short time, began to give way and fall back, and continued to do so for two hours, under a heavy and effective fire from the advancing batteries of General Lovell's division.

At 9½ o'clock, the enemy having made a stand one-half mile in front of his fortifications, Gen. Lovell advanced his infantry and poured a destructive musketry fire into the ranks of the Yankees, who replied with spirit; and now, Gen. Price having ordered up his divisions under Generals Maury and Herbert, the battle raged all along the line—the enemy suffering terribly. At length a charge was ordered, Gen. Lovell's division leading. In double-quick time our soldiers, pressing forward with loud cheers, drove the enemy behind his entrenchments. Simultaneously almost, the divisions of Generals Maury and Herbert, the one after the other, charged the enemy in front of them with equal success.

There was now a strange lull in the battle. The Yankees had withdrawn entirely behind their fortifications, their fire had dropped off, and the tumult of the fierce strife died away. The unexpected quiet lasted for a whole hour. By that time, the Yankees having brought several field batteries in front, opened from these, and at the same time from his heavy artillery, a most tremendous cannonade. This fire was directed chiefly, if not wholly, against the right wing under General Lovell, and, though so tremendous in sound, produced but little effect. Our soldiers remained silent and stood firm. They were waiting for orders. Presently the second charge was ordered. Gallantly was it made by Gen. Lovell's division, and as gallantly was it supported by charges all along the centre and right wing by the divisions of Generals Maury and Herbert. On, on our glorious columns swept through the leaden rain and iron hail; the first line of fortifications is reached and passed; and the Yankees do not stop until they have reached the next line of entrenchments.

On Friday night the news of a great victory was dispatched by Gen. Van Dorn to Richmond. This announcement was made with an exultation so hasty and extreme, that it is to be supposed that this commander was entirely unaware of the strength of the enemy's works at Corinth, and, consequently, of the supreme trial which yet remained for the courage and devotion of his troops.

The next morning the general relation of our troops to each other and to the enemy remained as it was on the previous day—Gen. Van Dorn, in supreme command, occupying the centre, Gen. Price the left wing, and Gen. Lovell the right wing. Gen. Lovell's division held ground west of Corinth and just south of the Memphis and Charleston railroad. General Maury's division was posted north of the Memphis and Charleston railroad, and between it and the Memphis and Ohio railroad. Gen. Herbert's division was on the left, east of the Memphis and Ohio railroad—thus advancing from the north upon Corinth.

The battle was commenced by Gen. Price early in the morning, one-half hour before daylight. The artillery having been moved forward, opened upon the enemy in his entrenchments at a distance of four hundred yards. The enemy replied, and a heavy cannonading, by both sides, ensued for one hour. Our troops suffered but little damage from this fire, and the artillery was withdrawn with the view of advancing the infantry. Now heavy skirmishing followed all along the line, which was kept up until about 10 o'clock. Then beginning with Gen. Lovell's division, who were immediately seconded by Gen. Price's army—Gen. Herbert's division first, and then Gen. Maury's—our whole line advanced upon the entrenchments of the enemy.

Here occurred one of the most terrible struggles of the war. The shock of the tremendous onset was terrible. One portion of our lines rushed pell mell into Corinth, losing in their confidence of victory almost every semblance of order, infantry and cavalry being crowded together in a dense mass, wild with excitement, and rending the air, with fierce and exulting yells. But the batteries of the enemy were situated to command the village as well as the approaches to it.

The serried ranks of the enemy, now prepared to receive us, afforded convincing proof that victory was yet distant from our grasp, and that a hard and bloody fight was at hand. A portion of Maury's division was ordered to charge the formidable fort on College Hill. This was the forlorn hope. Disappointed in gaining a lodgment in the village, we must confess to a defeat, if that battery be not taken. Once in our possession the town is ours. The men, massed in single column eight deep, moved forward in silence, regardless of the shower of bullets which whistled about their ears and decimated their ranks. The decisive moment—the turning point of the engagement—had arrived. Every battery of the enemy bearing on the column was double charged with grape and canister, which burst over the heads of our troops. Scores were killed at every discharge, but they moved steadily on, maintaining the silence of the grave. As fast as one soldier fell, his comrade behind stepped forward and took his place. They charged up to the battery, reserving their fire until they reached the parapets. Twice repulsed, the third time they reached the outer works, and planted their flag upon the escarpment. It was shot down and again planted, but shot down again.

These devoted troops now held partial possession of the works. But the triumph was of short duration. According to previous instructions, the enemy's gunners fell back behind the works, and the next instant from their batteries threw a murderous fire into our ranks at the shortest possible range. Nothing human could withstand such a fire; the confusion it produced was irretrievable; our men were driven back and the day lost.

But the attack was not abandoned without instances of wild and terrible courage that were almost appalling. In their madness and desperation, our men would rush up to the very mouths of the cannon, and many were blown to pieces by the rapid and constant discharges. Such spectacles of courage were curious and terrible to behold. An officer, standing a little way out from his men, was shouting, "Give it to the scoundrels." The words had but passed from his lips, when the first shell from a Parrott gun struck his left shoulder, tearing off his whole side. He turned his head a little to one side, his mouth opened, his eyes glared, and he fell dead.

The attack on the enemy's batteries was rash and magnificent. The intensity of the fight may be judged from the fact that two hundred and sixty dead bodies were found in and about the trenches within a distance of fifty feet of the works. It is impossible to enumerate the examples of daring which adorn the story of this attack. The second Texas infantry, under Col. Rogers, led the charge, and the Colonel himself fell on the enemy's breastworks with the colours of his regiment in his hand. A piece of paper was found under his clothing giving his name and rank and the address of his friends. As Gen. Cabell mounted the enemy's parapet, the first man he encountered was a Yankee colonel, who cried out, "Kill that d——d rebel officer." The next instant a blow from the General's sabre placed his antagonist at his feet. In the brigade of this brave officer, J. H. Bullock, Adjutant of the 13th Arkansas regiment—a noble specimen of the Southern soldier; for, though blessed in estate and family, a son-in-law of Chief Justice Parsons, of North Carolina, and the master of a beautiful and prosperous home,' he had volunteered as a private and been advanced for merit—made a display of courage to animate his men that was a splendid picture of heroism, as he stood out and exposed himself to the enemy's fire until his clothing was pierced by balls, his life being saved only by that unseen shield with which Providence protects its agents. The gallant commander of this ever-glorious regiment, Col. Daly, had fallen, while himself engaged in the animation of his men—cheering and leading them on to the attack.

Under the necessities of the case, our troops had fallen back; and, though in doing so they were exposed to a terrible and destructive fire, there was no panic, no rout—the wounded, except those who fell right at the entrenchments, having been nearly all brought away. Our army retired to the woods at a distance of only six hundred yards; and there, while our artillery resumed fire and kept it up for a short time, formed again in order of battle. But the enemy appearing indisposed to renew the conflict, Gen. Van Dorn, at three o'clock, drew off his whole force, being most ably supported in doing so by Gen. Price and the other general officers.

The next morning, at half-past eight o'clock, our advance, consisting of Gen. Phifer's brigade, and Col. Whitfield's Legion, with one battery—not exceeding one thousand five hundred in all—crossed the Davis bridge at Hatchie river, to engage the enemy, a large body of whom, from Bolivar, had the day before reached that point, and had there been held in check by Col. Slemmon's and Adams' cavalry, with one battery. Our advance having crossed the bridge and gone a little distance, received a heavy fire at short range from a concealed battery, which was followed directly by a charge from a largely superior force. Our troops retreated in a good deal of confusion across the bridge—having suffered a loss, perhaps, of three hundred killed, wounded and missing. The reinforcements arriving, our troops formed in line, and a fight with musketry ensued and was kept up for some time across the river, but with very little loss on our side. Meanwhile, our field pieces opened upon the enemy, and, they replying, cannonading was continued during the greater part of the day. During this time, our advance was gradually withdrawn, and following the other troops, with the long wagon train of supplies, wounded, &c.—the artillery having also been brought off—made a successful crossing of Hatchie river some miles higher up the stream. The retreat was eventually halted at a point little north of Ripley.

Our loss in all the three days' engagements was probably quite double that of the enemy. In killed and wounded it exceeded three thousand; and it was estimated, besides, that we had left more than fifteen hundred prisoners in the hands of the enemy.

The defeat of Corinth was followed by swift news of disaster and discouragement. The military prospect was not dark, but it had lost much of the brightness it had had only a few weeks before. Kentucky had been gloomily abandoned. In Virginia the hopes of conquering a peace on the Potomac had for the time been given up; the Kanawha Valley had again been mostly surrendered to the enemy; and Marshall's forces, back again in Southwestern Virginia, were consuming the substance of the country with but little return of other service. In other parts of the Confederacy, the prospect was not much relieved.

THE DEPARTMENT OF THE TRANS-MISSISSIPPI.

The events in the department of the Trans-Mississippi were too distant to affect the general fortunes of the war; they were but episodes to the great drama of arms that passed over the broad and imposing theatres of Virginia, Kentucky and Tennessee; but they were replete with romance, and if their interest is at present partial, it is so, perhaps, for the reason that they are imperfectly known.

Missouri had the better of other seats of hostility for the real romance of war. The remote geography of the country, the rough character of the people, the intensity and ferocity of the passions excited, and the reduction of military operations to a warfare essentially partisan and frontier, gave to the progress of the war in this quarter a wild aspect, and illustrated it with rare and thrilling scenes.

Gen. Schofield, the Yankee commander, who had been left by Halleck with the brief and comprehensive instructions "to take care of Missouri," found the power of the Confederates broken in nearly three fourths of that State, but the Southwestern portion threatened by the active movements of Gen. Hindman, in command of State forces raised in Arkansas and Texas. But in no part of Missouri was the spirit of the people broken. Guerrilla bands made their appearance in all parts of the State; and their numbers rapidly augmented under the despotic edict of Schofield, calling out the militia of the State to murder their own countrymen.

The dark atrocities of the Yankee rule in Missouri, enacted as they were in a remote country, and to a great extent removed from observation, surpassed all that was known in other parts of the Confederacy of the cruelty and fury of the enemy. The developments on this subject are yet imperfect; but some general facts are known of the inordinate license of the enemy in Missouri, while others of equal horrour have escaped the notice of the public.

In other parts of the Confederacy many of the excesses of the enemy were performed under certain formalities, and to some extent regulated by them. But in Missouri there was no "red tape," no qualification of forms; the order of the day was open robbery, downright murder, and freedom to all crimes of which "rebels" were the victims. Citizens were plundered with bare-faced audacity. Those citizens of St. Louis county alone, who were suspected by Gen. Schofield to sympathize with the South, were taxed five hundred thousand dollars to arm, clothe and subsist those who were spilling the blood of their brothers, and threatening their own homes with the torch and with outrages to which death is preferable.

The sanguinary guerrilla warfare in Missouri may be said to have commenced in the month of July by the assembling of bands under Porter, Poindexter, Cobb and others. The principal theatre of guerrilla operations was at this time the Northeastern division of Missouri, where the almost devilish cruelties of the Yankee commander, the notorious Colonel McNeil, had lashed the people into incontrollable fury.

On the 6th of August, Porter's band was attacked at Kirksville by McNeil with a large force of cavalry and six pieces of artillery. This gallant partizan made a resistance of four hours against overwhelming numbers, and retired only after such a demonstration of valour; leaving the Yankees to claim as a victory an affair in which they had sustained a loss of more than five hundred in killed and wounded, probably double our own.

The day after the action, a party of Yankee scouts succeeded in capturing near Edina Col. F. McCullough, who was attached to Porter's command, and at the time of his capture was quite alone. The next morning a train with an armed escort proceeded from Edina to Kirksville. McCullough was sent along. On arriving at Kirksville, the news of the capture of this famous partisan excited the most devilish feeling among the Yankee troops. He was confined a brief time with the other prisoners. Meantime a court-martial was held and he was sentenced to be shot that very afternoon. He received the information of his fate with perfect composure, but protested against it. Leaning against the fence, he wrote a few lines to his wife. These, with his watch, he delivered to the officer, to be given to her. Upon the way to his execution, he requested the privilege to give the command to fire, which was granted. All being ready, he said :. "What I have done, I have done as a principle of right. Aim at the heart. Fire!"

The command taking the soldiers by surprise, one fired sooner than the rest. The ball entering his breast, he fell, while the other shots passed over him. Falling with one leg doubled under the body, he requested to have it straightened out. While this was being done he said: "I forgive you for this barbarous act." The squad having reloaded their pieces, another volley was fired—this time into his body, and he died.

On the 15th of August occurred the more important action of Lone Jack. Large Yankee forces were moved from Lexington, with orders to effect a junction near Lone Jack and attack the forces under Hughes and Quantrell, supposed to be somewhere in Jackson county. The disaster which met the Yankees here was the most serious of the guerrilla campaign. Their command was defeated, with a loss of three hundred killed and wounded, two pieces of their artillery captured on the field, their routed forces turned back upon Lexington and that place put in imminent peril. The timely reinforcement of Lexington by all the available forces of the enemy in Northeastern Missouri alone saved the place from capture by the Confederates, and disconcerted their plans of relieving their comrades north of the river.

The guerrilla campaign of Missouri is made memorable by the fearful story of the "Palmyra massacre." The important incidents of this tragedy are gathered from the enemy's own publications, and it was from Yankee newspapers that the people of the South first learned the barbarous and exultant news that McNeil had executed ten Confederate prisoners because a tory and spy had been carried off a captive by our forces.

From the enemy's own accounts, it appears that the missing man, Andrew Allsman, was a legitimate prisoner of war; that on the descent of the Confederate forces upon Palmyra he was captured by them; that he belonged to the Federal cavalry, but that being too old to endure all the hardships of active duty, he was detailed as a spy, being "frequently," as one of the Yankee papers states, "called upon for information touching the loyalty of men, which he always gave to the extent of his ability."

When McNeil returned to Palmyra in October, he caused a notice to be issued that unless Allsman was returned in ten days he would shoot ten Confederate prisoners as "a meet reward for their crimes, among which was the illegal restraining of said Allsman of his liberty." The ten days elapsed, and the prisoner was not returned. The following account of what ensued, is condensed from the Palmyra *Courier*, a "Union" journal, without any variation from the language in which it describes the deed of the demons with whom it was in sympathy:

"The tenth day expired with last Friday. On that day ten "rebel prisoners, already in custody, were selected to pay "with their lives the penalty demanded. A little after 11 "o'clock, A. M., the next day, three government wagons drove "to the jail. One contained four, and each of the others three "rough board coffins. The condemned men were conducted "from the prison and seated in the wagons, one upon each "coffin. A sufficient guard of soldiers accompanied them, and "the cavalcade started for the fatal grounds. The ten coffins "were removed from the wagons and placed in a row, six or "eight feet apart, forming a line north and south. Each coffin "was placed upon the ground with its foot west and head east. "Thirty soldiers of the 2d M. S. M. were drawn up in a single "line, extending north and south, facing the row of coffins. "The arrangements completed, the men knelt upon the grass "between their coffins and the soldiers. At the conclusion of "a prayer by the army chaplain, each prisoner took his seat "upon the foot of his coffin, facing the muskets which in a "few moments were to launch them into eternity. They were "nearly all firm and undaunted. The most noted of the ten "was Captain Thomas A. Sidner of Monroe county, whose "capture at Shelbyville, in the disguise of a woman, we related "several weeks since. He was now elegantly attired in a suit "of black broadcloth, with a white vest. A luxuriant growth "of beautiful hair rolled down upon his shoulders, which, with "his fine personal appearance, could not but bring to mind the "handsome but vicious Absalom. There was nothing espe- "cially worthy of note in the appearance of the others. A "few moments after 1 o'clock the chaplain in attendance shook "hands with the prisoners. Two of them accepted bandages "for the eyes, the rest refused. A hundred spectators had "gathered around the amphitheatre to witness the impressive "scene. The stillness of death pervaded the place. The "officer in command now stepped forward, and gave the word "of command—'Ready! aim! fire!' The discharges, how- "ever, were not made simultaneously—probably through want "of a perfect understanding of the orders to fire. Two of the "rebels fell backwards upon their coffins and died instantly. "Capt. Sidner sprang forward and fell with his head towards "the soldiers, his face upwards, his hands clasped upon his "breast, and the left leg drawn half way up. He did not "move again, but died immediately. He had requested the "soldiers to aim at his heart, and they obeyed but too "implicitly. The other seven were not killed outright; so the "reserves were called in, who dispatched them with their "revolvers."

The "Palmyra massacre" was destined to a long and painful remembrance by the people of the South, not only because of its tragic interest, but because it was a comment scrawled in blood on that weak and remiss policy of our government, which had so long submitted to the barbarous warfare of the enemy and hesitated at the rule of retaliation.

### THE MILITARY AND POLITICAL SITUATION.

A slight survey of the military situation at this time adds something to the list of our disasters, and is necessary to understand the proportions of the crisis at which the fortunes of the South had arrived.

The capture of Galveston on the coast of Texas, on the 9th of October, was another repetition of the almost invariable story of disaster at the hands of the enemy's naval power. It was made almost without resistance. In the early part of the war, the defenceless condition of Galveston had been represented to the government, as in fact there was no ordnance available there but a lot of old cannon captured from the United States. These representations in the letters and petitions of the people of Galveston were made without effect, until at last, some time in the summer of 1861, a deputation of citizens waited upon the authorities at Richmond, begging piteously a few cannon to defend them from the enemy. The whole extent of the response of the government to this and other appeals was to send to Galveston eleven or thirteen guns, two of which were rifled; and transportation for these was only given to New Orleans, whence they had to be dragged over piney hills and through swamps to their destination. The consequence was, that the enemy had made an easy prize of one of our principal seaports; when, after threatening it for eighteen months, he at last found it practically defenceless.

The fall of Galveston again turned the perplexed attention of the people of the South to the enormous and rapid increase of the enemy's naval power in this war as one of its most painful subjects of interest. This arm had grown to such size as to threaten us in many respects more seriously than the enemy's land forces. It was calculated, that with the completion of their vast number of naval structures already on the stocks, the Yankees would have 388 vessels, mounting 3,072 guns—nearly nine guns to the vessel. Of these, thirty were iron-clad, mounting ninety of the heaviest guns in the world, each weighing 42,240 pounds, and throwing a solid shot, fifteen inches in diameter, weighing 480 pounds.

It is not wonderful that in view of these vast preparations in the North, the people of the South should have watched with intense interest the long lines of their sea-coast, and been on the tiptoe of expectation for the fleets of the Yankees, which were to sweep upon them in numbers and power yet unequalled by any naval demonstration of the enemy in this war. It was easy to see that the South would have to look to its foundries to set off the naval power of the enemy. When we could match their naval armaments with our batteries on shore, we might expect to hold our sea-coast against their fleets. The authorities at Richmond were instructed that there was but one way of replying to the Yankee iron-clads on equal terms; and that was by iron-clad batteries, with powerful guns in them, and with the use of steel-pointed or wrought-iron projectiles.

In the Southwest, the strong tenure which we maintained of Vicksburg was a stumbling-block to the Yankee schemes for the conquest of Mississippi. The fate of that State was also confidently entrusted to the brave troops under the command of General Pemberton, who was assisted by Van Dorn and Price and an increasing army.

But it was to Tennessee that the minds of the intelligent were turned to look for the earliest and severest conflict of the campaign in the West. The enemy already held the western portion of the State and a part of the middle, and evidently desired to obtain possession of the eastern portion. He was reported to be coming down from Kentucky for the purpose, in heavy columns, under Gen. Rosecranz, by way of Nashville; and there was reason to suppose that he would endeavour to make a flank movement on Knoxville, and, at the same time, capture Chattanooga, as the key of North Alabama and Georgia.

In Virginia a lull had followed the famous summer campaign, and our army in the northern part of the State quietly recruited, and was daily improving in organization and numbers. The only incident that had broken the monotony of our camps was the renewal in the North of the phantom of "invasion by the rebels" by a raid into Pennsylvania, accomplished by the rapid and brilliant commander of our cavalry, Gen. J. E. B. Stuart, with about two thousand men. The expedition penetrated to Chambersburg, which was occupied for a short time by our troops on the 10th of October. It met with no resistance, accumulated no stores, and accomplished nothing beyond the results of a reconnoissance, and the wonder of one of the most rapid marches on record.

This expedition left to the Yankees a remarkable souvenir

of Southern chivalry. Private property was uniformly respected by our troops; Yankee civilians were treated with scrupulous regard; and many kindnesses were shown the alarmed people in a knightly style, which would have been creditable to us had it not been made ridiculous by excess of courtesy and a tender and ceremonious politeness which was in very absurd contrast to the manners of our enemy. On entering Chambersburg, "the soft-mannered rebels," as Colonel McClure, the Yankee commander of the post, described them, treated him with the most tender politeness. Indeed, the narrative of this officer's experience furnishes a curious leaf in the history of the war. To the great amusement of the people of the North, Col. McClure gave a long account in the newspapers of the strained chivalry of our troops. He related how they had "thanked him for being candid," when he told them that he was a Republican; how he was politely asked for food by the officers; and how a private in Stuart's terrible command had, "with a profound bow, asked for a few coals to light a fire."

The story of these courtesies and salaams to our enemy is not one for our amusement. It affords an instructive illustration that is valuable in history, of the over-amiable disposition and simple mind of the South; and it places in stark and horrible contrast an agreeable picture with that of the devilish atrocities and wanton and mocking destruction of the Yankee armies on the soil of the Confederacy.

While the war lagged, we are called upon to notice new sources of resolution and power in the South, which were perhaps more valuable than victories in the field. In this department of interest, which is quite equal to that of battles and sieges, it will be necessary to pass in review some political acts of the rival governments, and some events of moral importance.

At last the Abolitionists of the North had had their wild and wicked will. On the 22d day of September, President Lincoln issued his celebrated proclamation of "emancipation"* of the slaves of the South, to take effect after the first of next January, thus unmasking the objects of the war, and exhibiting to the world the sublime of administrative madness.

---

* The following is a copy of this remarkable document:

BY THE PRESIDENT OF THE UNITED STATES—A PROCLAMATION.

*Washington,* Sept. 22, 1862.

I, Abraham Lincoln, President of the United States of America, and Commander-in-Chief of the army and navy thereof, do hereby proclaim and declare, that hereafter, as heretofore, the war will be prosecuted for the object of practically restoring the constitutional relation between the United States and the people thereof, in which States that relation is, or may be, suspended or disturbed; that it is my purpose, upon the next meeting of Congress, to again recommend the adoption of a practical measure tendering pecuniary aid to the free acceptance or rejection of all the slave States, so called, the people whereof may not then be in rebellion against the United States, and which States may then have voluntarily adopted or thereafter may voluntarily adopt the immediate or gradual abolishment of slavery within their respective limits; and that the efforts to colonize persons of African descent, with their consent, upon the continent or elsewhere, with the previously obtained consent of the governments existing there, will be continued; that on the first day of January, in the year of our Lord one thousand eight hundred and sixty-three, all persons held as slaves within any State, or any designated part of a State, the people whereof shall then be in rebellion against the United States, shall be thenceforward and forever free; and the executive government of the United States, including the naval and military authority thereof, will recognize and maintain the freedom of such persons, and will do no act or acts to repress such persons, or any of them, in any efforts they may make for their actual freedom; that the Executive will, on the first day of January aforesaid, by proclamation, designate the States and parts of States, if any, in which the people thereof respectively shall then be in rebellion against the United States; and the fact that any State, or the people thereof, shall on that day be in good faith represented in the Congress of the United States by members chosen thereto at elections wherein a majority of the qualified voters of such State shall have participated, shall, in the absence of strong countervailing testimony, be deemed conclusive evidence that such State and the people thereof have not been in rebellion against the United States.

And I do hereby enjoin upon and order all persons engaged in the military and naval service of the United States to observe, obey and enforce within their respective spheres of service the act and sections above recited.

And the Executive will in due time recommend that all citizens of the United States, who shall have remained loyal thereto throughout the rebellion, shall (upon the restoration of the constitutional relation between the

Since the commencement of the war, the Abolitionists had gradually compassed their ends at Washington, or rather the real objects and inherent spirit of the war had been gradually developed. They had legislated slavery forever out of the territories; they had abolished it in the District of Columbia; they had passed laws confiscating the property of "rebels" and emancipating their slaves, and declaring all fugitive slaves free within their military lines; they had made it a crime on the part of their military officers to restore or aid in restoring any fugitive slave to his master; and finally, they had procured from President Lincoln a proclamation declaring all the slaves in the Confederate States beyond the lines of their land and naval forces "henceforward and forever free."

This infamous proclamation, while regarded by the South as a fulmination of exasperated passion, was in the North a source of weakness and division. It divided the North and strengthened the enemies of Mr. Lincoln's administration without creating any enthusiasm among its friends. The few in the North who still had some regard for the written constitution under which they lived, contended that the President could not proclaim emancipation except under the pressure of military necessity, and what sort of a military necessity, it was asked, was that which admitted of a delay of a hundred days. The *fulmen brutum* issued to appease the anti-slavery party proved a fire-brand at home. Many even of this party were dissatisfied and decried the proclamation because of its tardiness. "There was a time," said the New York *Tribune*, "when even this bit of paper could have brought the negro to our side; but now slavery, the real rebel capital, has been surrounded by a Chickahominy swamp of blunders and outrages against that race which no *paper spade* can dig through."

---

United States and their respective States and people, if the relation shall have been suspended or disturbed) be compensated for all losses by acts of the United States, including the loss of slaves.

In witness whereof, I have hereunto set my hand and caused the seal of the United States to be affixed.

ABRAHAM LINCOLN.

To the South the fulmination of Lincoln was a crowning proof of the true principles of the party that had elevated him to the Presidency, and that on its accession to power had made perfidious use of the most solemn pledges.* It was a public confession of the fact that conquest, extermination and emancipation were the real objects of the war—a fact which the enemy for a while had affected to deny. It attempted to accomplish by the horrours of servile insurrection what our enemy had failed to accomplish by military operations. It

---

* One of the most singular juxtapositions between the professions of the North at the commencement of hostilities and its present ideas, is afforded in Mr. Seward's famous letter, written to the French Government on the 22d April, 1861, and his subsequent circular to the Yankee ministers in Europe. It is one of the most singular of all the juggleries and summersaults of Yankee diplomacy.

In the first pronunciamento of Secretary Seward, written "by the direction of the President," occurs the following passage:

"The condition of slavery in the several States will remain just the same, "whether it succeeds or fail. The rights of the States, and the condition of "every human being in them, will remain subject to exactly the same laws "and form of administration, whether the revolution shall succeed or whether "it shall fail. Their constitutions and laws and customs, habits and institu-"tions in either case will remain the same. It is hardly necessary to add to "this incontestable statement the further fact that the new President, as well "as the citizens through whose suffrages he has come into the administration, "has always repudiated all designs whatever, and wherever imputed to him "and them, of *disturbing the system of slavery as it is existing under the Con-"stitution and laws*. The case, however, would not be fully presented were "I to omit to say that any such effort on his part would be *unconstitutional*, "and all his acts in that direction would be prevented by the judicial "authority, even though they were assented to by Congress and the people."

Within eighteen months after Seward declares officially to one of the ministers of the government that the President has no wish and no right to interfere with the institutions of the "rebellious" States, he writes another letter, also directed to the ministers abroad, announcing the adoption of a policy which, if it could be carried out, would make a complete revolution in the social organization of the South. Utterly regardless of his former position and declaration, he undertakes to justify the "emancipation" proclamation of the Yankee President. But this is not all. What shall we say of the effrontery of the lie, when Seward asserts that the abolition proclamation is not only a just and proper act, but avows his belief that the world will recognize *"the moderation and magnanimity with which the government proceeds in a matter so solemn and important!"*

confessed to the world his inability and failure to accomplish his purposes by regular and honorable hostilities. It was, in short, the diabolical attempt of an infatuated ruler, unworthy of authority, in a fit of disappointed malice, to inflict the worst horrours known to human nature upon eight millions of people who had wisely rejected his authority.

The "emancipation" proclamation not only strengthened the South and nerved her to greater exertions in the war, but it fortunately gave occasion to the world for a more interested observation and closer study of the peculiar institution of the Confederacy. The sympathies of Europe with the anti slavery party in America were depressed by the conduct of that party, its exhibitions of ferocity and by the new manifestations which the war had made of the nature and moral condition of negro slavery in the South.

Indeed, the war had shown the system of slavery in the South to the world in some new and striking aspects, and had removed much of that cloud of prejudice, defamation, falsehood, romance and perverse sentimentalism through which our peculiar institution had been formerly known to Europe. It had given a better vindication of our system of slavery than all the books that could be written in a generation. It had shown that slavery was an element of strength with us; that it had assisted us in our struggle; that no servile insurrections had taken place in the South in spite of the allurements of our enemy; that the slave had tilled the soil while his master had fought; that in large districts unprotected by our troops, and with a white population consisting almost exclusively of women and children, the slave had continued at his work quiet, cheerful and faithful; and that, as a conservative element in our social system, the institution of slavery had withstood the shocks of war and been a faithful ally of our arms, although instigated to revolution by every art of the enemy, and prompted to the work of assassination and pillage by the most brutal examples of the Yankee soldiery.*

---

* The missionary settlements of the Yankees on the coast of South Caro-

Since the commencement of the war the North had had almost exclusive access to the ear of the world, and had poured into it whatever of slander or of misrepresentation human ingenuity could suggest. This circumstance, which was at first thought to be a great disadvantage to us, had not only proved a harmless annoyance, but had resulted in invaluable benefit. It had secured sympathy for us; it had excited the inquiries of the intelligent, who, after all, give the law to public opinion; and it had naturally tempted the North to such lying and bravado as to disgust the world.

At the beginning of the war the North had assured the world that the people of the South were a sensual and barbarous people, demoralized by their institution of slavery, and depraved by self-will and licentiousness below the capacity for

---

lina were an acknowledged failure, so far as the proposed education and exaltation of the blacks were concerned. The appearance of the ancient town of Beaufort, since it had fallen into the enemy's possession, indicated the peculiarities of Yankee rule, and afforded an interesting exhibition of their relations with the negro. The inhabitants had taken nothing away with them but their personal property and their valuable domestic slave servants. The furniture was left untouched in the houses. These houses were owned by the Barnwells, the Rhetts, the Cuthberts, the Phillipses, and other distinguished families of North Carolina. The elegant furniture, the libraries, the works of art, had nearly all disappeared. They had been sent North from time to time by Yankee officers, and many of these officers of high rank. The elegant dwelling-houses had been converted into barracks, negro quarters, hospitals and store-houses. The best houses had been put in complete order, and were occupied by the officers of the department and the abolitionist missionaries from Boston and elsewhere. The efforts of these missionaries to teach the negroes their letters and habits of cleanliness met with no success. Beaufort was full of negroes, well clothed, at government expense, fat, saucy and lazy. The town looked dirty and disorderly, and had the appearance of a second class Mexican village. Some of the missionaries had been elevated to the position of planters, and occupied the estates of the old Carolinians. The labor on these estates was performed by contraband negroes. These abolition lords assumed all the hauteur and dignity of the Southern planter. The only difference to the black labourer was that he had the name of freeman; his labour was as unrelenting as ever. Massachusetts missionaries and Massachusetts speculators enjoyed the larger share of government patronage here. The department of Hunter appeared to be experimenting in attempts to elevate a negro to equality with the white man. Military operations were secondary considerations.

administrative government. The best reply to these slanders, was our conduct in this war. Even the little that was known in Europe of the patriotic devotion, the dignity and cultivated humanity of the people of the South, as shown in the war, had been sufficient to win unbounded encomiums for them. We had not only withstood for nearly two years a power which had put thirteen hundred thousand men in the field; but we had shown that we were a people able in public affairs, resolute, brave and prudent.

Another characteristic Yankee misrepresentation, made to the world about this time on the subject of the war, was, that it was to be concluded at an early day by the force of destitution and suffering in the South. The delusion of conquering the "rebels" by famine easily caught the vulgar ear. The North made it a point to exaggerate and garble everything it could find in Southern newspapers, of the ragged condition of our armies, the high prices of the necessaries of life, and the hardships of the war. The Yankees were pleasantly entertained with stories of our suffering. Their pictorials were adorned with caricatures of "secesh" in skeleton soldiers and gaunt cavalrymen with spurs strapped to their naked heels. Their perfumed fops and dainty ladies had the fashion of tittering at the rags of our prisoners. They had an overwhelming sense of the ludicrous in the idea of Southern women cutting up the carpets in their houses to serve for blankets and garments for the soldiers.

The fact was that our sufferings were great; but their mute eloquence which the enemy misinterpreted as a prospect of craven submission, was truly the sign of self-devotion. Whatever was suffered in physical destitution was not to be regretted. It practiced our people in self-denial; it purified their spirit; it brought out troops of virtues; it ennobled our women with offices of charity; it gave us new bonds of sympathy and love, and it trained us in those qualities which make a nation great and truly independent.

In the whirl of passing events, many strange things were

daily happening around us that at a remoter period of history will read like romance. The directions of our industry were changed. Planters raised corn and potatoes, fattened hogs and cultivated garden vegetables, while cotton was by universal consent neglected. Our newspapers were of all sizes and colours, sometimes containing four pages, sometimes two, and not a few were printed on common brown wrapping paper. Politics were dead. A political enemy was a curiosity only read of in the records of the past. Our amusements had been revolutionized. Outside of Richmond, a theatre was remembered only as an institution of bye-gone times. Most of our people did their own playing and their own singing; and the ladies spent the mornings in sewing coarse shirts or pantaloons for the soldiers to wear, and sung in public at night to gain money for the soldiers' equipments.

The footprints of the enemy, in Virginia especially, had marked lines of desolation such as history seldom records. Starting from Fortress Monroe and running westward to Winchester, scarcely a house within fifty miles of the Potomac but bore evidence of Yankee greed and spoliation. In nearly every county the court-house in which the assizes for each county used to be held, was rudely demolished, doors and windows torn down, while within, upon the white walls in every phase of handwriting, were recorded the autographs of the vandals, whose handiwork surrounded the beholder.

While the people of the South suffered, the resources of the country were developed by harsh necessity; and about the period where our narrative reaches, we are called upon to notice that happy change in the administration of our government, in which short-sighted expectations of peace were replaced by the policy of provision and an amassment of stores for a war of indefinite duration. Measures were adopted to afford adequate supplies of ordnance, arms and munitions for the army. Of small arms the supply was more adequate to the regiments of the army than at any other time. They had increased from importation and capture not less than eighty thousand. Establishments for making ordnance were founded in different parts of the South; a nitre corps was organized for service; and former dread of deficiency of the munitions of war no longer existed. The manufacturing resources of the country, especially in iron, were liberally patronized by the government, by large advances and liberal contracts; but in this the public service met great embarrassment from the temptations constantly offered to contractors to prefer the superiour profits which they could command by supplying the general market. The quartermaster's department was under the direction of Gen. Myers, of South Carolina, whose contributions to the cause of the South, in the zeal and ability which he brought into his important office, must take a high rank in all the histories of the war. He contended against the great obstacles of the blockade, the difficulties of railroad transportation and the constant losses in the enemy's ravages of the country, and performed wonders under the most unfavorable circumstances. Woolens and leather were imported from Europe through trains of difficulties; the most devoted exertions were made to replenish the scant supplies of blankets and shoes in the army; and by using to the utmost our internal resources, by the establishment of factories and the organization of workshops; and by greater economy in the use of our supplies, the sufferings of our soldiers were alleviated and their zeal refreshed for the campaign.

## CHAPTER VII.

The Heroism of Virginia...Her Battle-Fields...Burnside's Plan of Campaign...Calculations of his Movement upon Fredericksburg...Failure to Surprise Gen. Lee...THE BATTLE OF FREDERICKSBURG...The Enemy Crossing the River...Their Bombardment of the Town...Scenes of Distress...The Battle on the Right Wing...The Story of Marye's Heights...Repulse of the Enemy... The Old Lesson of Barren Victory...Death of Gen. Cobb...Death of General Gregg...Romance of the Story of Fredericksburg...Her Noble Women...Yankee Sacking of the Town...A Specimen of Yankee Warfare in North Carolina...Designs of the Enemy in this State...The Engagements of Kinston... Glance at other Theatres of the War...Gen. Hindman's Victory at Prairie Grove...Achievements of our Cavalry in the West...The Affair of Hartsville... Col. Clarkson's Expedition...Condition of Events at the Close of the Year 1862.

Virginia had borne the brunt of the war. Nearly two-thirds of her territory had been overrun by the enemy, and her richest fields had been drenched with blood or marked by the scars of the invader. The patriotic spirit and the chivalrous endurance of this ancient and admirable commonwealth had not only supported these losses and afflictions without a murmur, but these experiences of the war were the sources of new inspiration, and the occasions of renewed resolution and the reinforcement of courage by the sentiment of devotion. When we add to the consideration of the grand spirit of this State the circumstances that the flower of the Confederate army was naturally collected on this the most critical theatre of the war, and that the operations in Virginia were assisted by the immediate presence of the government, we shall naturally look here for the most brilliant and decisive successes of the war.

When the Confederate army fell back into Virginia, after its short but eventful campaign in Maryland, Gen. Lee, by the skillful disposition of his forces in front of Winchester, rendered it impracticable for McClellan to invade the Valley of the Shenandoah, and forced him to adopt the route on the east side of the Blue Ridge. The Federal commander accepted this alternative the more readily, since he hoped, by an ostentatious display of a part of his forces near Shepherdstown, to deceive Gen. Lee and gain his flank and rear at Warrenton. On his arrival at this latter place, however, much to his surprise and dismay, he found the forces of Lee quietly awaiting him on the south bank of the Rappahannock.

McClellan having been superseded by Burnside, that officer undertook a plan of campaign entirely on his own responsibility, in opposition to the suggestions of Halleck and to what were known to be the predilections of the military authorities at Washington. The plan of Gen. Burnside was to concentrate the army in the neighbourhood of Warrenton, to make a small movement across the Rappahannock as a feint, with a view to divert the attention of the Confederates and lead them to believe he was going to move in the direction of Gordonsville, and then to make a rapid movement of the whole army to Fredericksburg, on the North side of the Rappahannock.

In moving upon Fredericksburg, Gen. Burnside calculated that his army would all the time be as near Washington as would the Confederates, and that after arriving at Fredericksburg it would be at a point nearer to Richmond than it would be even if it should take Gordonsville.

This novel enterprise against the Confederate Capital was hailed by the Northern newspapers with renewed acclamations of "on to Richmond;" and the brazen and familiar prophecy of the fall of the city "within ten days" was repeated with new emphasis and bravado. In the meantime the plans of Burnside, so far as they contemplated a surprise of the Confederates, had failed, and at Fredericksburg, as at Warrenton, his army found itself, by the active movements of Gen. Lee, confronted by a force sufficient to dispute its advance and to deliver battle on a scale commensurate with the stake.

## THE BATTLE OF FREDERICKSBURG.

Gen. Burnside having concentrated his army at Fredericksburg, employed himself for several days in the latter part of November in bringing up from Aquia Creek all the pontoons he could for building the bridges which were necessary to throw his forces across the river. Several councils of war were called to decide about crossing the Rappahannock. It was finally determined to cross at Fredericksburg, under the impression that Gen. Lee had thrown a large portion of his force down the river and elsewhere, thus weakening his defences in front.

On the night of the 10th December the enemy commenced to throw three bridges over the Rappahannock—two at Fredericksburg, and the third about a mile and a quarter below, near the mouth of Deep Run. In the prosecution of this work, the enemy was defended by his artillery on the hills of Stafford, which completely commanded the plain on which Fredericksburg stands. The narrowness of the Rappahannock, its winding course, and deep bed, afforded opportunity for the construction of bridges at points beyond the reach of our artillery, and the banks had to be watched by skirmishers. The houses of Fredericksburg afforded a cover for the skirmishers at the bridges opposite the town, but at the lowest point of crossing no shelter could be had.

The 17th Mississippi regiment, Barksdale's brigade, being on picket within the town, were ordered to the bluff overlooking the site of the old railroad bridge. The moon was brilliant, and by its light our men could distinguish the enemy's forces working on a pontoon bridge stretching from the Stafford bank towards the foot of the bluff. In the course of an hour the bridge had been stretched within sixty yards of the southern shore. The work was going bravely on, when the two companies of the 17th, who were lying on the extreme verge of the bluff, were ordered to fire. The order was deliberately given and executed. At the crack of our rifles, the bridge-builders scampered for the shore; but the next moment there was opened upon the bluff a terrific fire of shell, grape and musketry, which was kept up until our troops retired. Twice again, at intervals of half an hour, the enemy renewed the attempt to complete the bridge, but was in each instance repulsed. After the third repulse of the enemy, the whole of Barksdale's brigade was ordered to the support of the 17th regiment, and were put into position, some in the rear of the bluff and others higher up and lower down the stream. At this juncture the enemy's fire from cannon and small arms became so tremendous and overwhelming that our troops were only preserved from destruction by lying flat on their faces. In every instance in which a man ventured to raise his head from the earth, he was instantly riddled by bullets or torn to pieces by grapeshot. The emergency may be understood when it is borne in mind that the position occupied by our men was swept by the enemy's batteries and sharpshooters not two hundred yards distant on the opposite heights.

Towards five o'clock in the afternoon of the 11th December, three rousing cheers from the river bank beneath the bluff announced that the enemy had completed the bridge, and that his troops had effected a landing on the southern bank. About this time the order for a retreat was received by our men. The regiments of the brigade fell back by different streets, firing as they retreated upon the enemy, who closely followed them. The brigade rendezvoused at the market-house and faced the enemy. A sharp skirmish ensued, but our troops, acting under orders, again fell back and left the town in possession of the enemy.

It having become evident to Gen. Lee that no effectual opposition could be offered to the construction of the bridges or passage of the river, it only remained that positions should be selected to oppose the enemy's advance after crossing. Under cover of the darkness of the night of the 12th and of a dense fog, a large force passed the river, and took position on the right bank, protected by their heavy guns on the left.

The effects of the enemy's bombardment upon the unfortunate town were deplorable. The majority of the population had long ago fled the city at the prospect of its destruction; and the touching spectacles of their misery and suffering were seen for miles around the city, where houseless women and children were camped out or roaming shelterless and hungry through the fields. A number of citizens who had returned to the town under the delusion that it would not be attacked, left it during the day the enemy crossed the river, single or in families, and sought for refuge and safety in the country. They were scattered about—some in cabins, some in the open air, and others wandering vacantly along the railroads. Little children with blue feet trod painfully the frozen ground, and those whom they followed knew as little as themselves where to seek food and shelter. Hundreds of ladies wandered homeless over the frozen highway, with bare feet and thin clothing, knowing not where to find a place of refuge. Delicately nurtured girls, with slender forms, upon which no rain had ever beat, which no wind had ever visited too roughly, walked hurriedly, with unsteady feet, upon the road, seeking only some place where they could shelter themselves. Whole families sought sheds by the wayside, or made roofs of fence-rails and straw, knowing not whither to fly, or to what friend to have recourse. This was the result of the enemy's bombardment. Night had settled down, and though the roar of the batteries had hushed, the flames of burning houses still lit up the landscape.

The sun of the 13th of December rose clear, but a dim fog shrouded the town of Fredericksburg and the circumjacent valleys, and delayed the opening of the antagonistic batteries. At two o'clock in the morning our troops were all under arms, and batteries in position to receive the expected attack of the enemy.

The Rappahannock, in its course from west to east, is skirted, just at the point where Fredericksburg stands on its southern bank, by low crests of hills, which on the northern bank run parallel and close to the river, and on the southern bank trend backward from the stream, and leave a semi-circular plain six miles in length and two or three in depth, enclosed within their circumference before they again approach the river in the neighborhood of Massaponax creek. Immediately above the town, and on the left of the Confederate position, the bluffs are bold and bare of trees; but south of the railroad, beginning near the town and running to a point at Hamilton's Crossing, and also parallel with the river, is a range of hills covered with dense oak forest fringed on its northern border by pine thickets. Our forces occupied the whole length of this forest. Longstreet's corps occupied the highlands above, opposite and for a mile below the town. Jackson's corps rested on Longstreet's right, and extended away to the eastward, the extreme right under A. P. Hill crossing the railroad at Hamilton's crossing, and stretching into the valley towards the river. Our front was about six miles in length. Most of the batteries of both corps were posted in the skirts of the forest, along the line of the railroad, the seven batteries in Colonel Lindsey Walker's regiment and Stuart's horse artillery being stationed in the valley, between the railroad at Hamilton's Crossing and the river. The enemy's forces occupied the valley north of the railroad from Fredericksburg to within half a mile of our extreme right. His light batteries were posted over the southern extremity of the valley, at from a quarter of a mile to a mile from the railroad, while the hills on the northern banks of the river from Falmouth to Fitzhugh's farm, five miles below Fredericksburg, were studded at intervals of half a mile with his batteries of heavy guns.

At noon the fog had cleared away, but there was a thick haze in the atmosphere. About this time the enemy's infantry moved forward from the river towards our batteries on the hills. As they pressed forward across the valley, Stuart's horse artillery from our extreme right opened upon them a destructive enfilading fire of round shot. This fire, which annoyed them sorely, was kept up in spite of six batteries which were directed against the horse artillery as soon as it was unmasked. By one o'clock the Yankee columns had crossed the valley and entered the woods south of the railroad. The batteries on both sides slackened their fire, and musketry, at first scattering, but quickly increasing to a crash and roar, sounded through the woods. Dense volumes of smoke rose above the trees, and volley succeeded volley, sometimes so rapidly as to blend into a prolonged and continuous roar. A. P. Hill's division sustained the first shock of battle. The rest of Jackson's corps were in different lines of reserves. D. H. Hill's division was drawn up in J. L. Marye's field, under a long hill, in rear of our line of battle. Here they remained during the most of the day, being moved from time to time to the right or left, as the exigencies of battle dictated. Shortly after the infantry fight began, a brigade of this division was moved at a double-quick a mile and a half to the right, and posted in a dense clump of pines in supporting distance of Stuart's horse artillery. In ten minutes they were brought back to their original position.. The celerity of this movement made a singular and exciting spectacle. A long black line shoots from the position of the reserves, crosses the railroad at Hamilton's station, skims across the valley, and in a few moments is lost in the pines nearly two miles away. After scarcely a breathing spell, the same line emerges from the pines and retraces its steps to its original position. As this brigade resumed its position in reserve, the fire of musketry directly in its front slackened. A few crackling shots were heard to our left, along Longstreet's division, and then a succession of volleys, which were kept up at intervals during the remainder of the evening. The musketry fire on our right was soon renewed, and the battle raged with increased fury. Our batteries along our whole front again re-opened, and Col. Walker's artillery regiment, composed of Latham's, Letcher's, Braxton's, Pegram's, Crenshaw's, Johnson's and McIntosh's batteries, stationed in the open low grounds to the east of the railroad at Hamilton's station, moved forward several hundred yards in the direction of Fredericksburg. Hill's and Early's troops had driven the enemy from the woods and across the railroad in the direction of their pontoon bridges near Deep Run. Our men pursued them a mile and a half across the bottom land, and fell back only when they had gotten under the shelter of their batteries. Again the enemy rallied and returned to renew the contest, but were again driven back. All the batteries of Jackson's corps were at this time in full play, and in the approaching twilight the blaze of the guns and the quick flashes of the shells more distinctly visible, constituted a scene at once splendid and terrific.

On the right wing the enemy had been driven back with great loss. General Stuart had well redeemed his grim despatch—that he was "going to crowd 'em with artillery." The enormous strength of this military arm, had been used with desperation on one side and devoted courage on the other. The enemy had twenty thousand men engaged on this wing; while, altogether, from first to last, we had not more than ten thousand in the line of fire.

But while the battle was dashing furiously against the lines of Jackson, the enemy was crossing troops over his bridges at Fredericksburg and massing them in front of Longstreet, in the immediate neighbourhood of the town.

On reference to the positions of the battle-field, it will be apparent that the left of the Confederate army—a portion of it stationed not more than four hundred yards from Fredericksburg—occupied a much stronger position than the centre and right. There was not sufficient room for the Yankee troops destined for the attack of the nearest Confederate batteries to deploy and form, except under a deadly Confederate fire, whereas, the Yankee troops who attacked the Confederate centre and right had a large plain on which to deploy, and had much fewer disadvantages of ground to contend with, inasmuch as they advanced against lower hills and had the long spurs of copse to assist them as points of attack, calculated to protect and serve as *points d'appui* to the Yankees if they could once have succeeded in carrying and holding them.

In this part of the field the enemy displayed a devotion that is remarkable in history. This display does not adorn the Yankees: it was made by a race that has left testimonies of its courage in such stories as Waterloo and Fontenoy. To the Irish division, commanded by Gen. Meagher, was principally committed the desperate task of bursting out of the town of Fredericksburg, and forming under the withering fire of the Confederate batteries, to attack Marye's Heights, towering immediately in their front. The troops were harangued in impassioned language by their commander, who pointed to the heights as the contested prize of victory.

The heights were occupied by the Washington Artillery and a portion of McLaws' division. As the enemy advanced, the artillery reserved their fire until he arrived within two hundred and fifty yards, when they opened on the heavy masses with grape and canister. At the first broadside of the sixteen guns of the battalion, hundreds of the enemy went down, and at every successive discharge great furrows were plowed through their ranks. They staggered repeatedly, but were as often rallied and brought forward. Again and again they made frantic dashes upon our steady line of fire, and as often were the hill-sides strewn for acres with their corpses. At last, no longer able to withstand the withering fire, they broke and fled in confusion. They were pressed into town by our infantry. Our victory was complete all along the line. When the voices of our officers in the darkness ordered the last advance, the combat had terminated in the silence of the foe.

The enemy left behind him a ghastly field. Some portions of it were literally packed with his dead. At the foot of Marye's Heights was a frightful spectacle of carnage. The bodies which had fallen in dense masses within forty yards of the muzzles of Col. Walton's guns, testified to the gallantry of the Irish division, and showed what manner of men they were who pressed on to death with the dauntlessness of a race whose courage history has made indisputable. The loss of the enemy was out of all comparison in numbers with our own; the evidences of its extent do not permit us to doubt that it was at least ten thousand; while our own killed and wounded, during the operations since the movements of the enemy began at Fredericksburg, amounted to about eighteen hundred.

At the thrilling tidings of Fredericksburg the hopes of the South rose high that we were at last to realize some important and practical consequences from the prowess of our arms. We had obtained a victory in which the best troops of the North—including Sumner's grand division—had been beaten; in which defeat had left the shattered foe cowering beneath the houses of Fredericksburg; and in which he had been forced into a position which left him no reasonable hope of escape, with a river in his rear, which, though threaded by pontoon bridges, would have been impassable under the pressure of attack. It is remarkable that, so far as the war had progressed, although fought on an almost unparalleled scale in numbers, it was yet not illustrated by the event so common in the military history of Europe, of the decisive annihilation of any single army. But it was thought that Fredericksburg, at least, would give an illustration of a decisive victory in this war. The Southern public waited with impatience for the completion of the success that had already been announced, and the newspapers were eagerly scanned for the hoped-for intelligence that Gen. Lee had, by the vigour of a fresh assault, dispatched his crippled enemy on the banks of the river. But no such assault was made. While the public watched with keen impatience for the blow, the announcement came that the enemy, after having remained entirely at his leisure one day in Fredericksburg, had the next night crossed the Rappahannock without accident or a single effort at interruption on our part, and that the army of Burnside, which was a short while ago thought to be in the jaws of destruction, was quietly re-organizing in perfect security on the north bank of the river. It was the old lesson to the South of a barren victory. The story of Fredericksburg was incomplete and unsatisfactory; and there appeared no prospect but that a war waged at awful sacrifices was yet indefinitely to linger in the trail of bloody skirmishes.

The victory, which had only the negative advantage of having checked the enemy without destroying him, and the vulgar glory of our having killed and wounded several thousand men more than we had lost, had been purchased by us with lives, though comparatively small in numbers, yet infinitely more precious than those of mercenary hordes arrayed against us. Two of our Brigadier-Generals—General Thomas R. R. Cobb of Georgia and Gen. Maxcy Gregg of South Carolina—had fallen on the field. The loss of each was more conspicuous from extraordinary personal worth than from mere distinctions of rank. Gen. Cobb was the brother of Gen. Howell Cobb, and was an able and eloquent member of the Provisional Congress, in which body he had served in the important capacity of chairman of the committee on military affairs.

Of the virtues and services of Gen. Maxcy Gregg it is not necessary to remind any portion of the people of the South by a detailed review of incidents in his career. His name was familiarly coupled with the first movements of the war, he having been appointed to the command of the First South Carolina regiment, the first force from the State which arrived in Virginia, and whose advent at Richmond had been hailed with extraordinary demonstrations of honour and welcome. The term of the service of this regiment having expired, it returned to South Carolina, but its commander, Colonel Gregg, remained in Virginia, and subsequently re-organized the regiment, which had since been constantly and conspicuously in service. Its commander was subsequently made a Brigadier General.

Gen. Gregg, although the occupations of his life were principally professional, had a large and brilliant political reputation in his State. He was a leading member of the bar, and practiced his profession with distinction and success for a period of more than twenty years in Columbia. In politics he was an extreme State Rights man, and stood, with others, at the head of that party in South Carolina. He took a prominent part in favour of the policy of re-opening the Slave Trade, which had been the subject of some excited and untimely discussion in the South some years ago; he and ex-Governor Adams, of South Carolina, being associated as the leading representatives of that idea in the Cotton States.

Gen. Gregg was remarkable for his firm and unflinching temper. In the army he had an extraordinary reputation for self-possession and *sang froid* in battle. He was never disconcerted, and had the happy faculty of inspiring the courage of his troops, not so much by words as by his cool determination and even behaviour.

The romance of the story of Fredericksburg, is written no less in the quiet heroism of her women than in deeds of arms. The verses of the poet rather than the cold language of a mere chronicle of events are most fitting to describe the beautiful courage and noble sacrifices of those brave daughters of Virginia, who preferred to see their homes reduced to ashes, rather than polluted by the Yankee, and who in the blasts of winter, and in the fiercer storms of blood and fire, went forth undismayed, encouraging our soldiers, and proclaiming their desire to suffer privation, poverty and death, rather than the shame of a surrender or the misfortune of a defeat. In all the terrible scenes of Fredericksburg, there were no weakness and tears of women. Mothers, exiles from their homes, met their sons in the ranks, embraced them, told them their duty, and with a self-negation most touching to witness, concealed their want, sometimes their hunger, telling their brave boys they were comfortable and happy, that they might not be troubled with domestic anxieties. At Hamilton Crossing, many of the women had the opportunity of meeting their relatives in the army. In the haste of flight, mothers had brought a few garments, or perhaps the last loaf of bread for the soldier boy, and the lesson of duty whispered in the ear gave to the young heart the pure and brave inspiration to sustain it in battle. No more touching and noble evidence could be offered of the heroism of the women of Fredericksburg than the gratitude of our army; for, afterwards, when subscriptions for their relief came to be added up, it was found that thousands of dollars had been contributed by ragged soldiers out of their pittance of pay to the fund of the refugees. There could be no more eloquent tribute than this offered to the women of Fredericksburg—a beautiful and immortal souvenir of their sufferings and virtues.

What was endured in the Yankee sacking of the town, finds scarcely anywhere a parallel in the history of civilized races. It is impossible to detail here the murderous acts of the enemy, the arsons, the robberies, the torture of women, and the innumerable and indescribable villanies committed upon helpless people. The following extract from the New York *Tribune*, written by one of its army correspondents in a tone of devilish amusement, affords a glimpse of Burnside's brigands in Fredericksburg, and of the accustomed barbarities of the enemy.

"The old mansion of Douglas Gordon—perhaps the wealth-
"iest citizen in the vicinity—is now used as the headquarters
"of General Howard, but before he occupied it, every room
"had been torn with shot, and then all the elegant furniture
"and works of art broken and smashed by the soldiers, who
"burst into the house after having driven the rebel sharp-
"shooters from behind it. When I entered it early this morn-
"ing, before its occupation by Gen. Howard, I found the sol-
"diers of his fine division diverting themselves with the rich
"dresses found in the wardrobes; some had on bonnets of the
"fashion of last year, and were surveying themselves before
"mirrors, which, an hour or two afterwards, were pitched out
"of the window and smashed to pieces upon the pavement;
"others had elegant scarfs bound round their heads in the
"form of turbans, and shawls around their waists.

"We destroyed by fire nearly two whole squares of build-
"ings, chiefly used for business purposes, together with the
"fine residences of O. McDowell, Dr. Smith, J. H. Kelly, A.

"S. Cott, William Slaughter, and many other smaller dwell- "ings. Every store, I think, without exception, was pillaged "of every valuable article. A fine drug store, which would "not have looked badly on Broadway, was literally one mass "of broken glass and jars."

The records of the Spanish and Moorish struggles, the wars of the Roses and the thirty years war in Germany, may be safely challenged for comparisons with the acts of barbarity of the Yankees. Their worst acts of atrocity were not committed in the mad intoxication of combat, but in cold and cowardly blood on the helpless and defenceless. While the lawless and savage scenes in Fredericksburg, to which we have referred, were still fresh in the public mind, the enemy in another department of the war, was displaying the same fiendish temper, stung by defeat and emboldened with the prospect of revenging her fortunes on the women and children of the South. The Yankee incursions and raids in North Carolina in the month of December are companion pieces to the sack of Fredericksburg.

"On entering Williamstown, North Carolina," says an eye-witness, "the Yankees respected not a single house—it mat- "tered not whether the owner was in or absent. Doors were "broken open and houses entered by the soldiers, who took "everything they saw, and what they were unable to carry "away they broke and destroyed. Furniture of every des- "cription was committed to the flames, and the citizens who "dared to remonstrate with them were threatened, cursed and "buffeted about. \* \* \* \* The enemy stopped "for the night at Mr. Ward's mill. Mr. Ward was completely "stripped of everything, they not even leaving him enough "for breakfast. While on a sick bed his wife was, in his pre- "sence, searched and robbed of five hundred dollars. The "Yankees went about fifteen miles above Hamilton, when, for "some cause, they suddenly turned and marched back, taking, "with some slight deviations in quest of plunder, the same "route they had come. The town of Hamilton was set on

"fire and as many as fifteen houses laid in ashes. During the
"time the Yankees encamped at Williamstown everything
"which they left unharmed when last there, was demolished.
"Every house in town was occupied and defaced. Several
"fine residences were actually used as horse stables. Iron
"safes were broken open, and in the presence of their owners
"rifled of their contents. Several citizens were seized and
"robbed of the money on their persons. *   *   *   *
"On Sunday morning Williamstown was fired and no effort
"made to arrest the flames until several houses were burnt.
"No attempt was made by the Yankee officers, from General
"Foster down, to prevent the destruction of property. On
"the contrary, they connived at it, and some of the privates
"did not hesitate to say that they were instructed to do as
"they had done. Two ladies at Williamstown went to Gen.
"Foster to beseech protection from his soldiers, and were
"rudely and arrogantly ordered from his presence."

Referring to the same scenes, a correspondent writes: "Fa-
"milies who fled in dismay at the approach of the invader, re-
"turned and found, as well as the few who remained at home,
"clothes, beds, bedding, spoons and books abstracted; costly
"furniture, crockery, doors, harness and vehicles demolished;
"locks, windows and mirrors broken; fences burned; corn,
"potatoes and peas gathered from the barns and fields con-
"sumed; iron safes dug to pieces and thrown out of doors,
"and their contents stolen."

The object of the enemy's movements in North Carolina, long a subject of anxious speculation, was at last developed, in time for a severe check to be given it. At the time that the enemy assaulted our lines in front of Fredericksburg, following his favorite policy of simultaneous attack in different departments, he had planned a movement upon the Wilmington and Weldon railroad; and on the same day that the battle of Fredericksburg was fought, occurred an important passage of arms in North Carolina.

On the thirteenth of December, Brigadier General Evans

encountered, with two thousand men, the advancing enemy, and with this small force held him in check at Southwest creek, beyond Kinston. The Yankee force, commanded by Foster, consisted of fifteen thousand men and nine gunboats. Having delayed their advance for some time, General Evans succeeded in withdrawing his force, with small loss, to the left bank of the Neuse river at Kinston. He held the Yankees at bay until the 16th, when they advanced on the opposite side of the river, and made an attack at Whitehall bridge, about eighteen miles below Goldsboro'; in which they were driven back by General Robertson, with severe loss.

The important object on our side was to protect the railroad bridge over the Neuse and the county bridge about half a mile above; and to effect this, reinforcements having reached us, a rapid disposition of our forces was made. During the 17th, the enemy appeared in force before General Clingman's three regiments, and he withdrew across the county bridge to this side of the river. The artillery of the enemy was playing upon the railroad bridge; and Evans' brigade had at last to move forward by the county road, and cross, if at all, the bridge a half mile above the railroad. About two o'clock in the afternoon one bold and daring incendiary succeeded in reaching the bridge, and covered by the wing wall of the abutment, lighted a flame which soon destroyed the superstructure, leaving the masonry, abutments and pier intact.

It was very important for us now to save the county bridge, the only means remaining of crossing the river in the vicinity. Evans' and Clingman's brigades were ordered to cross, supported by Pettigrew's brigade; and the Mississippi brigade, just coming in, was ordered to move forward at once. The enemy were driven back from their position on the line of the railroad, but on account of the lateness of the hour, the nature of the ground, and the fact that our artillery, cavalry and a large portion of the reinforcements had not yet arrived, it was not deemed advisable to attack their strong second position that evening. During the night the enemy made a hurried retreat to their fortifications and gunboats, moving with such celerity that it was useless to attempt pursuit with any other arms than cavalry, of which at that time, unfortunately, we had none.

Our loss in these engagements was inconsiderable—seventy-one killed and two hundred and sixty-eight wounded. The enemy's occupation of Kinston and the bridge there prevented a body of our men, about five hundred in number, from escaping. The greater part were taken prisoners and paroled, and some few succeeded in escaping higher up on the river.

The substantial achievements of the grand army of invasion were, that they burned the superstructure of two bridges, which cost originally less than ten thousand dollars. They had utterly failed to attempt to take advantage of the temporary and partial interruption of our railroad line, for the purpose of striking a decisive blow at any important point before we could thoroughly re-establish our communication without it.

In other quarters of the war less important than Virginia or North Carolina, the early months of the winter were distinguished by some combats of various importance. The feeble campaign in the country west of the Mississippi was marked by one engagement, the dimensions of which were large for that campaign, but the situation of which was too distant to affect the general condition of the Confederacy.

On the 27th of November Gen. Hindman came up with the enemy at Prairie Grove, near Fayetteville, Arkansas, with a force of about nine thousand men. The enemy, under the command of Gen. Blount, was already largely superiour in numbers; and it was the object of Hindman to cut off reinforcements of seven or eight thousand, which were on the march. In this he failed; but, nothing daunted, brought on the attack at daylight, capturing, in the first charge of Gen. Marmaduke's cavalry, a whole regiment, and twenty-three wagons heavily laden with quartermaster and medical stores. Soon after sunrise the fight commenced in good earnest, and with no cessation the artillery continued until night-fall. Our whole line of infantry were in close conflict nearly the whole day with the enemy, who were attempting with their force of eighteen thousand men to drive us from our position. In every instance they were repulsed, and finally driven back from the field; Gen. Hindman driving them to within eight miles of Fayetteville, when our forces fell back to their supply depot, between Cane Hill and Van Buren. We captured three hundred prisoners and vast quantities of stores. The enemy's loss in killed and wounded was about one thousand; the Confederate loss in killed, wounded and missing, about three hundred. In one of the charges of the engagement, Gen. Stein, of the Missouri State Guard, was killed, a ball passing directly through his brain.

The close of the year 1862 leaves little to record of events of importance sufficient to affect the fortunes of the war, beyond what has been related in these pages with more or less particularity of detail. In that large expanse of country between the Mississippi and the tributaries of the Atlantic, events, since our last reference to these theatres of the war, were of little apparent importance, although they were preparing for a grand tragedy of arms upon which we shall find that the first page of the new year opens. There were daring forays, brilliant skirmishes and enterprises of our cavalry, to which a brief reference is only possible in these pages. Such were the exploits of Gens. Forrest and Morgan, our distinguished cavalry commanders in West Tennessee, in which they annoyed the enemy, destroyed railroad bridges and Federal property, and captured several towns in successful raids. On the 7th of December a single expedition, sent out under Morgan from Gen. Bragg's lines, attacked an outpost of the enemy at Hartsville on the Cumberland, killed and wounded two hundred, captured eighteen hundred prisoners, two pieces of artillery and two thousand small arms, and all other stores at the position. Nor in our slight record of indecisive but gallant incidents of the war, must we neglect to mention the brave enterprise of Col. Clarkson, another choice spirit of Southern chivalry, who, with a detachment of the Virginia State line, penetrated into Kentucky, captured the town of Piketon on the 8th of December, secured a large amount of stores, and nipped an important enterprise of the enemy in the bud.

In the meantime some important new assignments of military command had been made in preparation for the winter campaign, and happily inspired the country with renewed confidence in the fortunes of the war. Gen. Gustavus W. Smith, whose patriotism was as enthusiastic as his military genius was admirable, (for he had broken ties as well as restraints in escaping from the North to join the standard of his native South,) had taken command in North Carolina. Gen. Beauregard had been assigned to the important care of the defences of Charleston and Savannah, threatened by the most formidable armadas that the warlike ingenuity and lavish expenditure of the enemy had yet produced. Gen. Pemberton had relieved Van Dorn of the army of the Southwest at Holly Springs, which had been taken by surprise on the 20th of December, and was now in our possession; and that latter officer, ill-starred by fortune, but whose gallantry and enterprise were freely acknowledged, was appropriately appointed to take command of the cavalry forces in the West. The command of all the forces between the Alleghany and the Mississippi was entrusted to Gen. Joseph E. Johnston, whose matchless strategy had more than once enlightened the records of the war, and whose appointment to this large and important command was hailed with an outburst of joy and enthusiastic confidence in all parts of the South.

## CHAPTER VIII.

The Eastern Portion of Tennessee...Its Military Importance...Composition of Bragg's Army—THE BATTLE OF MURFREESBORO'...The Right Wing of the Enemy Routed—Bragg's Exultations...The Assault of the 2d January..."The Bloody Crossing of Stone River"...The Confederates Fall Back to Tullahoma...Review of the Battle Field of Murfreesboro'...Repulse of the Enemy at Vicksburg....THE RE-CAPTURE OF GALVESTON....The Midnight March... Capture of "the Harriet Lane"...Arkansas Post Taken by the Yankees...Its Advantages...The Affair of the Rams in Charleston Harbour...Naval Structure of the Confederacy...Capture of the Yankee Gunboat "Queen of the West"... Heroism of George Wood...Capture of "the Indianola"...The War on the Water...The Confederate Cruisers...Prowess of the Alabama."

The eastern portion of Tennessee abounds in hills, rocks, poverty and ignorance. But its military situation was one of great importance to the Confederacy. The enemy already held West and Middle Tennessee. It required but to occupy East Tennessee to have entire possession of one of the most valuable States of the Confederacy. They also felt bound in honour and duty to render the long promised assistance to the Unionists of East Tennessee. Tennessee would be more thoroughly theirs than Kentucky, when once they filled this eastern portion of it with their armies. The essential geographical importance of this country to the Confederacy was too obvious to be dwelt upon. It covered Georgia and involved the defences of the cotton region of the South. Through it ran a great continental line of railroad, of which the South could not be deprived without unspeakable detriment. The importance of this road to the supply of our armies was no less considerable than to the supply of our general population.

The gallant and heroic army of the Confederacy, commanded by General Braxton Bragg, composed of Floridians, Louisianians, South Carolinians, Georgians and Kentuckians, numbering between thirty and forty thousand men, had occupied Murfreesboro' for over a month, in confidence and security, never dreaming of the advance of the enemy. President Davis had visited and reviewed the brave veterans of Fishing Creek, Pensacola, Donelson, Shiloh, Perryville and Hartsville, and, satisfied of their ability to resist any foe who should have the temerity to attack them, he withdrew from our forces Stevenson's division, of Kirby Smith's corps, numbering about eight thousand men, leaving scarcely thirty thousand men to defend what was left to us of Tennessee.

Balls, parties and brilliant festivities relieved the ennui of the camp of the Confederates. On Christmas eve scenes of revelry enlivened Murfreesboro', and officers and men alike gave themselves up to the enjoyment of the hour, with an abandonment of all military cares, indulging in fancied security.

The enemy's force at Nashville, under command of Rosecranz, was not believed to have been over forty thousand, and the opinion was confidently entertained that he would not attempt to advance until the Cumberland should rise, to afford him the aid of his gunboats. Indeed, Morgan had been sent to Kentucky to destroy the Nashville road and cut off his supplies, so that he might force the enemy to come out and meet us. Yet, that very night, when festivity prevailed, the enemy was marching upon us!

THE BATTLE OF MURFREESBORO'.

The grounds in front of Murfreesboro' had been surveyed and examined a month before, in order to select a position for battle in case of surprise, and our troops were thrown forward to prevent such a misfortune. Polk's corps, with Cheatham's division, occupied our centre, Maney's brigade being thrown forward towards Lavergne, where Wheeler's cavalry was annoying the enemy. A portion of Kirby Smith's corps, McCown's division, occupied Readyville, on our right, and Hardee's corps occupied Triune, on our left, with Wharton's cavalry thrown out in the vicinity of Franklin.

Festival and mirth continued on Christmas day, but the day following, Friday, the 26th, was a most gloomy one. The rain fell in torrents. That same evening couriers arrived and reported a general advance of the enemy. All was excitement and commotion, and the greatest activity prevailed. The enemy had already driven in our advance front. Hardee's corps fell back from Triune. Major-Gen. McCown's division was ordered to march to Murfreesboro' at once, having received the order at midnight. Heavy skirmishing by Wheeler and Wharton's cavalry had continued since the 25th. On the 27th the ground for our line of battle was selected in front of the town, about a mile and a half distant on Stone's River. The enemy had now advanced beyond Triune, his main body occupying Stuart's Creek, ten miles from town. On the 28th our troops took up their position in line of battle. Polk's corps, consisting of Withers' and Cheatham's divisions, formed our left wing, and was posted about a mile and a half on the west side of Stone's River, its right resting on the Nashville road, and its left extending as far as the Salem pike, a distance of nearly six miles. Hardee's corps, consisting of Breckinridge's and Cleburne's divisions, was formed on the east bank of the river, its left resting near the Nashville road, and its right extending towards the Lebanon pike, about three miles in length, making our line of battle about nine miles in length, in the shape of an obtuse angle. McCown's division formed the reserve, opposite our centre, and Jackson's brigade was held in reserve on the right flank of Hardee. Stone's River crosses the Salem pike about a mile and a half on the south side of the town, making a curve below the pike about a mile further south, and then runs nearly north and south in front of Murfreesboro', crossing the Nashville pike and extending towards the Lebanon pike, some half a mile, when it makes another turn or bend and runs nearly east and west, emptying into the Cumberland River. The river, at the shoals, where it crosses the Nashville pike, was fordable and not over ankle deep. The banks above and below were rather steep, being some five to eight feet high, with rocky protusions. The nature of the country was undulating, but mostly level in our front, with large, open fields. To the right or the west side the ground was more rolling, with rocky upheaval and croppings of limestone and thick cedar groves. On the side of the river towards the Lebanon pike were thin patches of woods and rocky projections.

On the 29th there was continued skirmishing by our cavalry forces, the enemy gradually advancing. On the 30th the enemy had advanced by three columns and took up his position about a mile in our front. At noon he shelled our right and centre in order to feel our reserves. At 3 P. M. the enemy made an advance on our left, and attempted to drive us back in order to occupy the ground for his right wing. A spirited engagement immediately commenced, General Polk having ordered forward a portion of Withers' division. Robinson's battery held the enemy in check, keeping up a most deadly and destructive fire. Three times the enemy charged this battery, but were repulsed by the gallant one hundred and fifty-fourth Tennessee. Colonel Loomis, commanding Gardner's brigade, and the brigade formerly Duncan's, with the South Carolinians, Alabamians and Louisianians, were most hotly engaged, and though suffering considerably, succeeded in driving back the enemy with great slaughter. It was now clear that the enemy intended to mass his forces on our left, in order to make a flank movement the next day, and obtain, if possible, the Salem pike, which, if successful, would give him possession of the Chattanooga railroad. Cleburne's division, of Hardee's corps, and Major-General McCown's division, were immediately ordered over towards the Salem pike to reinforce our extreme left wing. Wheeler's cavalry had already gained the enemy's rear, and had captured a train of wagons and a number of prisoners. A cold, drizzling rain had set in, and our troops were greatly exposed, being without shelter and bivouacking by their camp fires.

On the morning of the 31st, the grand battle was opened.

At the break of day on the cold and cloudy morning, General Hardee gave the order to advance, and the fight was opened by McCown's division, with Cleburne, advancing upon the enemy's right wing under Gen. McCook. The charge was of the most rapid character. The alarm given by the enemy's pickets scarcely reached his camp before the Confederates were upon it. The sight of our advance was a most magnificent one. Two columns deep, with a front of nearly three-fourths of a mile, the line well preserved and advancing with great rapidity, on came the Confederate left wing, the bayonets glistening in a bright sun, which had broken through the thick fog.

The enemy was taken completely by surprise, their artillery horses not even being hitched up. Such was the impetuosity of the charge, that the enemy fell back in dismay, our troops pouring in a most murderous fire. With such rapidity did our men cross the broken ploughed fields, that our artillery could not follow them. Wharton's cavalry had charged a battery, the horses not being harnessed, and driving back the infantry supporting it, succeeded in capturing it. The enemy having gradually recovered, now disputed our further advance, and the battle raged with terrific violence. They continued to fall back, however, under our fire, until we had swung round nearly our whole left on their right, as if on a pivot, driving the enemy some six miles towards his centre, when Withers and Cheatham also hurled their divisions on the foe with such terrible effect, that battery after battery was taken, and their dead lay in heaps upon the field. The enemy was now driven towards the Nashville road, about a mile in front of our centre, and took a commanding position on an eminence overlooking the plain, and which was protected by rocks and a dense cedar wood.

The battle had been terrific; crash upon crash of musketry stunned the ear; the ground trembled with the thunder of artillery; the cedars rocked and quivered in the fiery blast, and the air was rent with the explosion of shells. The enemy at several points offered a most gallant resistance, but nothing human could withstand the impetuosity of that charge. A spirit of fury seemed to possess our men, from the commanders down to the common soldiers, and on they swept, shot and shell, canister, grape and bullets tearing through their ranks, until the way could be traced by the dead and dying. Still on they went, overturning infantry and artillery alike, driving the enemy like the hurricane scatters the leaves upon its course, capturing hundreds of prisoners, and literally blackening the ground with the dead. Such a charge was never before witnessed. For miles, through fields and forests, over ditches, fences and ravines, they swept. Brigade after brigade, battery after battery, were thrown forward to stay their onward march; but another volley of musketry, another gleaming of the bayonet, and like their predecessors they were crushed into one common ruin.

It was now about noon. Our charge had been one of splendid results. We had already captured some five thousand prisoners, nearly thirty pieces of cannon, some five thousand stand of arms, and ammunition wagons. We had broken the enemy's right, having driven him for nearly five hours on a curve, a distance of over five miles from our extreme left to the enemy's centre, and backwards about three miles from our centre. The Yankees had made a stand only where the natural advantages of the ground sheltered them.

Rosecranz had not been dismayed by the events of the morning, and had watched them with an air of confidence which his subordinate officers found it difficult to understand. Referring to his adversary, he said: "I'll show him a trick worth two of his." Gen. Rosecranz was well aware of the danger of advancing reinforcements from his left or centre. The Confederates lay in his front within sight and almost within hearing. He knew that they were anxiously watching his movements, and waiting to see which part of his line would be weakened. But though he declined to send McCook reinforcements, Rosecranz employed himself in so preparing his line as to aid

McCook to get safely on his right. His preparations were to halt the Confederates on his defeated right without exposing his left and centre to imminent danger. For this purpose he quickly determined to mass his artillery on the position occupied by the centre. These movements were masked by immense cedar forests. Thus prepared, at the proper moment the centre of the enemy was advanced a few hundred yards, and soon after the Confederates appeared in force pursuing his right wing.

The position of the enemy was on an oval-shaped hill not very high, but furnishing an excellent position for his artillery. It was determined to carry this stronghold at all hazards, and the brigades of Chalmer and Donelson, supported by Manley's and Stewart's brigades, with Cobb's, Byrne's, Chas. Smith's and Slocomb's batteries, were ordered to prepare for the charge. It was a forlorn hope, but our men faced the mighty whirlwind of shot and shell with heroic firmness, and did not fall back until they had captured two batteries. The brigades of Generals Adams and Jackson, of Breckinridge's division, who held our right, were now ordered across the river to relieve our broken columns, and advanced towards the enemy's grand battery with a like coolness and heroism, but they were also repulsed and fell back under the enemy's terrible fire.

A portion of Gen. Hardee's command bivouacked for the night in the cedars, within five hundred yards of the enemy's lines. That night it was cold to freezing. Upon the battlefield lay thousands of the enemy's dead and wounded, who froze stiff, presenting a ghastly scene by moonlight.

The scene in the cedars was fearful and picturesque. A brilliant winter moon shed its lustre amid the foliage of the forest of evergreens, and lighted up with silver sheen the ghastly battle field. Dismounted cannon, scattered caissons, glittering and abandoned arms strewed the forest and field. The dead lay stark and stiff at every step, with clenched hands and contracted limbs in the wild attitudes in which they fell, congealed by the bitter cold. It was the eve of the new year.

Moans of the neglected dying, mingled with the low peculiar shriek of the wounded artillery horses, chanted a misere for the dying year.

Amid the dim camp fires, feebly lighted to avoid attracting the artillery of the enemy, groups of mutilated and shuddering wounded were huddled, and the kneeling forms of surgeons bending in the firelight over the mangled bodies of the dying, added to the solemnity of the night.

The appearance of the dead on the field was remarkable, for the large proportion was evidently slain by artillery. The bodies of many of the confederates who had advanced to the assault on the enemy's masked batteries were literally torn to pieces. The cross-fire of the artillery had had this terrible effect. "I saw," says a spectator of this terrible scene, "an officer, whose two legs, one arm and body lay in separate parts of the field. I saw another whose dislocated right arm lay across his neck, and more than half his head was gone."

On the day succeeding the fight, Gen. Bragg telegraphed to Richmond the news of a great victory, presented his compliments to the authorities, and wrote, "God has granted us a happy new year." His exultations were over hasty, for though we had routed on the morning of the preceding day the right wing of the enemy, the final contest was yet to be decided.

In the meantime, Rosecranz fearing that his position might be flanked, or from some suspicion that it was not secure, abandoned it that night, only to take up a still stronger one in the bed of the river, towards the Lebanon pike, on a couple of hillocks, which he again crowned with his strongest batteries.

Many of his generals felt despondent; some favoured retreat; but the constancy of Rosecranz remained untouched. One of his staff officers remarked, "Your tenacity of purpose, General, is a theme of universal comment." "I guess," he replied, "that the troops have discovered that Bragg is a good dog, but hold-fast is better."

The first of the year found the enemy strongly entrenched,

with his right drawn up a little on the south side of the Nashville pike, while his left remained fortified in the bend of the river, already described. Our position was greatly advanced on the left and centre, but otherwise remained the same. On that day General Bragg issued the following address to his army:

"The General commanding is happy to announce to the troops the continued success of our arms yesterday. Generals Wheeler and Wharton, with the cavalry, again assaulted the enemy's line of communication, capturing over two hundred wagons and other stores. Twice have we now made the circuit of the enemy's forces, and destroyed his trains, and not less than six hundred wagons, and three thousand mules have fallen into our hands. * * * * Our success continues uninterrupted. One more struggle, and the glorious victory already achieved will be crowned by the rout of the enemy, who are now greatly demoralized. The General commanding has every confidence that his gallant troops will fully meet his expectations."

It was confidently believed that the enemy would have retreated on the night of the 31st, but as he did not, it was concluded to wait and see if he would make any attack. The day consequently passed off quietly, excepting some slight skirmishing.

On the second of January, the ill-omened Friday, the attitude of the two armies remained the same during the morning, and without incident, except some shelling on our right.

By three o'clock it was determined to assault the enemy's stronghold on the bend of the river. It was a desperate determination. Unfortunately, Gen. Bragg had given the enemy nearly two days to re-organize and concentrate his baffled army, so that he might the more effectually make a stubborn resistance.

The enemy had taken up a position at a point near the bend of the river where it takes a westerly course. Here rises a high ridge covered by a skirt of woods, on which the enemy had planted their artillery, supported by a line of infantry. Behind this ridge and in the woods and rocky ravines lay concealed also a large force of the enemy. Further to the enemy's left was another skirt of woods, which the enemy also occupied, outflanking our front nearly one thousand yards. Near the first skirt of woods mentioned, is a ford of the river, the opposite banks of which, from its elevated position, overlooks and commands the ridge above described on this side, or the south and east bank of the river, while one mile further down the river is another ford. It was at this commanding position in the river bend where the enemy had made his citadel, having massed his batteries of artillery and infantry in such a skillful manner as to protect his centre on the Nashville pike, and his extreme left, which now extended on our side of the river. Such was the position of the enemy on our extreme right on the morning of that memorable day of slaughter, the 2d of January.

Gen. Breckenridge was ordered to carry by assault, the position of the enemy on the ridge already described. He formed his division in two lines, changing front from his former position to nearly a right angle, and facing in the direction of the river. General Hanson's brigade, with Palmer's, now commanded by Gen. Pillow, formed the first line, with Pillow on the right; the second line being formed by Preston's and Gibson's, two hundred yards in the rear. Colonel Hunt's regiment, of Hanson's brigade, was left to support Cobb's battery on the hill. From the enemy's commanding position across the river, he was enabled to see all of our movements, and, consequently, prepared to resist us. Between General Breckenridge's division and the enemy's batteries on the ridge was an intervening space of eight hundred yards, extending over an open field skirted by woods, along which the enemy's skirmishers were in such force as almost amounted to a line of battle.

The attack was to be made at 4 o'clock, and a signal gun was to announce the hour. In those battalions stood the noble soldiers of Florida, Alabama, Kentucky, Louisiana, Tennessee and North Carolina in battle array, firm and inflexible, awaiting the signal for combat. The report of a cannon had not died upon the ear before the bugle from Hanson's brigade sounded a charge. The brigades moved rapidly forward through the thinned woods until gaining the open fields, the men having been instructed not to deliver their fire until close upon the enemy, and then to charge with the bayonet. On came Pillow, followed by Preston; forward hurried Hanson, followed by Gibson. From the moment of gaining the field the enemy's artillery from the ridge opened a sweeping fire, and a whirlwind of Minnie balls from their infantry, with shot and shell, filled the air. Our men were ordered to lie down for a few minutes to let the fury of the storm pass. Then the cry from Breckenridge—" Up, my men, and charge!"—rang out. With the impetuosity of a torrent they rushed forward to the woods sloping the ridge. On dashed Wright's battery of Preston's brigade at a furious gallop, and soon opened fire upon one of the enemy's batteries about three hundred yards to our right. The enemy, awed by the mad bravery of our men, recoiled; their ranks thinned rapidly, notwithstanding they received reinforcement after reinforcement. Their left wing, which already outflanked us on our right, was driven back towards the river bank, the 20th Tennessee capturing some two hundred prisoners. The contest now raged fierce and bloody. It was one continuous roar of musketry and artillery. Facing the storm of death, our heroes charged with fury, and so effective was the firing of our lines, that we carried the ridge with a wild demoniac yell, driving the enemy from it, with his artillery, down the hill side and across the river. Captain Wright soon reached the top of the ridge with his battery, and opened on the enemy with spherical case. At this time the concentrated fire of the enemy became terrible and appalling. A sheet of flame was poured forth from their artillery on the hills on the opposite side of the river overlooking our left and front and from their batteries on the river bank, while the opposite side also swarmed with their infantry, who poured in on us a most murderous fire. Still our men never quailed, but pressed forward and crossed the river, the enemy making frightful gaps in our ranks, but which were immediately closed up. Here it was that in less than half an hour over two thousand of our brave soldiers went down! The utter hopelessness of carrying the opposite heights, and of contending against the overwhelmingly superior numbers of the enemy without artillery or reinforcements to support us, having been fully tested, General Breckenridge ordered his division to fall back. It was nearly dark when the conflict closed, and during the night he occupied a portion of the field in advance of that he occupied during the day.

"It was after the capture of the enemy's position on the ridge, when our men drove him across the river with terrible slaughter of his forces, that the noble Hanson fell mortally wounded, exclaiming: "Forward—forward, my brave boys, to the charge;" and afterwards, when brought from the field, he said with his flickering breath: "I am willing to die with such a wound received in so glorious a cause." We had held the enemy's position on the ridge for about half an hour, Captain E. E. Wright's battery doing admirable execution, when that gallant officer fell at his guns mortally wounded, the enemy having charged within seventy-five yards of his pieces.

The final repulse of Breckenridge was a sad blow to our hopes. The prudence of this terrible attack upon the impregnable position of the enemy has been seriously questioned, and military critics of the battle of Murfreesboro' have also found room for censuring the neglect of Gen. Bragg in not previously securing the hillocks in the bend of Stone's River, which he permitted the enemy to occupy. As it happened, it was a bad repulse, and the vivid recollections of the "bloody crossing of Stone's River," in which in less than one hour two thousand of our men were killed and wounded, long survived in our army. It lost us the vantage ground we had gained over the enemy on the 31st and greatly depressed our troops. But for this, we would still have held Murfreesboro'. On the 3d the rain fell in torrents, and as our troops were worn out and nearly exhausted, it was determined to fall back that night, and not run the risk of meeting the enemy's reinforcements, which, it was reported, he was receiving. Everything had previously been provided for the retreat. It was conducted with order and composure.*

Sunday morning Rosecranz moved into Murfreesboro', and Gen. Bragg retired to the position of Tullahoma. This place is in Coffee county, Tennessee, situated on Rock creek, and offers admirable means of defence. It is seventy-one miles

---

\* In his official report of the battle, Gen. Bragg makes the following statement on the subject of the first day's operations, relative to their check and the failure to break the enemy's centre:

"To meet our successful advance, and retrieve his losses in the front of his left, the enemy early transferred a portion of his reserve from his left to that flank, and by two o'clock had succeeded in concentrating such a force in Lieutenant-General Hardee's front as to check his further progress. Our two lines had by this time become almost blended, so weakened were they by losses, exhaustion and extension to cover the enemy's whole front. As early as 10 o'clock, A. M., Major-General Breckenridge was called on for one brigade, and soon after for a second, to reinforce or act as a reserve to Lieut. Gen. Hardee. His reply to the first call represented the enemy crossing Stone's river in heavy force, in his immediate front, and on receiving the second order, he informed me that they had already crossed in heavy force, and were advancing to attack his lines. He was immediately ordered not to await attack, but to advance and meet him. About this same time a report reached me that a heavy force of the enemy's infantry was advancing on the Lebanon road, about five miles in Breckenridge's front. Brigadier-General Pegram, who had been sent to that road to cover the flank of the infantry with his cavalry brigade, save two regiments detached with Wheeler and Wharton, was ordered forward immediately to develop any such movement. The orders for the two brigades from Breckinridge were countermanded, whilst dispositions were made, at his request, to reinforce him. Before they could be carried out, the movements ordered disclosed the fact that no force had crossed Stone's river; that the only enemy in our immediate front then was a small body of sharpshooters; and that there was no advance on the Lebanon road. These unfortunate misapprehensions on that part of the field, which with proper precaution could not have existed, withheld from active operations three fine brigades until the enemy had succeeded in checking our progress, had re-established his lines, and had collected many of his broken battalions.

from Nashville and thirty-two from Murfreesboro', and lies immediately on the Nashville and Chattanooga railroad, where it is intersected by the McMinnville and Manchester road. As a base of operations and as a position of defence, the place offered great advantages.

So far as the relative amount of carnage affects the question of victory, no doubt can be entertained to which side in the battle of Murfreesboro' is to be ascribed the superiority. In the first day's fight, the number of the enemy's killed and wounded was probably six or seven thousand; in the engagement which succeeded, our loss was disproportionate to the enemy's; but at the close of the whole affair, the Yankees were doubtless greater losers in life than ourselves. In point of captures and with respect to the number of prisoners taken, the battle of Murfreesboro' may be accounted a Confederate success. The ground which the North has for claiming a victory is, that our forces fell back and that their positions were occupied. But the occupation of Murfreesboro' was no important consideration; the works were neither extensive nor strong; and the new line of defence reorganized by General Bragg was, as we shall see, quite sufficient to hold the enemy in check. The truth is, that the Yankees, although their claims to the victory of Murfreesboro' are questionable, had great reasons to congratulate themselves that an army which, in the first day's battle, had its right wing broken and one-third of its artillery lost, should have escaped destruction and extricated itself in a manner to assure its further safety.

But however the issue of Murfreesboro' is to be decided, the South had reason to expect considerable material advantages from events in other parts of the West. The siege of Vicksburg by land was for the time virtually abandoned. Some engagements had taken place before this town, which were exaggerated by the telegraph; but they were mere skirmishes, intended to feel the strength of the defences. Being satisfied that they were too strong to be attacked with safety, and probably learning that Grant's army would never effect a junction with it, the Yankee force before Vicksburg re-embarked, with a great loss of material employed in the entrenchments preparatory to the siege.

## THE RECAPTURE OF GALVESTON.

While the new year had doubtfully opened in Tennessee, a brilliant success marked the same period in the distant State of Texas. An expedition was skillfully planned and gallantly executed by the brave and energetic Magruder, the results of which were the capture of the city and harbour of Galveston, a large quantity of arms, ammunition, stores, &c., the famous Yankee steamer Harriet Lane, and some other craft of less importance.

On the night of the 31st of December, General Magruder silently marched along the road to Galveston city. Our forces consisted of several regiments of infantry and about twenty-two pieces of artillery, though the principal attack was to be made by the artillery, as there were only about three hundred of the enemy in the city, and they were behind a barricade at the outer end of the wharf.

Our troops reached the suburbs of the city about three o'clock. The streets were completely deserted; the few inhabitants who had remained in the city were sleeping soundly, and had our men not awaked and warned them of their danger, they would have slept on until the cannon's roar had startled them. The march of our troops through the city was a quiet procession.

The scene, the dead hour of night, and the fact that this was to be the first battle of many of them, all conspired to make them serious. Then, too, the great heavy waves came tumbling and roaring in from the Gulf, chanting out upon the still night air, as they dashed along, something that sounded like a funeral dirge. But onward our men stole, through long, lonely streets, now around this corner and now turning that, until at length they reached Strand street, which runs parallel with the water, and is the next one to the wharves. The moon was now down, and every thing was enveloped in darkness; the guns were noiselessly placed in position and loaded, the men looking like so many shadows as they took their places in the gloom. There, within three hundred yards, lay the Harriet Lane, the Owasso, the Clifton, and two other boats, with their broadsides turned towards our troops, and ready to open upon them the moment they fired. This they knew, for the Yankees had been ashore the day before and told the people that they knew all about the plans of the "rebels," and were waiting for them. In fact, they were so certain of victory that they allowed our men to place their guns in position without firing upon them.

Gen. Magruder opened the attack by firing the first gun. In a few moments the bright flashes, the booming reports and whizzing shells told plainer than words that the action had begun in earnest; for the next hour the roar of cannon was incessant. The clear, keen crack of our little rifled guns, the dull sound of our sea-coast howitzers, and the mighty thundering bass of the columbiads and 100-pound Parrott guns on the gunboats, combined to form a piece of music fitted for Pandemonium.

The fight raged furiously on both sides, but it was fast becoming evident that our land forces alone were no match for the Yankee boats, with their great guns and mortars, which vomited a half bushel of grape and canister at every discharge. Early in the engagement a charge was made by three hundred of our infantry on three companies of the forty-second Massachusetts regiment, stationed behind a barricade at the end of Kuhn's wharf. The enemy had torn up the planks from the wharf, and made a breastwork of them. Our men rushed out into the waters with their scaling ladders and dashed up to them, but the position was too strong and they had to retire, leaving our artillery to shell them out. We lost some ten or fifteen in this charge, and would have lost more, but it was pitch dark and the Yankees fired very wildly.

Daylight at length arrived, and every one was anxiously

looking for our boats, which ought to have been up two hours before. They had come down within sight at about 12 o'clock, and, hearing nothing of our troops, retired five or six miles, under the impression that the land attack had been postponed. There they waited until about three o'clock, when the land attack began. As soon as Major Smith, who commanded the expedition, saw that the work had begun, he ordered all steam to be put on and started back. He was then a considerable distance from the city, and was unable to reach it until daylight. At that time the Bayou City and Neptune, followed in the distance by the John F. Can and Lucy Gwin, hospital boats, bore steadily down upon the Harriet Lane, then lying at the end of the wharf, opposite the Cotton Press.

The Harriet Lane had for some time directed her fire at them, but fortunately without effect; but when within about fifty yards, the Neptune received several balls, damaging her considerably. She kept steadily on her way, however, and in a few moments more ran into the Lane amidship. The enemy's decks were soon cleared with the buck-shot from the double-barrel guns of the Neptune's crew, who would have boarded her, but it was discovered that the Neptune was rapidly sinking in consequence of the damages she had received. She was accordingly run into shoal water, about fifty yards from the Lane, where she sunk immediately. In the mean time the Yankee crew, seeing the predicament of the Neptune, came up on deck again, and were preparing to give her a broadside, when the Bayou City fortunately interfered with their preparations by running into the Lane's wheel-house. Another volley of buck-shot again cleared her decks. The next instant the crew of the Bayou City were aboard of her, Major Smith gallantly leading the way, and shooting the Lane's commanding officer (Capt. Wainwright) as he leaped upon the deck. The vessel was immediately surrendered, and down came the stars and stripes and up went our flag. It was found that the captain and first lieutenant of the boat were both killed and about thirty of her crew killed or wounded. Our loss on the boats was about sixteen killed and thirty wounded.

The Yankee boats, the Clifton and Owasso, saved themselves by beating out of the harbour, while the Bayou City was in some way entangled with her prize. The Westfield was burnt as she was fast aground. Our prize was one of which we might well be proud. The Harriet Lane was a vessel of six hundred tons burden, was originally built for the revenue service, but at the beginning of the war with the South she was turned over to the navy, and at once underwent such alterations as were thought necessary to adapt her to her new service. At the time of her capture, she mounted eight guns of heavy calibre, her bow gun being a fifteen inch rifle.

The re-capture of Galveston and the advantages which ensued, were perhaps outbalanced by a disaster which shortly followed and overshadowed much of the prospect in the remote regions west of the Mississippi. This was the forcible occupation by the Yankees of Arkansas Post and the surrender of its entire garrison.

The troops garrisoning Arkansas Post at the time of attack, consisted of three brigades, mostly Texans, and commanded respectively by Colonels Garland, Deshler and Dunnington, the whole forming a division under the command of Brigadier General T. J. Churchill, and numbering on the day of the fight not more than thirty-three hundred effective men. On the 9th day of January a scout from below brought intelligence to General Churchill of a Yankee gun boat having made its appearance in the Arkansas river, some thirty miles below the Post; some hours later on the same day another scout brought news of other gun-boats, followed by transports, making their way up the river. Upon the receipt of this intelligence, Gen. Churchill ordered every thing in readiness for an attack, and ere night closed in all the troops were distributed along the line of entrenchments, where they remained all night in a pelting storm of rain. The enemy, in the mean time, had landed a force about two miles below the fort, but they made no demonstration until about nine or ten o'clock the next morning, when they commenced shelling the fort from their advance gun-boats that were cautiously and slowly feeling their way up the river.

Our troops held the position first taken by them until about four o'clock, P. M., when the General, fearing a flank movement on our left, ordered the men to fall back to a line of entrenchments near the yet unfinished fort, which line was speedily completed and all the troops properly distributed before night set in. Just as darkness was drawing near, four gun-boats approached the fort and commenced their bombardment, our guns from the fort answering gallantly, and after two hours' terrific shelling, the gun-boats retired, one of them, the Eastport, badly disabled. Our loss up to this time consisted of only three killed and some three or four wounded.

The next morning at ten o'clock the enemy renewed the attack with gun-boats and land forces combined. They had also erected a battery on the opposite side of the river, by means of which they kept up a terrible cross-fire that swept the whole area of ground occupied by our men. The firing continued until about four o'clock in the evening, when General Churchill, seeing his defences exposed to a raking fire and storming parties closing upon his rear, surrendered, General McClernand taking the whole force, making more than three thousand men prisoners. Our loss in killed and wounded was not two hundred men.

The results of this success of the Yankees were many thousand prisoners of war, and a fortified point guarding the navigation of the Arkansas river, and shutting out its commerce from the Mississippi. But the prospect which they indulged of ascending without interruption to Little Rock and taking full possession of the Arkansas capital, was rather premature.

There is nothing yet important to record of the operations of the immense fleets of the enemy collected on our coast in the winter of 1862. The armadas were as yet silent. For months a large fleet of the enemy had been at the mouth of Charleston harbour or picketed off the coast.

On the 30th of January the Confederate rams in the harbour of Charleston, under command of Capt. Ingraham, had made a sally towards the enemy's fleet. The success of this sally was ignorantly exaggerated by the Confederates, and a claim made that the blockade had been raised, which pretension was afterwards abandoned. The fact was that one of the Yankee vessels—the Mercedita—was seriously injured, and another—the Keystone State—got a shot through her steam drum, causing the death of twenty-one persons. The Mercedita was saved by the treachery of the Yankees, who represented the ship to be in a sinking condition, thus deceiving the Confederates as to the extent of the damage they had inflicted. She steamed down to Port Royal, after our rams had left her, under the supposition that she was sinking in shoal water. Her commander had called out, "We are in a sinking condition," and the reply of Capt. Ingraham was, that she could only sink as far as her rails, and we could not take her crew aboard. A mean and cowardly falsehood saved the vessel; but in Yankee estimation the triumphs of such villainy were quite equal to the congratulations of a victory.

Our victory at Galveston, of which we have given some account, was the precursor of other captures of the enemy's vessels, which were important accessions to our little navy. That arm of service, in which we were so deficient, and had shown such aptitude for self-destruction, was not entirely powerless; for we not only had rams for harbour defences and three fleet privateers at sea, but our power on the water was enlarged even beyond our expectations, as we shall see, by captures from the enemy.

The Yankee gun-boat Queen of the West, having succeeded in running our batteries at Vicksburg, had for some weeks been committing ravages, penetrating the country of the Red river. On the 14th of February she encountered in this river and captured a small Confederate steamer, the Era. The crew and passengers of the Era were taken prisoners, and all were guarded on board the Era by a band of soldiers, save Mr. George Wood, the pilot, who was ordered aboard the Queen of the West, and, with threats, directed to her pilot wheel to assist her pilot in directing her onward to the capture of our fort on the river. On they glided, but not distrustful, and much elated at their success, till they came in reach of our battery at five P. M., when the vessel commenced firing, still advancing. She had come within a quarter of a mile of our battery and on the opposite shore in full range for our guns, when the gallant Wood, who directed her wheel, had her rounded, ran her aground, breaking her rudder and thus crippling her and turning her broadside to give our guns a fair chance. This gallant man, in the confusion, made good his escape. Thus crippled and disabled by the hand that drove her on to her destiny; she lay like a wounded falcon, at the mercy of her adversaries.

. The night was dark and stormy, the heavens overhung with clouds, which now and then pealed forth their muttering thunder, and drenched the earth with rain. Thus in the rain storm this crippled Queen lay beaten by the tempest. She was well barricaded with cotton bales. On seeing all hope of success gone, the commanding officer, Colonel Ellett, made his escape, with nearly all his crew, by getting on cotton bales and floating down the river. She raised the white signal; as the storm abated, as it was seen by the light of a burning warehouse, but it was not answered till next morning. Thirteen of the crew remained in silence till day-light, then her white banner was still afloat, and then, and not till then, our soldiers crossed the river and took possession of her.

. The fog which had enabled the Queen of the West to get by Vicksburg had also availed for the passage of another gunboat, the Indianola. This vessel had also continued for weeks to go at large, preying on the boats that were transporting our supplies, and harassing our forces in every way. Seeing the great injury and havoc that she might do, a council was held, and the capture of the Indianola at every sacrifice was determined upon.

Accordingly an expedition was fitted out, consisting of two gun-boats—the Queen of the West and the Webb—and two steamers—the Era and Dr. Batey. The expedition was commanded by Major Walker, with Captain Hutton as executive officer of the fleet. All being ready, the expedition started out from the mouth of the Red river in pursuit of the Indianola. Coming up the Mississippi to Grand Gulf, it was learned that the Indianola was not far off, and a halt was ordered that all the vessels might come up. All being in line, the expedition put up the river and on the 24th of February came upon the Indianola, overhauling her about five miles below New Carthage, and some thirty below Vicksburg. It was about nine o'clock at night. The enemy had received no information of the movement, and was not aware of our approach until we were within a half mile of her. Seeing the rapid approach of the vessels, the Indianola at once knew that it was an attempt to capture her, and she immediately rounded her broadside to, lashing a coal barge alongside her to parry the blows that might be made to run in and sink her. On the vessels nearing, fire was opened, and a most terrific and desperate engagement ensued, lasting over an hour. Putting on all her steam, the Queen of the West made a blow at the Indianola, cleaving the barge in two and striking her with such tremendous force that the Indianola's machinery was badly injured. Here the action on both sides became desperate. The blow of the Queen of the West was quickly followed up by the Webb with a terrific "butt" at full speed. This finished the work. The Indianola was discovered to be in a sinking condition, and was put for the shore on the Louisiana side. Seeing this, the Dr. Batey was ordered to board her. On beating alongside her, the Indianola surrendered, and all her officers and crew—numbering in all about one hundred and twenty men—were made prisoners.

These additions to our naval structures on the Mississippi were important. We now possessed some power in the interior waters of the Confederacy; to our harbour defences we had already added some rams; and our deficiency in a navy was not a laughing stock to the North as long as our few privateers were able to cruise in the Atlantic and carry dismay to the exposed commerce of the Gulf.

The few ships the North possessed that were the equals in point of speed of the Confederate privateers, the Alabama and Florida, were, with a single exception, purchased vessels, built for the merchant service, and exceedingly liable to be disabled in their machinery on account of its being nearly all above the water line. Taking, as samples of vessels of this class, the Vanderbilt, Connecticut and Rhode Island, the North had three ships which, for the purpose they were intended, were without superiours; but the chances were that, if coming under the fire of the Alabama or Florida, they would be, by a well directed shot or shell at close quarters, crippled and become an easy prize.

The exploits of our cruisers were sufficient to show the value and efficiency of the weapon of privateering, and to excite many regrets that our means in this department of warfare were so limited. One national steamer alone—the Alabama—commanded by officers and manned by a crew who were debarred by the closure of neutral ports from the opportunity of causing captured vessels to be condemned in their favour as prizes, had sufficed to double the rates of marine insurance in Yankee ports, and consigned to forced inaction numbers of Yankee vessels, in addition to the direct damage inflicted by captures at sea. The Northern papers paid a high tribute to the activity and daring of our few privateers in the statement that, during one month of winter, British steamers had carried from San Francisco to Europe six and a quarter millions of gold, whilst during the same time from the same port there had arrived in New York only two hundred and fifty thousand dollars of the precious metal. In view of such results, it would be difficult to over-estimate the effects, if we had had a hundred of private armed vessels, and especially if we could have secured from neutral Europe the means of disposing of such prizes as we might make of the commerce of the enemy.

## CHAPTER IX.

An Extraordinary Lull in the War...An Affair with the Enemy on the Blackwater...Raids in the West...Van Dorn's Captures...THE MEETING OF CONGRESS...Character of This Body...Its Dullness and Servility...Mr. Foote and the Cabinet...Two Popular Themes of Confidence...Party Contention in the North...Successes of the Democrats There...Analysis of the Party Politics of the North...The Interest of New England in the War...How the War Affected the Northwestern Portions of the United States...Mr. Foote's Resolutions Respecting the Northwestern States...How They Were Received by the Southern Public...New War Measures at Washington...Lincoln a Dictator...Prospect of Foreign Interference...Action of the Emperor Napoleon... Suffering of the Working Classes in England...The Delusions of an Early Peace...The Tasks Before Congress...Prostrate Condition of the Confederate Finances...President Davis' Blunder...The Errours of Our Financial System... The Wealth of the South...The Impressment Law of Congress...Scarcity of Supplies...Inflated Prices...Speculation and Extortion in the Confederacy... Three Remarks About These...The Verdict of History.

The battle of Murfreesboro' was followed by an extraordinary lull of the movements of the war. For months the great armies in Tennessee and Virginia were to stand agaze of each other. The events of this period are slight and easily recounted.

While the lines of the Rappahannock remained undisturbed, our forces on the Blackwater had an engagement of outposts on the 31st of January, which was unduly magnified into a battle. The success of the affair was not wholly unimportant, as a loss of some hundreds was inflicted upon the enemy before our forces fell back to Carrsville, which they were compelled to do in the face of superiour numbers.

In Tennessee there was a series of exploits of our cavalry, the details of which it is impossible now to recount. The most remarkable of these successes was probably that of Van Dorn, who, on the first day of March, at Thompson's Station, between

Columbia and Franklin, captured five regiments of the enemy's infantry, comprising twenty-two hundred officers and men.

### THE MEETING OF CONGRESS.

The reader will be interested in turning from the unimportant military events of this period to notice the re-assembling of the Confederate Congress and its proceedings in the early months of 1863. It is not to be disguised that this body fell below the spirit and virtue of the people, and was remarkable for its destitution of talents and ability. Not a single speech that has yet been made in it will live. It is true that the regular Congress elected by the people was an improvement upon the ignorant and unsavory body known as the Provisional Congress, which was the creature of conventions, and which was disgraced in the character of some of its members; among whom were conspicuous corrupt and senile politicians from Virginia, who had done all they could to sacrifice and degrade their State, who had "toadied", in society, as well as in politics, to notabilities of New England, and who had taken a prominent part in emasculating, and, in fact, annulling, the Sequestration Law, in order to save the property of relatives who had sided with the North against the land that had borne them and honoured their fathers.

But the regular Congress, although it had no taint of disloyalty or Yankee toadyism in it, was a weak body. It had made no mark in the history of the government; it was destitute of originality; its measures were, generally, those which were recommended by the Executive or suggested by the newspapers; it had produced no great financial measure; it made not one stroke of statesmanship; it uttered not a single fiery appeal to the popular heart such as is customary in revolutions. It afforded, perhaps, a proof of the frequent assertion that our democratic system did not produce great men. The most of the little ability it had was occupied with servility to the Executive and demagogical displays.

It is difficult, indeed, for a legislative body to preserve its independence, and to resist the tendency of the Executive to absorb power in time of war, and this fact was well illustrated by the Confederate Congress. One of the greatest political scholars of America, Mr. Madison, noticed this danger in the political constitution of the country. He said:—"War is in fact the true nurse of Executive aggrandizement. In war a physical force is to be created, and it is the Executive will which is to direct it. In war the public treasures are to be unlocked, and it is the Executive hand which is to dispense them. In war the honours and emoluments of office are to be multiplied, and it is the Executive patronage under which they are to be enjoyed. It is in war, finally, that laurels are to be gathered, and it is the Executive brow they are to encircle."

There was but little opposition in Congress to President Davis; but there was some which took a direction to his cabinet, and this opposition was represented by Mr. Foote of Tennessee—a man of acknowledged ability and many virtues of character, who had re-entered upon the political stage after a public life, which, however it lacked in the cheap merit of partisan consistency, had been adorned by displays of wonderful intellect and great political genius. Mr. Foote was not a man to be deterred from speaking the truth; his quickness to resentment and his chivalry, which, though somewhat Quixotic, was founded in the most noble and delicate sense of honour, made those who would have bullied or silenced a weaker person, stand in awe of him. A man of such temper was not likely to stint words in assailing an opponent; and his sharp declamations in Congress, his searching comments, and his great powers of sarcasm, used upon such men as Mallory, Benjamin and Northrop were the only relief of the dulness of the Congress, and the only historical features of its debates.

Mr. Foote was of a temperament that easily indulged the prospects of peace which so generally existed when Congress resumed its session in the opening of the new year. At an early period of the session resolutions were introduced by him inviting the Northwestern States to abstention from the war, and expressing a lively and friendly confidence in the negotiation which the Emperor of the French had just undertaken for a qualified mediation in the war in America. Of these two popular themes of confidence some explanation is due.

Since the commencement of the war, there had been some few people in the North who had opposed its prosecution, and many more who were averse to its policy and measures. The removal of McClellan added a bitter feud to animosities already existing, and the enunciation at Washington of the policy of emancipation contributed to the party divisions in the North. The result of the Northern elections in the fall of 1862 was apparently an emphatic and impressive popular verdict against the Abolition party which had ruled the government at Washington. In the face of a majority of 107,000 against them in 1860, the Democrats had carried the State of New York. The metropolis of New York was carried by a Democratic majority of 31,000—a change of 48,000 votes in twelve months. Within the great States of New Jersey, New York, Pennsylvania, Ohio, Indiana and Illinois, the results of the popular elections were a more or less emphatic avowal of opposition to the schemes of those who were using the power of the government to advance and fasten upon the country their political vagaries, regardless of right and written constitutions. These six States contained a majority of the free State population. They furnished the majority of the troops in the field against us. They had two-thirds of the wealth of the North. It was clear that the Washington government needed men and money to carry on the war, and to have a united North the Democratic States must furnish more than half of either.

Under these circumstances, it is not surprising that the people of the South should have convinced themselves that an important reaction was taking place in public sentiment in the North, and that it naturally tended to a negotiation for peace. But in one-half of this opinion they were mistaken. There was a reaction in the North; but it had scarcely any thing more than a partisan significance. It was a struggle between those in power and those out of power; the issues of which were feigned and exaggerated; in which much that was said against the war was not really meant; and at the close of which the passions it had excited suddenly evaporated. Mr. Van Buren, who, in the Democratic campaign in New York, had made speeches quite warm enough for Southern latitudes, was after the elections an advocate of the war and a mocker of "the rebellion." Many more followed the distinguished lead of the demagogue in raising a clamour about the administration merely for party purposes, and having served those purposes, in returning to the advocacy of a war, in which, by giving false encouragement to the North, and holding out hopes of "reconstruction," they were enemies more fatal to the South than the blind and revengeful radicals who sought her destruction.

It is probable that the movements, in the Northwestern States against the administration were better founded in principle than those that had taken place in other parts of the North, and that they denoted a sincere aversion to the war. The opposition of Mr. Vallandigham, who assumed to represent this sentiment of the Northwest in Congress, was apparently superiour to the demagogical clamour of such men as Van Buren and Seymour of New York. The sentiment was undoubtedly sincere, whatever the merits or demerits of its officious representative.*

*There is unavoidable reason for doubting the virtue of Mr. Vallandigham. It is difficult to discover the motives of the Yankee. The people of the South have reason to know, from former political association with this faithless race, how indirect are their courses and how affected their zeal. What appears to be the inspiration of virtue, may be the deep design of a selfish ambition; singularity of opinion may prove nothing but an itch for a cheap reputation; and an extraordinary display of one's self before the public may, at best, be but the ingenious trick of a charlatan.

When Mr. Vallandigham was exiled for obstructing enlistments in the North, he had an opportunity in his travels in the Confederacy of learning the sentiments of the people, and of these he gave the following report in an address to the people of Ohio:

"Travelling a thousand miles and more through nearly one-half of the

The pecuniary interest of New England in the war was plain enough. The demand for the products of her ———— for objects of this war was greater than at any former period in the history of this continent. Her workshops were in full blast. Ships and locomotives were to be built, the weapons of war were to be created, and the ironmongers of New England found a vast and profitable employment in answering these demands. The spinners and weavers and blanket-makers and artisans were kept busy at their avocations, and everywhere in these avaricious districts of the North arose the hum of profitable industry.

But while New England rioted in the gains of the war, it was stark ruin to the agricultural States of the Northwest. The people there were growing poorer every day, in the midst of plenty. The great Southern market which their resources supplied had been closed, and there was no new demand for their agricultural products. The corn, wheat and bacon of Indiana and Illinois was scarcely worth the cost of transportation to the Atlantic coast. The railroads connecting the West with the seaboards were principally in the hands of the Eastern capitalists, and the rates of freight were so enormous, that the surplus agricultural product of the Northwestern farmers was in many instances left to rot on their lands or be used as fuel.

This violent contrast between New England and the West in the effects on each of the war, was developed in a formidable opposition of opinion. Indications of this opposition had already been given in the press of St. Louis and Chicago.

---

" Confederate States, and sojourning for a time at widely different points,
" I met not one man, woman or child, who were not resolved to perish rather
" than yield to the pressure of arms, even in the most desperate extremity.
" * † * * . Neither, however, let me add, did I meet any one, what-
" ever his opinion or station, political or private, who did not declare his readi-
" ness, when the war shall have ceased, and invading armies be withdrawn, to
" consider and discuss the question of reunion. And who shall doubt the issue
" of the argument?"

A man who can be guilty of such a deliberate falsehood, and one evidently planned to catch votes for his political lobby, can certainly make no pretension to heroism, and may even have his claims to honesty justly doubted.

The jealousy of the agricultural States of the North was being inflamed by the unequal profits of the war, and the selfish policy of the Abolitionists; and the opinion plainly grew in the press and public discussion that the West had not a single interest in the war beyond securing the free navigation of the Mississippi.

How far statesmanship in the South might have profited by this disaffection in the Northwestern States is left a matter of conjecture and controversy. The efforts made in the Confederate Congress by Mr. Foote in this direction, tendering to these States a complete assurance of the free navigation of the Mississippi, and proposing an alliance with the Confederacy, without political complications, met with feeble encouragement in that body, a doubtful response from the army and divided comments of the press. Whatever may have been the merits of Mr. Foote's proposition, it admitted of no delay. While our government treated it with hesitation, the authorities at Washington were making anxious and immense preparations to overcome the disaffection of the people and to carry on the war; and the means to do this were supplied by an act suspending the *habeas corpus* and making Lincoln absolute dictator; by new measures of finance, and by a conscription law which called into the field three million of men.

The prospect of a termination of the war by any action of foreign governments was more distant than that afforded by party elections and movements in the North. This action was limited to the French Emperor alone; it had not progressed further at this time than an invitation to England and Russia, made in November 1862, to unite in proposing an armistice to the Washington Government, which should merely give an opportunity for discussion, without affecting in any way the present military interests and positions of the belligerents. Mild as the French proposition was, it was rejected by Russia and England. Lord Russell replied for his government that the time was not ripe for such mediation as was proposed, and that it would be better to watch carefully the progress of opinion in America and wait for some change in which the three Courts could offer their friendly counsel with a prospect of success. The British statesman had nothing to plead for the mass of suffering humanity in his own land which the war he was implored to stop or to ameliorate had occasioned; for humanity was easily outweighed by political reasons, which are as often worked out through the blood and tears of its own people as through the misfortunes of others.*

---

* In a letter of Mr. Cobden, published during the early winter in an English journal, he declares that in travelling from Manchester to Blackburn over a country covered with snow, he found hundreds of wasted victims of cold and want. He says: "Hitherto the distressed population have felt little more than the want of food. Now and from henceforth blankets, fuel and clothing are as essential to health as bread and soup." He argues that it is useless to save people from dying by hunger, only that they may perish by fever, or by the exhaustion consequent on cold and insufficient food.

The early advent of winter enhanced the misery of the suffering. In many districts there was no fuel, no means of warmth except the scanty allowance of coals distributed in some places by the Relief Committees. Everywhere the people had too little to eat, and that little was not sufficiently nutricious; everywhere they suffered from cold yet more cruelly than from hunger; and nowhere was there a fund sufficient to provide for their necessities.

The humane shuddered with horror as they read the frightful accounts of the suffering of the poor published day after day in the London *Times*. A letter from Stockport described the people there as "suffering all the horrours of a protracted famine." The same writer says: "One poor man upon whom I called this morning, having stripped the walls of every little ornament to purchase bread for his wife and three little children, took the fender and sold it for a shilling." The cases of distress reported in the newspapers merely represented the average condition of the unemployed. An aged couple, we are told, had saved thirty-six pounds; this is gone, their furniture is pawned, the husband is in the infirmary, and the old woman living on a charitable dole of half a crown per week, with some soup and bread. In another case five persons, among them a sick woman, are living on seven shillings a week. One family of six—considered to be particularly well off—have seven shillings, an allowance of coals and some soup and bread from their former employer. Another family of six or seven had lived for twelve months on six shillings a week.

The University of Oxford had subscribed about £4000 towards the relief of the suffering people. A meeting was held to promote further action, at which the following facts were stated by the Hon. E. L. Stanley of Balliol College:

"They received from America before the blockade five-sixths of their

But while the prospect of an early peace dissolved before the eyes of Congress, a subject of instant and practical importance was sorely pressing upon its attention. The vast volume of Treasury notes issued by the government had occasioned a rapid depreciation of our currency, inflated prices and produced serious financial difficulties. So crude and short-sighted had been our notions of public finance, that at the meeting of Congress in August 1862, we find President Davis recommending to it that the public creditors should not be paid in bonds, but that unlimited issues of currency should be made. He then said in his written message to Congress: "The legislation of the last session provided for the purchase of supplies with the bonds of the government, but the preference of the people for Treasury notes has been so marked that legislation is recommended to authorize an increase in the issue of Treasury notes, which the public service seems to require. No grave inconvenience need be apprehended from this increased issue, as the provision of law by which these notes are convertible into eight per cent. bonds, forms an efficient and permanent safeguard against any serious depreciation of the currency."

---

"cotton; five days of the week they worked on what came from America; "only one day on what came from other countries. That supply was now "practically at an end. The few ships that ran the blockade made no notice- "able difference, and even if other countries should double their production, "we should be only supplied with material for one-third of our usual work. "The country, then, was losing two-thirds of the industry engaged in this "trade, and two-thirds of the capital were making no return. And this "trade was such a main part of the industry of the nation that what affected "it must affect all. A Parliamentary return gave the persons actually "engaged in the mills at near 500,000. If they reckoned their families, the "traders who supplied them, the colliers, machinists, builders, and shipping "interest engaged in supplying cotton, they would probably not overstate the "number of dependents on cotton only at 3,000,000. These people were now "deprived of fully two thirds of their subsistence."

Such is a picture of the "Cotton Famine" in England. The most remarkable circumstance in connection with it was the profound indifference of the English Ministry to the distress of near a million of those for whose lives and happiness they were responsible.

The consequences of this ignorant and wild financial policy were that, by the next meeting of Congress, the volume of currency was at least four times what were the wants of the community for a circulating medium; that prices were inflated more than an equal degree, for want of confidence in the paper of the government had kindled the fever of speculation; that the public credit, abused by culpable ignorance and obstinate empiricism, had fallen to an ebb that alarmed the country more than any reverse in the military fortunes of the war; and that the government was forced to the doubtful and not very honourable expedient of attempting to restore its currency by a system of demonetizing its own issues.

The redundancy of the currency was the chief cause of its depreciation. The amount of money in circulation in the South in time of peace, was $80,000,000. In January 1863, it was $500,000,000. In September 1861, Confederate notes were about equal to specie; before December, specie was at 20 per cent. premium; before April 1862, it was at 50 per cent.; before last September, at 100; before December, at 225; before February, at 280, and in the spring of 1863, at the frightful premium of four hundred per cent., while bank bills were worth one hundred and ninety cents on the dollar.

Since the foundation of the Confederate Government, its finances had been grossly mismanaged: The Treasury note was a naked promise to pay; there was no fund pledged for its redemption; and the prospect of the rigid liquidation of the enormous debt that this class of paper represented six months after the restoration of peace, depended solely on the speculative prospect of a foreign loan to the amount of many hundred millions of dollars. At the commencement of the war the South had the elements for the structure of one of the most successful and elastic schemes of finance that the world had seen. The planters were anxious to effect the sales of their cotton and tobacco to the Confederate States: these would have supplied the government with a basis of credit which would have been extended as the prices of these staples advanced, and therefore kept progress with the war; but this scheme was opposed by the Secretary of the Treasury, Mr. Memminger, and defeated by his influence. He was unfortunately sustained by an Executive grossly incompetent on subjects of finance; which was ignorant of the principle of political economy, that there are no royal ways of making money out of nothing, that governments must raise money in the legitimate way of taxation, loans, &c.; which relied upon the manufacture of a revenue out of naked paper obligations; and which actually went to the foolish extremity of recommending that the creditors of the government should take their payment in currency rather than in the public stocks. It appears, indeed, that our government was ignorant of the most primitive truths of finance, and that it had not read in history or in reason the lesson of the *fatal connection between currency and revenue.*

It is true that some appreciation of this lesson was at last shown by Congress in its new tax bill; for the theory of that bill was, by an enormous weight of taxation, to pay, at least measurably, the expenses of the war as it progressed, and to risk no further connection between the two distinct financial concerns of revenue and currency. But on the other hand its system of forcing the funding of treasury notes by arbitrary reductions of interest, betrayed the ignorance of Congress; left incomplete and embarrassed a system of finance which might have otherwise been carried to a point of extraordinary success; and aimed a direct blow at the integrity of the public credit.

It was easy to see that slight differences in rates of interest would afford but feeble inducements for the conversion of the treasury note into the bond, when money was easily doubled or quadrupled in the active commercial speculations peculiar to the condition of the South in the war, unless the bond could be readily used as a medium of exchanges; and in that event there would only be a change in the form of the paper, the volume of the currency would be undiminished, and its depreciation therefore remain the same. But while the analysis of this system of funding shows it to be a transparent juggle, it was by no means certain that it did not contain the germ of many positive evils. The right of a government to make arbitrary changes in any of the terms of its obligations which affect their value, is questionable, and the commercial honour of such an expedient is more than doubtful. While it introduced the shadow of repudiation only to weak and suspicious minds, it is yet to be regretted that even whispers on that subject were ever heard in the South. But as far as our foreign credit was concerned, there is no doubt that the empirical action of Congress, which involved, even to the smallest extent, the integrity of our obligations, was of serious prejudice. It might indeed have been logically and certainly expected that the general confidence in Europe in the military fortunes of the Confederacy would have been productive of unlimited credit to us abroad, had the faith of Europe in the management of our finances equalled that in the success of our arms.*

On the subject of the financial management of the new Confederacy, one general reflection at least admits of no doubt. The attentive reader will recognize as the most remarkable circumstance of this war, that within two years the public finances of the Confederacy should have been brought

---

* It is true that a small foreign loan has been negotiated in Europe; but it affords no test of our credit in present circumstances, as it was made on a pledge of cotton. It shows, however, what might have been done, if the cotton had been purchased by the government and mobilized, for the whole crop might have been secured in 1861 at seven cents a pound. But against this scheme the government had set its face as flint, and when it did become distrustful of its former conclusion, it had only the nerve to make a very limited experiment in the application of this staple to support a credit almost hopelessly abused by paper issues.

It was estimated that there remained in the States of the Confederacy at this time 3,500,000 bales of cotton, which would be exported in the event of the ports being opened to trade. This estimate is made after deducting from the crops of 1861 and 1862 the quantity of cotton which had run the blockade, the amount destroyed to prevent capture by the Yankees, and the quantity used for home consumption, which, since the commencement of the war, had enormously increased, being now fully 500,000 bales per annum.

to the brink of ruin. The sympathy of the people with the revolution was unbounded. The disposition of all classes towards the government was one of extreme generosity. The property of the States of the Confederacy was greater per capita than that of any community on the globe. No country in the world had export values comparable in magnitude to those of the South, and the exports of all other countries were produced at a cost in labour four times that of ours. In such circumstances it is highly improbable that the government of the Confederacy could, within two years, have wrecked its credit with its own people, unless by the most ignorant trifling with great questions and the childish management of its treasury.

At an early period of the war it had been our boast that we had spent only fifteen millions, while the Yankees had spent ten or fifteen times that amount. But we find that the debt of the general government of the Confederate States in January last was $556,000,000, with the prospect, at the current rate of expenditure, that it would reach nine hundred millions by the close of the fiscal year on the first of July; and it is curious to observe what miscalculations were made of public debt both in the North and in the South. The newspapers of the two nations flourished the estimates of their debt in enumerations only of the obligations of the general government of each, and made complacent comparisons of these sums with the debts of European governments. But according to the estimates of Europe and the calculations of plain reason, the true volume of the debt of each of these nations was represented not only by what was owed by the Richmond and Washington governments, but by the aggregate amount of the indebtedness of the several States composing each confederation. Here could be the only true and just measure of the national debt of either the South or the North in comparison with the debts of other governments, to which the system of the division of powers between a central authority and States was unknown. The debt of each member of the Southern

Confederacy, as well as that of a central authority, was a burden on the nation, for the problem of its payment was at last to resolve itself into a tax upon the people. It is only by a calculation of these aggregates that just comparisons could be made between our financial condition and that of the North or European nations; and although such comparisons on our side were to the disadvantage of our enemies, yet they exhibited facts which were unpleasant enough to ourselves.

The law of impressment enacted by Congress affords the evidence of the scarcity of supplies in the South. The question of food with that of finance divided the attention of the government. The grain-growing and provision-raising country, which stretches from the Potomac at Harper's Ferry to Memphis on the Tennessee, was now exhausted of its provisions. Much of the productive portions of North Carolina and the Gulf States had been also exhausted. The great and true source of meat supply, the State of Kentucky, which contained more hogs and cattle, two or three to one, than were left in all the South besides, had fallen into the undivided possession of the Yankees. The general scarcity of all sorts of supplies was attested by the high prices of everything eatable. The advance in prices induced by the scarcity of supplies, was still further enormously enhanced by the greedy commercial speculation which distressed the South, and threw a shadow of dishonour upon the moral aspects of our struggle.

It is a subject of extraordinary remark, that the struggle for our independence should have been attended by the ignoble circumstances of a commercial speculation in the South unparalleled in its heartlessness and selfish greed. War invariably excites avarice and speculation; it is the active promoter of rapid fortunes and corrupt commercial practices. But it is a matter of surprise that more than an ordinary share of this bad, avaricious spirit should have been developed in the South during a war which involved the national existence, which presented so many contrasts of heroic self-sacrifice, and which was adorned with exhibitions of moral courage and devotion such as the world had seldom seen.

But of this social and moral contradiction in our war for independence, some explanation may be offered. It may, in some measure, be found in three facts: first, that a distrust of the national currency prevailed in the country; secondly, that the initiative (for it is the first steps in speculation which are more responsible) was made by Jews and foreign adventurers who everywhere infested the Confederacy; and, thirdly, that the fever of gain was greatly inflamed by the corruptions of the government, the abuse of its pecuniary patronage, and a system of secret contract, in which officials who were dishonest shared the profits, and those who were incompetent were easily overreached in the negotiation. The only serious blot which defaced our struggle for independence was, at least to some extent, the creature of circumstances; and that is lost to the eye of humane and enlightened history in the lustre of arms and virtues shed on the South in the most sublime trials of the war.

## CHAPTER X.

Character of Military Events of the Spring of 1863...Repulse of the Enemy at Fort McAllister...THE SIEGE OF VICKSBURG...The Yazoo Pass Expedition...Confederate Success at Fort Pemberton...The Enemy's Canals or "Cut Offs"...Their Failure...BOMBARDMENT OF PORT HUDSON...Destruction of "The Mississippi"...A Funeral Pyre...Happy Effects of our Victory...A Review of the Line of Inland Hostilities...Hooker's Hesitation on the Rappahannock...The Assignment of Confederate Commands West of the Mississippi...The Affair of Kelly's Ford...Death of Major Pelham...NAVAL ATTACK ON CHARLESTON...Destruction of "The Keokuk"...Scenery of the Bombardment...Extent of the Confederate Success...Events in Tennessee and Kentucky...Pegram's Reverse...The Situation of Hostilities at the close of April 1862.

Although but little is to be found of a decisive character in the military events of the Spring of 1862, there was yet a series of interesting occurrences which went far to prove the inefficiency of the most boasted naval structures of the enemy and the progress we had made in defensive works on the lines of our harbours and the banks of our rivers.

The first of these may be mentioned as the repulse of the enemy at Fort McAllister on the third of March. This fort is on the outer line of the defences of Savannah. Off the Georgia coast, and eighteen miles to the southward of the Savannah river, is Ossabaw Sound. Into this sound flows the Ogeechee river, a stream navigable some distance up—some thirty miles—to vessels of a larger class. On the Ogeechee river, four miles above the sound, is situate Fort McAllister. The fort stands on the main land, directly on the river bank, and commands the river for a mile and a half or two miles.

The attack of the enemy on this fort was made with three iron-clads and two mortar-boats. The result of a whole day's bombardment was, that one gun was dismounted, but the fort remained uninjured, and no loss of life was sustained on our side. The iron-clad Montauk was struck with solid shot seventy-one times, and was lifted clear out of the water by the explosion of a torpedo under her bow, but the Yankees stated that she was not seriously injured. Indeed, they declared that the whole affair was nothing more than an *experimentum crucis*, to ascertain the power of their new iron-clads to resist cannon-shot, and that the result of the encounter was all that they had hoped: "If the enemy was pleased with the result, the Confederates had certainly no reason to dispute his satisfaction, as long as they had the solid gratification of having resisted a bombardment of eight hours, without injury to their works or the loss of a single life.

While the enemy menaced the seaboard, he had found another theatre for his naval power on the waters of the Mississippi river. His operations there were even more important than those on our sea lines, for they were an essential part of the campaign in the West. In fact, Vicksburg was for a long time the point on which depended the movements in Tennessee and the resolution of the great crisis in the West.

### THE SIEGE OF VICKSBURG.

The siege of Vicksburg furnishes a most remarkable instance of the industry and physical perseverance of the Yankees. Ever since December 1862, they had been busily engaged in the attempt to circumvent our defences, even to the extremity of forcing our internal navigation of swampy lagoons and obstructed creeks for a distance of four hundred and fifty miles.

The enemy's operations in other directions kept him quiet directly in front of Vicksburg, but his purpose was all the same—the capture and occupation of the place. The enemy had three distinct projects for compassing the capture of Vicksburg: First, the canal across the isthmus opposite the city; secondly, the project of getting through the Yazoo Pass; third, the Lake Providence canal project. It had been all the time the principal aim of the Yankees to get in the rear or below Vicksburg. Their present plan, and one on which they were now at work, was to get through the Yazoo Pass in the hope of getting in our rear and cutting off our supplies. Their idea was to flank Vicksburg, capture Jackson, cut off Grenada, and destroy all possibility of our obtaining supplies throughout that rich country, by this one bold stroke. The route mapped out by the Yankees commences near Helena, Arkansas, where the Yazoo Pass connects the Mississippi with the Coldwater river, through Moon lake. The distance from the Mississippi to the Coldwater by this pass is about twenty miles—a very narrow and tortuous channel, only navigable when the Mississippi is quite high and its waters overflow the low lands of this region. The Coldwater river empties into the Tallahatchie, and the Tallahatchie into the Yazoo. The whole distance by this route from the Mississippi to the mouth of the Yazoo, in the neighbourhood of Vicksburg, is some five hundred miles, and over one-half of it, or to the mouth of the Tallahatchie, it is easily obstructed. The Yankees met with no obstruction on their ascent of the Tallahatchie, except the overgrowth and tortuousness of the stream —which prevented the gunboats, in some instances, from making more than three and four miles a day—until reaching the mouth of the Tallahatchie, or its neighbourhood, where they encountered the batteries known as Fort Pemberton, which stood as the barrier against the entrance of their fleet into the Yazoo river, formed by the confluence of the Tallahatchie and Yallobusha rivers.

This fort was nothing more than an indented line of earthworks, composed of cotton bales and mud, thrown up on the neck of a bend of the Tallahatchie river, where the river was only two hundred and fifty yards wide. The site was selected by Major General Loring as the best position on the Yazoo or Tallahatchie river.

It was here on the 13th of March, that the Yazoo expedition was intercepted and driven back by our batteries, which achieved a splendid victory over the Yankee gunboats. The Yallabusha river unites with the Tallahatchie in the bend, forming the Yazoo, so that the right flank of our works rested upon the Tallahatchie, and the left upon the Yazoo, both, however, being really the same stream. The left flank was opposite Greenwood, which is situated on the east side of the Yazoo. The Tallahatchie, under the guns of the fort, was obstructed by an immense raft, behind which the Star of the West was sunk in the channel. The intervention of the point above the bend masked the whole of our line except the left, upon which, consequently, the fire of the enemy's boats was directed. The fire was terrific, uninterrupted for four hours, from ten to sixteen heavy calibre guns on gunboats, two heavy guns on land, and one mortar. Yet the line of our batteries was maintained. The loss of the enemy in this unsuccessful attack is not known; but his gunboats and batteries were constantly hit and large quantities of burning cotton were struck from them.

The defeat of the enemy at Fort Pemberton prevented his fleet from passing by to the lower Yazoo. But this was not the only canal project of the Yankees. One at Lake Providence, was intended to afford a passage from the Mississippi to the headwaters of the Red river, by which they might command a vast scope of country and immense resources. This canal, which it was said was to change the bed of the Mississippi and turn its mighty current in the Atchafalaya river on its way to the Gulf of Mexico, was also a failure. The canal had been opened and an enormous extent of country submerged and, ruined, but it was found that no gunboats or transports could ever reach the Mississippi below Vicksburg by that route. Snags and drift choked up the tortuous streams formed by the flood from the cut levees, and even if navigation had been possible, the channel might have been rendered impassable in a hundred places by a score of active guerrillas.

In the meantime, there was every reason to believe that the Yankees were content to abandon the project of cutting a ditch through the main land opposite Vicksburg, by which it was hoped to force the current of the Mississippi into an unaccustomed course through which to pass their vessels without going within range of our batteries.

It was thus that the enemy was apparently brought to the point of necessity of either attacking our fortifications at Snyder's Bluff on the Yazoo, or our batteries in front of the city. These were the only two points left against which he could operate, and they were the same which he had been trying to avoid for the last three months. When he first arrived these were the only points susceptible of assault, but wishing to flank them he had wasted three months' time, lost a number of gunboats and transports, and many thousands of his troops.

An attack directly in front of the city plainly threatened the most serious disaster to the enemy. From a point of the river above, where high land begins, there is a high and precipitous bluff, which would not afford any landing place for the troops—only about two acres of ground are to be found where a landing could be effected, and upon this a formidable battery was ready to receive them, and in the rear there were numberless other batteries to protect it. The whole bluff, extending a distance of two miles, was also frowning with guns, all of which would bear upon an enemy in the river.

The expedition of the enemy on the Tallahatchie, which met such unexpected and disgraceful defeat from the guns of a hastily made fort, is memorable as another of those Yankee raids which, unable to accomplish military results, was left to gratify itself with the plunder of citizens and the cowardly atrocities of marauders. From the barbarity of the Yankee, Mississippi was a distinguished sufferer as well as Virginia. Two-thirds of Sherman's army was composed of new troops from Indiana, Illinois and Wisconsin, and they had come down the Mississippi with the intention of burning and destroying everything they could lay their hands on. The whole line of their march was one continued scene of destruction. Private dwellings were burned, women and children driven out of their houses, and even the clothes stripped from their backs, to say nothing of acts committed by the soldiery which might make the blackest hearted libertine. blush for shame.*

Another attempt of the enemy to force our strongholds on the Mississippi, which we have to relate at this time, was made on Port Hudson on the 15th of March. We have seen how fatal, so far, had been the enemy's attempts to run our batteries and to get to the south of Vicksburg. His first attempt was with the Queen of the West, his second with the Indianola; but though successful in these two cases in running our batteries, the boats were soon captured by our men, and the enemy completely foiled in his design. It was now proposed that the enemy's fleet should attack Port Hudson and attempt to force a passage up the river.

### THE BOMBARDMENT OF PORT HUDSON.

Port Hudson is a strongly fortified position on the lower Mississippi—about sixteen miles above Baton Rouge and three hundred below Vicksburg. It is situated on a bend in the river, and its great strength as a place of defence against a fleet consists in the height of its cliffs and the peculiar formation of the river at that place. The cliffs are very high

---

\* The following is a private confession taken from the letter of a Yankee officer, attached to Sherman's command: "I have always blamed Union Generals for guarding rebel property, but I now see the necessity of it. Three weeks of such unbridled license would ruin our army. I tell you the truth when I say we are about as mean a mob as ever walked the face of the earth. It is perfectly frightful. If I lived in this country, I never would lay down my arms while a 'Yankee' remained on the soil. I do not blame Southerners for being secessionists now. I could relate many things that would be laughable if they were not so horribly disgraceful. For instance, imagine two privates in an elegant carriage, belonging to some wealthy Southern nabob, with a splendid span of horses riding in state along the road we are marching over, with a negro coachman holding the reins in all the style of an English nobleman, and then two small drummer boys going it at a two forty pace, in an elegant buggy, with a fast horse, and the buggy loaded with a strange medley of household furniture and kitchen utensils, from an elegant parlor mirror to a pair of fire-dogs, all of which they have 'cramped' from some fine house, which, from sheer wantonness, they have rifled and destroyed."

and also very steep—in fact, almost perpendicular. The river just at the bend opposite the town suddenly narrows, so that the rapid current strikes against the west bank, and then sweeps through a narrow channel just at the base of the cliff. Our batteries were located on a bluff at the elbow of the river, and commanded a range of three miles above and below, compelling any vessel which might attempt the passage to run the gauntlet of a plunging fire.

Six vessels were to comprise the enemy's expedition, divided into two divisions. The vanguard was to consist of the flag ship Hartford, a first class steam sloop-of-war, carrying twenty-six eight and nine inch Paixhan guns, leading, followed by the Monongahela, a second class steam sloop, mounting sixteen heavy guns, and the Richmond, a first class steam sloop of twenty-six guns, principally eight and nine inch columbiads. The rear guard was composed of the first class steam sloop Mississippi, twenty-two guns, eight and nine inch, and the gunboats Kinnes and Gennessee, each carrying three columbiads and two rifled thirty-two pounders. The Mississippi was a side-wheel steamer. All the others were screw propellers. The vanguard was commanded by Admiral Farragut in person, on board the Hartford. The rear was under command of Capt. Melancthon Smith, flying his pennant from the Mississippi. They were to proceed up the stream in single file, the stern of one following close upon the stern of another, and keeping their fires and lights well concealed until they should be discovered by our batteries, when they were to get by the best they could, fighting their passage, and once above they believed they would have the stronghold on both sides, their guns covering every part of the encampment.

Shortly before midnight, the boats, having formed the line of battle as described, their decks cleared for action, and the men at their quarters, the Hartford led the way and the others promptly followed her direction. At the moment of their discovery, a rocket was to be sent up from the admiral's flagship, as the signal for the Essex and her accompanying mortar-boats to commence work.

Although there had been no indications of such a determined night attack by Farragut, the usual vigilant precautions were in force at our batteries. Every gun was ready for action, and around each piece slept a detachment of gunners. So dark was the night, however, and so slightly had the armed craft nosed their way up, that the flag-ship had passed some of our guns and all the fleet were within easy range before their approach was known. Almost at the same time a rocket from our signal corps, and the discharge of muskets by an infantry picket, aroused our line. Quick as a flash, while the falling fire of our alarm rocket was yet unextinguished, there shot up into the sky, from the Hartford's deck, another. Then came one grand, long, deafening roar, that rent the atmosphere with its mighty thunder, shaking both land and water, and causing the high battery-crowned cliffs to tremble, as if with fear and wonder.

The darkness of the night gave extraordinary sublimity to the scene of bombardment. The sheets of flame that poured from the sides of the sloops at each discharge lit up nearly the whole stretch of river, placing each craft in strong relief against the black sky. On the long line of bluff, the batteries but a moment before silent as the church-yard, now resounded to the hurrying tread of men, while the quick, stern tones of command were heard above the awful din, and the furtively glancing rays of light from the battle lanterns revealed the huge instruments of death and destruction, and showed the half-covered way to magazines.

Minute after minute passed away, and the fleet kept its unchecked course up the stream. The feeling of its officers was one of amazement at the silence of the batteries. The question was seriously propounded, had not the Confederates deserted them? But only too soon did the enemy discover that we were but waiting to bring their whole fleet irretrievably under our guns before we went to work.

For fifteen minutes had they plied at their monster cannon, and now they were commencing to relax, from sheer vexation, when a flash of light from the crest of a cliff lights the way for a shell to go plunging through the Hartford's deck. This was the monitor, and at once the enemy saw a cordon of vivid light as long as their own.

Now commenced the battle in all its terrible earnestness. Outnumbered in guns and outweighed in metal, our volleys were as quickly repeated and the majority of them unerring in their aim. As soon as the enemy thus discovered our batteries, they opened on them with grape and canister, which was more accurately thrown than their shells, and threw clouds of dirt upon the guns and gunners; the shells went over them in every conceivable direction, except the right one.

The Hartford, a very fast ship, now made straight up the river, making her best time, and trying to divert the aim of our gunners by her incessant and deafening broadsides. She soon outstripped the balance of the fleet. Shot after shot struck her, riddling her through and through, but still she kept on her way.

Every craft now looking out for itself and bound to make its very best time to get by, the fleet lost its orderly line of battle, and got so mixed up, it was difficult, and sometimes impossible, to distinguish one from another. It was speedily apparent to the enemy, that the fire was a great deal hotter and more destructive than had been expected, and the captains of the two gunboats and of the Monongahela, doubtless resolved quickly that it would be madness to attempt to run such a terrific gauntlet of iron hail. Whether the commanders of the Richmond and Mississippi had already arrived at the same determination, or came to it soon after, is not known; but they all, except the Hartford, undertook to put about and return the way they came.

For this purpose the Richmond came close in to the left bank, under the batteries, and then circled round, her course reaching nearly up to the opposite point. In executing this manœuvre, she gave our batteries successively a raking position, and they took excellent advantage of it, seriously damaging her, as the crashing of her timbers plainly told.

The Mississippi undertook to execute the same manœuvre of turning round and making her escape back to the point she started from. She had rounded and just turned down stream, when one of our shots tore off her rudder, and another went crushing through her machinery. Immediately after came the rushing sound of steam escaping from some broken pipe, and the now unmanageable vessel drifted aground directly opposite our crescent line of batteries. Her range was quickly gained, and she was being rapidly torn to pieces by our missiles, when her commander gave the order for all hands to save themselves the best way they could. At the same time fire broke out in two places. At this time her decks were strewn with dead and wounded. Some fifty-five or sixty persons saved themselves by jumping overboard and swimming to the shore.

The dead and wounded were left upon the Mississippi, which soon floated off and started down with the current. All the other vessels were now out of range, and the spectacle of the burning ship was a grand and solemn one, yet mingled with painful thoughts of the horrible fate of those mangled unfortunates who were being burned to death upon this floating funeral pyre. As the flames would reach the shells lying among her guns, they exploded one by one, adding to the novel grandeur of the sight. The light of the burning wreck could be seen, steadily increasing its distance, for two hours and a half. At five minutes past five o'clock, when the Mississippi was probably within five miles of Baton Rouge, a sudden glare lit up the whole sky. The cause was well known to be the explosion of the magazine. After a considerable interval of time, a long rumbling sound brought final proof that the Mississippi, one of the finest vessels of the United States navy, which had earned an historical fame before the commencement of the present war for her usefulness in the Gulf during the Mexican war, and as the flag-ship of the Japan expedition, was a thing of the past.

The victory of Port Hudson forms one of the most satisfactory and brilliant pages in the history of the war. The fleet, with the exception of the Hartford, had been driven back by our batteries, and a grateful surprise had been given to many of our people who had acquired the disheartening conviction that gunboats could treat shore batteries with contempt. So far our strongholds on the Mississippi had bid defiance to the foe, and months of costly preparation for their reduction had been spent in vain.

While these events were transpiring on the Mississippi, the long line of inland hostilities remained unvaried and almost silent. In Virginia and in Tennessee, the powerful armies of Lee and Hooker, Bragg and Rosecranz, had camped for months in close proximity without a cannonade, and almost without a skirmish. To some extent the elements had proclaimed a truce, while the hesitating temper of the enemy betrayed a policy strangely at variance with the former vigorous campaign in the same season of the last year. Especially was the hesitation remarkable in Virginia, where the new commander-in-chief of the enemy—Hooker—was a violent member of the Abolitionist party. He was the chief of that clique among the Yankee officers who made the war not to realize the dream of a restored Union, but for the subjugation and destruction of the Southern social system, the massacre or exile of the inhabitants of the Southern country, and the confiscation of their entire real and personal property.

Beyond the Mississippi there was scarcely any thing to remark but a new assignment of military commands. We had now west of the Mississippi Lieutenant-General Kirby Smith, General Price, General Magruder and General Sibley. Gen. Smith had been placed at the head of the department, and had already issued an order announcing that fact; General Price was assigned to lead the field movements for the redemption of Arkansas and his own State, Missouri; Gen. Sibley was moving to other important points; and Gen. Magruder's field of operations was Texas.

We have to record but a single incident in the spring of 1863, to break the long silence of the lines of the Rappahannock. On the morning of the 17th of March the enemy crossed the river at Kelly's Ford, with both a cavalry and artillery force, numbering probably three thousand men. They advanced within six miles of Culpeper Court-House, where they were engaged by the brigade of Gen. Fitzhugh Lee. The fight was severe and lasted several hours. The Yankees were finally repulsed, and fell back routed and panic-stricken, after having inflicted a loss upon us of about one hundred in killed and wounded. They had fought with some advantages at first, bravely contesting their ground, and it is not improbable that a report of reinforcements coming up to us was the occasion of their retreat. When the retreat was ordered, they fled in dismay and confusion.

This affair—if it was worth any thing—cost us the life of one of the most brilliant artillery officers in the army. Major Pelham, of Alabama, who had acquired the title of "the gallant Pelham" from the hands of Gen. Lee in the official report of the battle of Fredericksburg, was killed by the fragment of a shell. At Fredericksburg he had distinguished himself by sustaining the concentrated fire of a number of the enemy's batteries. In that terrible trial he had stood as a rock. In the affair which cost him his life, he had just risen in his saddle to cheer a troop of cavalry rushing to the charge, when the fatal blow was given. He was only twenty-two years of age, and had been through all the battles in Virginia. Unusual honours were paid his remains, for they were laid in the capitol, and tributes of rare flowers strewn upon the bier of "the young Marcellus of the South."

### NAVAL ATTACK ON CHARLESTON.

The city of Charleston had long been the object of the enemy's lust; it was considered a prize scarcely less important than the long-contested one of Richmond; and with more than their customary assurance, the Yankees anticipated the glory and counted the triumphs of the capture of the cradle of the revolution. It was thought to be an easy matter for Admiral Dupont's iron-clad fleet to take the city, and the Yankee newspapers for months had indulged the prospect of the capture of Charleston as a thing of the future that only awaited their pleasure.

On Sunday morning, the 5th of April, four "monitors," the Ironsides (an armour-plated frigate with an armament of twenty-two 10, 11 and 15-inch guns) and thirty vessels of various sizes were seen off the bar. Four monitors and thirty-five wooden vessels were added to the fleet on the following day; thirty-five vessels, for the most part transports, appeared in the Stono, and the enemy landed a force of about six thousand men on Coles' and Battery Islands. These facts, with other indications, led Gen. Beauregard to count upon an attack on Tuesday, and the expectations of that sagacious and vigilant commander were not disappointed.

The atmosphere early on Tuesday morning, 7th of April, was misty, but as the day advanced the haze lightened, and the monitors and the Ironsides were seen lying off Morris Island. Between two and three o'clock in the afternoon, a dispatch from Colonel Rhett, commandant of Fort Sumter, informed Gen. Beauregard that five monitors and the Ironsides were approaching the fort. The fleet were seen rounding the point of Morris Island, the Keokuk in the advance. It was a happy moment for the defenders of Charleston. So long had suspense reigned in that city, that the booming of the signal gun and the announcement that at last the battle had begun was a positive relief. A thrill of joy came to every heart, and the countenances of all declared plainly that a signal victory over the mailed vessels was reckoned upon without doubt or misgiving. The long roll beat in Fort Sumter; the artillerists in that work rushed to their guns. The regimental flag of the 1st South Carolina Artillery and "the stars and bars" of the Confederate States flaunted out from their flagstaffs on the fort, and were saluted as the enemy advanced with an outburst of "Dixie" from the band, and the deep-mouthed roar of thirteen pieces of heavy artillery.

On came the mailed monitors. Their ports were closed, and they appeared deserted of all living things. They moved northwardly towards Sullivan's Island, and at a distance from its batteries about 1200 yards they began to curve around towards Sumter. A flash, a cloud of smoke, a clap of thunder herald a storm of heavy shot which bursts from the island upon the side of the frigate. The ships move on silently. The deep-mouthed explosions of Sumter in the next instant burst upon the advancing ships, and hurl tremendous bolts of wrought iron against the armour of the Ironsides. The frigate halts. At a distance of about twelve hundred yards from that work she delivers from seven guns a broadside of 15-inch shot that dashes against the sea-face of Sumter with a heavy crash. Bricks fly from the parapet and whirl from the traverse. A shell smashes a marble lintel in the officers' quarters, hustles through a window on the other side, and, striking the parapet, hurls a tornado of bricks far to the rear. The works on Morris Island burst into the deafening chorus. On land and on sea, from all the batteries of the outer circle, from all the turrets of the inner circle.

It was manifest that the Ironsides was appointed to test the strength of the fort. Fort Sumter acknowledged the compliment by pouring the contents of her biggest guns into that pride of the Yankee navy. Advancing on her circling course, the Ironsides made way for her attendant warriors; and one by one, as their turrets moved in the solemn waltz, they received the fire, sometimes diffused, sometimes concentrated, of the surrounding circle of batteries. The first division of the ships curved on its path under an iron storm that rended the air with its roar and bursted upon their mail in a quick succession of reports; sometimes with the heavy groan of crushing, sometimes with the sharp cry of tearing. Delivering a fire of shot and shell as they passed the works on Morris Island, the Ironsides and her monitors moved slowly out of range.

As the Ironsides withdrew from the action, taking position to the south of Fort Sumter, steam was seen issuing from her in dense volumes, and it was believed that she was seriously damaged.

The Keokuk, a double-turreted iron-clad, led into the fight four monitors. More bold than even the Ironsides, she advanced under a tornado of shot to a position within about nine hundred yards of Fort Sumter. Halting at that distance, she discharged her 15-inch balls from her turrets against the sea-face of that fort. Crushing and scattering the bricks on the line of her tremendous fire, she failed, however, to make any serious impression on the walls. A circle of angry flashes radiated towards her from all sides, while a tempest of iron bolts and round shot crashed against her sides. For about twenty minutes she stood still in apparent helplessness. At the expiration of that time she moved slowly on, and after receiving the fire of the works on Morris Island, passed out of range. She was fairly riddled, for she had been the target of the most powerful guns the Confederates could command. Great holes were visible in her sides, her prow, her after-turret and her smoke-stack. Her plates were bent and bolts protruded here and there all over her. She was making water rapidly, and it was plain to see that she was a doomed ship.

After the Keokuk and her companions had passed out of range, the circular movement was not renewed. The ships retired outside the harbour to their anchorage; and after about two hours and a half of a most terrible storm of shot and thunder of artillery, Fort Sumter and its supporting batteries settled down under sluggish clouds of smoke into triumphs of quiet.

Our victory was one of unexpected brilliancy, and had cost us scarcely more than the ammunition for our guns. A drummer-boy was killed at Fort Sumter and five men wounded. Our artillery practice was excellent, as is proved by the fact that the nine Yankee vessels were struck five hundred and twenty times. The Keokuk received no less than ninety shots. She did not outlive the attack on Fort Sumter twelve hours.

The next day her smoke-stack and one of her turrets were visible during low water off Morris Island, where she had sunk.

The battle had been fought on the extreme outer line of fire, and the enemy had been defeated at the very threshold of our defences. Whether his attack was intended only as a reconnoissance, or whether what was supposed to be the preliminary skirmish, was in fact the whole affair, it is certain that our success gave great assurances of the safety of Charleston; that it had the proportions of a considerable victory; and that it went far to impeach the once dreaded power of the iron-clads of the enemy.*

The month of April has but few events of military note beyond what has been referred to in the foregoing pages. The check of Van Dorn at Franklin, Tennessee, and the reverse of Pegram in Kentucky, were unimportant incidents; they did not affect the campaign, and their immediate disasters were inconsiderable. The raid of the latter commander into Kentucky again revived reports of the reaction of public sentiment in that unhappy State in favour of the Confederacy. It was on his retreat that he was set upon by a superiour force of the enemy near Somerset, from which he effected an escape across the Cumberland, after the loss of about one hundred and fifty men in killed, wounded and prisoners.

---

* It is a question of scientific interest whether, in the construction of iron-clads, the Confederate plan of slanted sides is not superiour to the Yankee plan of thick-walled turrets—the Virginia-Merrimac, and not the Monitor, the true model. The Yankee monitor is an upright, cylindrical turret. If a shot strikes the centre line of this cylinder, it will not glance, but deliver its full force. On the contrary, the peculiarity of the Virginia-Merrimac was its roof shaped sides, on which the shot glances. The inventor of that noble naval structure, Commander Brooke, claimed the slanted or roof-shaped sides as constituting the original feature and most important merit of his invention. We may add now that to the genius of this accomplished officer the Confederacy was variously indebted; for it was a gun of his invention—"the Brooke gun"—that fired the bolt which pierced the turret of the Keokuk and gave the first proof in the war that no thickness of iron, that is practical in the construction of such a machine, is sufficient to secure it.

This period, properly the close of the second year of hostilities, presents a striking contrast with the corresponding month of the former year with respect to the paramount aspects of the war. In April, 1862, the Confederates had fallen back in Virginia from the Potomac beyond the Rappahannock, and were on the point of receding from the vicinity of the lower Chesapeake before the advancing army of McClellan. Now they confronted the enemy from the Rappahannock and hovered upon his flank within striking distance to the Potomac, while another portion of our forces manœuvred almost in the rear and quite upon the flank of Norfolk. Twelve months ago the enemy threatened the important Southern artery which links the coast of the Carolinas with Virginia; he was master of Florida, both on the Atlantic and the Gulf; and Mobile trembled at every blast from the Federal bugles of Pensacola. Now his North Carolina lines were held exclusively as lines of occupation; he was repulsed on the seaboard; his operations in Florida were limited to skirmishing parties of negroes; and Mobile had become the nursery of cruisers in the very face of his blockading squadron. A year ago the grasp of the enemy was closing on the Mississippi from Cairo to the Gulf; but while Butler was enjoying his despotic amusements and building up his private fortunes in the Crescent City, the strongholds of Vicksburg and Port Hudson were created, and held at bay the most splendid expeditions which the extravagance of the North had yet prepared. A year ago the enemy, by his successes in Kentucky and Tennessee, held the way almost into the very heart of the Confederacy, through Eastern Tennessee and Western Virginia. Now the fortunes of the war in that whole region were staked upon the issues of impending battle.

For three months the "grand hesitation" of the North had continued. With some seven or eight hundred thousand soldiers in the field and countless cruisers swarming on our coasts, the enemy had yet granted us a virtual suspension of arms since the great battles of Fredericksburg and Murfreesboro', interrupted only by petty engagements and irresolute and fruitless bombardments. He had shown that he possessed no real confidence in the success of his arms; he had so far failed to reduce any one of "the three great strongholds of the rebellion," Richmond, Charleston and Vicksburg; and he had ceased to map out those plans of conquest of which he was formerly so prolific.

## CHAPTER XI.

Close of the Second Year of the War...Propriety of an Outline of Some Succeeding Events...Cavalry Enterprises of the Enemy...The Raids in Mississippi and Virginia...SKETCH OF THE BATTLES OF THE RAPPAHANNOCK...The Enemy's Plan of Attack...The Fight at Chancellorsville...The Splendid Charge of "Stonewall" Jackson...The Fight at Fredericksburg...The Fight at Salem Church...Summary of our Victory...DEATH OF "STONEWALL" JACKSON...His Character and Services.

The second year of the war, having commenced with the fall of New-Orleans, 1st of May, 1862, properly closes with the events recorded in the preceding chapter. Of succeeding events, which have occurred between this period and that of publication, we do not propose to attempt at this time a full narrative; their detail belongs to another volume. It is proposed at present only to make an outline of them, so as to give to the reader a stand-point of intelligent observation, from which he may survey the general situation at the time these pages are given to the public.

The next volume of our history will open on that series of remarkable raids and enterprises on the part of the enemy's cavalry which, in the months of April and May, disturbed many parts of the Confederacy. We shall find that the extent of these raids of Yankee horsemen, their simultaneous occurrence in widely removed parts of the Confederacy, and the circumstances of each, betrayed a deliberate and extensive purpose on the part of the enemy and a consistency of design deserving the most serious consideration.

We shall relate how the people of Richmond were alarmed by the apparition of Yankee cavalry near their homes. But we shall find causes of congratulation that the unduly famous expedition of Stoneman was not more destructive. The damage which it inflicted upon our railroads was slight, its hurried pillage did not amount to much, and the only considerable capture it effected was of a train of commissary wagons in King William county.

Other parts of the Confederacy, visited about the same time by Yankee cavalry, were not so fortunate. The State of Mississippi was ransacked almost through its entire length by the Grierson raid. Starting from Corinth, near the northern boundary of Mississippi, a body of Yankee horsemen, certainly not exceeding two thousand, rode down the valley of the Tombigbee, penetrated to a point below the centre of the State, and then making a detour, reached the Mississippi Gulf coast in safety. This force, so insignificant in numbers, made the entire passage of the State of Mississippi from the northeast to the southwest corner; and the important town of Enterprise was barely saved by reinforcements of infantry which arrived from Meridian just fifteen minutes before the Yankees demanded the surrender of the place.

We shall have to add here cotemporary accounts of another Yankee raid in Georgia. That adventure, however, was happily nipped in the bud by Forrest, who captured the Yankee commander, Stuart, and his entire party, at Rome, Georgia, after one of the most vigorous pursuits ever made of an enemy.

The interest of these raids was something more than that of the excursions of brigands. That of Stoneman was an important part of the great battle which signalized the opening of the month of May on the banks of the Rappahannock, and broke at last the "grand hesitation" of the enemy, which had been the subject of so much impatience in the South.

SKETCH OF THE BATTLES OF THE RAPPAHANNOCK.

The plan of attack adopted by Gen. Hooker may be briefly characterized as a feint on our right, and a flank movement in force on our left. It was determined to throw a heavy force across the river just below the mouth of Deep Run, and three miles below Fredericksburg, and pretend to renew the attempt in which Burnside had previously been unsuccessful. The object of this movement was two-fold—first, to hold the Confederate forces at that point; and second, to protect Hooker's communications and supplies, while the other half of the army should make a crossing above the fortifications, and sweeping down rapidly to the rear of Fredericksburg, take a strong position and hold it until they could be reinforced by the portion of the army engaged in making the feint, which was to withdraw from its position, take the bridges to the point of the river which had been uncovered by the flank movement, and the whole army was thus to be concentrated in the rear of Fredericksburg.

The execution of this plan was commenced on Monday, the 26th of April. Three *corps d'armee*—the Fifth, Eleventh and Twelfth—were ordered to march up the river with eight days' rations to Kelly's Ford, on the north bank of the Rappahannock, near the Orange and Alexandria railroad. This force, under the command of Gen. Slocum, of the Twelfth corps, reached the point at which it was to cross the Rappahannock on Tuesday night. On the same night three other corps—the First, Third and Sixth—were sent to the mouth of Deep Run, three miles below Fredericksburg, to be ready to undertake the crossing simultaneously with the other corps at Kelly's Ford on Wednesday morning before day. The movement was successfully conducted at both points, and without serious opposition from the Confederates.

The second corps, under Couch, which had remained at Banks' Ford, four miles above the town, was moved up to the United States Ford, just below the point of confluence of the Rappahannock and Rapidan, and crossed to join Gen. Slocum, who had crossed the Rappahannock several miles higher up at Kelly's Ford, and the Rapidan at Germanna Mills and Ely's Ford, and marched down to Chancellorsville. These movements occupied Wednesday and Thursday. Hooker now assumed command of the right wing of his army. He took his position across the plank road and turnpike at Chancellorsville, eleven miles from Fredericksburg, in order to cut off our anticipated retreat in the direction of Gordonsville, and strengthened his naturally formidable position by a series of elaborate abattis and field works.

The North eagerly seized upon the different circumstances of the existing situation as indicative of victory. General Hooker had made himself conspicuous in the eyes of the Yankees. He was confident, when examined before the Congressional Committee on the conduct of the war, that he could have marched into Richmond at any time at his ease had he been at the head of the Army of the Potomac instead of Gen. McClellan; and if he had had command instead of Burnside, he would have achieved wonders. He had recently stated that the army he led was "the finest on the planet," "an army of veterans," as the Tribune remarked, "superior to that of the Peninsula;" and so large was it that Northern journals asserted that Hooker had more troops than he knew what to do with. Nor was this all. He was allowed by Lee to cross the Rappahannock without opposition and without loss, and to secure a position deemed impregnable—one which, according to the order he issued on Thursday, the 30th of April, had rendered it necessary that "the enemy must either ingloriously fly or come out from behind his defences and give us (the Yankee army) battle on our own ground, where certain destruction waits him."

In the meantime, Gen. Lee was not slow to meet the dispositions of his adversary. The enemy continued to pour across the river at Deep Run, until three entire corps, numbering between fifty and sixty thousand men under Gen. Sedgwick, had crossed to the South side. Lee calmly watched this movement, as well as the one higher up the river under Hooker, until he had penetrated the enemy's design, and seen the necessity of making a rapid division of his own forces, to confront him on two different fields, and risking the result of fighting him in detail.

About noon on Wednesday, the 29th, information was received that the enemy had crossed the Rappahannock in force at Kelly's and Ellis Fords above, and were passing forward towards Germania Mills and Ely's Ford on the Rapidan. Two brigades of Anderson's division, Posey's Mississippians and Mahone's Virginians, numbering about 8,000 men, and one battery of four guns, were, and had been for several weeks, stationed in the neighborhood of Ely's Ford on the Rapidan, and United States Ford on the Rappahannock, guarding the approaches to Fredericksburg in that direction. It was apparent that this small force would be entirely inadequate to arrest the approach of Hooker's heavy column, and Wright's brigade was ordered up to their support. At daylight on Thursday morning, the head of Wright's brigade reached Chancellorsville, at which point Posey and Mahone had concentrated their forces with a view of making a stand. Major General Anderson having also arrived in the latter part of the night, and having obtained further information of the number of the Yankee forces, upon consultation with his brigade commanders, determined to fall back from Chancellorsville, in the direction of Fredericksburg, five miles, to a point where the Old Mine road leading from the United States Ford crosses the Orange and Fredericksburg turnpike and plank road. The turnpike and plank road were parallel to each other from Chancellorsville to the point where the Old Mine road crosses them, and from there to Fredericksburg they make one road.

Chancellorsville is eleven miles above Fredericksburg, and about four miles south of the point of confluence of the Rapidan with the Rappahannock, and consists of a large two story brick house, formerly kept as a tavern, and a few out-houses. It is situated on the plank road leading from Fredericksburg to Orange Court House, and is easily approached by roads leading from Germania Mills and Ely's, United States and Banks' Fords. Between Chancellorsville and the river and above lies the Wilderness, a district of country formerly covered with a scrubby black jack, oaks, and a thick, tangled undergrowth, but now somewhat cleared up. The ground around

Chancellorsville is heavily timbered, and favorable for defence. Seven miles from Chancellorsville, on the road to Fredericksburg, and four miles from the latter place, is Salem Church.

During the night of Thursday, General Lee ordered Jackson to march from his camp below Fredericksburg, with A. P. Hill's and Rhodes' (formerly D. H. Hill's division,) to the relief of Anderson. Gen. Lee brought up the divisions of Anderson and McLaws. He occupied the attention of the enemy in front, while Gen. Jackson with the divisions of Hill, Rhodes and Trimble moved by the road that leads from the Mine Road, behind the line-of-battle, to the road that leads to Germana Ford. This movement of General Jackson occupied nearly the whole of Saturday, May 2d, so that he did not get into position at the Wilderness Church until near sunset of that day.

While Jackson was gaining the enemy's rear, McLaws and Anderson had successfully maintained their position in front. Hooker had been felicitating himself upon his supposed good fortune in gaining our rear. What must have been his surprise, then, to find Stonewall Jackson on his extreme right and rear. Jackson's assault was sudden and furious. In a short time he threw Seigel's corps (the 11th) of Dutchmen into a perfect panic, and was driving the whole right wing of the Yankee army fiercely down upon Anderson's and McLaw's sturdy veterans, who, in turn, hurled them back, and rendered futile their efforts to break through our lower lines, and made it necessary for them to give back towards the river.

There was an intermission of about one hour in the firing from three until nine o'clock. It was at this time that Jackson received his death wound from his own men, who mistook him for the enemy. General Hill, upon whom the command now devolved, was soon afterwards wounded also; when General Rhodes assumed command until General Stuart could arrive upon that part of the field. Stuart renewed the fight at nine o'clock at night & it was, in accordance with General Jackson's original plan, and did not withhold his blows until the enemy's

18

right had been doubled in on his centre in and around Chancellorsville.

At daylight Sunday morning, our army, which now surrounded the enemy on all sides except towards the river, commenced advancing and closing in upon him from all points. The enemy had dug rifle pits and cut abattis in front and along his whole line, while his artillery, well protected by earthworks, covered every eminence and swell of rising ground, so as to get a direct and enfilading fire upon our advancing columns. But on our gallant men moved, their ranks played upon by an incessant fire of shell, grape and canister, from the front, the right and left. On they pressed through the wood, over the fields, up the hills, into the very mouths of the enemy's guns, and the long line of rifle pits. With a terrible shout they sprang forward, and rushing through the tangled abattis, they gained the bank in front of the rifle-pits, when the foe gave way in great confusion and fled.

An extraordinary victory appeared to be in our grasp. The capture or destruction of Hooker's army now appeared certain.

General Lee, finding the enemy still in force towards the river, ordered the army to form on the plank road above Chancellorsville, extending his line in a south-easterly direction down the turnpike below Chancellorsville, with his centre resting about the latter point. Just there news was received that Sedgwick, taking advantage of our weakness, had crossed the river at Fredericksburg, driven Barksdale from the town, and occupied Marye's Hill, after capturing several pieces of the Washington Artillery. It was also stated that Sedgwick was advancing up the plank road upon Lee's rear. This movement of the enemy was all that saved Hooker from destruction.

The story of the reverse at Fredericksburg is easily told. Our forces in defence of the line, commencing at Marye's hill, and terminating at Hamilton's Crossing, consisted of General Barksdale's brigade and General Early's division. General Barksdale held the extreme left. His line had its beginning at a point two hundred yards north of Marye's heights, and extended a mile and a half to a point opposite the pontoon bridge on the left of Mansfield. This brigade, on the morning of the battle, did not exceed two thousand in numbers, rank and file, and throughout the entire length of its line, had no other support than six pieces of the Washington Artillery, which were posted on Marye's heights, and Read's Battery, which was placed in position on the hill to the left of Howison's house.

Against this position the enemy brought to bear the command of Gibbins on the left flank, and about twenty thousand of Sedgwick's corps. The first assault was made in front of the stone wall, as in the case of last December, and was signally repulsed. This was repeated three times, and on each occasion the handful of men behind the wall, with shouts of enthusiasm and deadly volleys, drove back the assailants. The first charge was made before sunrise, and the others in as rapid succession as was possible after rallying and reinforcement. About nine o'clock in the morning, the enemy adopted the ruse of requesting a flag of truce for the alleged purpose of carrying off the wounded, but for the real object of ascertaining our force. The flag was granted, and thereby our insufficient defence was exposed, the bearer coming up on the left flank from a direction whence our whole line was visible. Immediately after the conclusion of the truce, the enemy reinforced their front, and threw the whole of Gibbins' division on our left, defended by the 21st Mississippi regiment alone, commanded by Colonel B. J. Humphreys. This regiment faced the advancing host without quailing, and, after firing until but a few feet intervened between them and the foe, they clubbed muskets and successfully dashed back the front line of their assailants. The enemy, by the force of overwhelming numbers, however, broke through our line, and Marye's hill was flanked about eleven o'clock Sunday morning.

The turn which events had taken in front of Fredericksburg made it necessary for General Lee to arrest the pursuit of Hooker, and caused him to send back to Fredericksburg the divisions of Anderson and McLaws to check the advance of Sedgwick. Gen. McLaws moved down the plank road to reinforce Barksdale and Wilcox, the latter of whom had been observing Banks' Ford, and who had been driven back to Salem Church. McLaws reaching Salem Church in time to relieve Wilcox from the pressure of overwhelming numbers, checked the advance of Sedgwick, and drove him back, with great loss to both parties, until night closed the conflict.

The enemy, however, was not yet defeated. One more struggle remained, and to make that the enemy during the night massed a heavy force against McLaws' left, in order to establish communication with Hooker along the river road. Anderson moved rapidly to the support of McLaws, and reached the church about 12 M., having marched fifteen miles. Gen. Lee, having arrived on the field, ordered Anderson to move round the church and establish his right on Early's left, (Early having come up from Hamilton's Crossing in rear of the enemy.) The enemy having weakened his left in order to force McLaws and gain the river road, Gen. Lee massed a heavy force upon this weakened part of the enemy, and at a concerted signal, Anderson and Early rushed upon the enemy's left.

The signal for the general attack was not given until just before sunset, when our men rushed upon the enemy like a hurricane. But little resistance was made, the beaten foe having fled in wild confusion in the direction of Banks' Ford. At dark a short pause ensued; but as soon as the moon rose, the enemy was speedily driven to Banks' Ford, and on that night of the 4th May ended this remarkable series of battles on the lines of the Rappahannock.

The enemy being driven from every point around Fredericksburg, Gen. Lee determined to make short work of Hooker at United States Ford. Therefore, Tuesday, noon Anderson was ordered to proceed immediately back to Chancellorsville, while McLaws was instructed to take up his position in front of United States Ford, at or near the junction of the old

Mine and River roads. But a drenching storm of wind and rain set in and continued without cessation until Wednesday forenoon, when it was discovered that Hooker, taking advantage of the darkness and the storm, had also retreated across the river the preceding night.

Our forces engaged in the fight did not exceed fifty thousand men. The enemy's is variously estimated at from one hundred thousand to one hundred and fifty thousand. Yet the greater gallantry of our troops, even despite the emergency into which their commander had brought them, enabled him not only to beat this immense army, but to capture several thousand prisoners, thirty or forty thousand small arms, several stands of colours, and an immense amount of personal property, and to kill and wound some twenty-five thousand men. It was a glorious week's work.*

We have not at present those lights before us necessary for a just criticism of the military aspects of these battles of the Rappahannock. They were undoubtedly a great victory for the Confederacy. But there were two remarkable misfortunes which diminished it. The breaking of our lines at Fredericksburg withdrew pursuit from Hooker. When thereupon our forces were turned upon Sedgwick, a second misfortune robbed

---

* The army which accomplished this work was, according to the Yankee description of it, a curiosity. Some of the military correspondence of the Yankee journals was more candid than usual, and admitted a shameful defeat by the "ragged rebels." One of these correspondents wrote:

"We had men enough, well enough equipped and well enough posted, to have devoured the ragged, imperfectly armed and equipped host of our enemies from off the face of the earth. Their artillery horses are poor, starved frames of beasts, tied on to their carriages and caissons with odds and ends of rope and strips of raw hide. Their supply and ammunition trains look like a congregation of all the crippled California emigrant trains that ever escaped off the desert out of the clutches of the rampaging Camanche Indians. The men are ill-dressed, ill-equipped and ill-provided—a set of ragmuffins that a man is ashamed to be seen among, even when he is a prisoner and can't help it. And yet they have beaten us fairly, beaten us all to pieces, beaten us so easily that we are objects of contempt even to their commonest private soldiers, with no shirts to hang out of the holes in their pantaloons, and cartridge-boxes tied round their waists with strands of rope."

us of a complete success; for he managed to secure his retreat by Banks' Ford, which exit might possibly have been cut off, and the exclusion of which would have secured his surrender. Of these events there is yet no official detail.

But a shadow greater than that of any partial misfortunes on the field rested on the Confederate victory of Chancellorsville. It was the death of Gen. Jackson. This event is important enough to require, even in the contracted limits of these supplementary pages, a separate title and a notice apart from our general narrative.

### THE DEATH OF "STONEWALL" JACKSON.

It was about eight o'clock on Saturday evening, 2d May, when Gen. Jackson and his staff, who were returning on the front of our line of skirmishers, were fired upon by a regiment of his own corps, who mistook the party for the enemy. At the time the General was only about fifty yards in advance of the enemy. He had given orders to fire at any thing coming up the road before he left the lines. The enemy's skirmishers appeared ahead of him and he turned to ride back. Just then some one cried out, "Cavalry!" "charge!" and immediately the regiment fired. The whole party broke forward to ride through our line to escape the fire. Capt. Boswell was killed and carried through the line by his horse, and fell amid our own men. The General himself was struck by three balls: one through the left arm, two inches below the shoulder joint, shattering the bone and severing the chief artery; another ball passed through same arm, between elbow and wrist, making its exit through the palm of the hand; a third ball entered the palm of the right hand about its middle, and passing through, broke two of the bones. As General Jackson was being borne from the field, one of the litter-bearers was shot down, and the General fell from the shoulders of the men, receiving a severe contusion, adding to the injury of the arm and injuring the side severely. The enemy's fire of artillery on the point was terrible. Gen. Jackson was left for five minutes until the fire slackened, then placed in an ambulance and carried to the field hospital at Wilderness Run. He lost a large amount of blood, and at one time told Dr. McGuire he thought he was dying, and would have bled to death, but a tourniquet was immediately applied. For two hours he was nearly pulseless from the shock.

Amputation of the arm was decided upon, and the operation was borne so well that hopes of a speedy recovery were confidently entertained. A few days had elapsed, and his physicians had decided to remove the distinguished sufferer to Richmond, when symptoms of pneumonia were unfortunately developed. The complication of this severe disease with his wounds left but little hope of his life, and on Sunday, the eighth day of his suffering, it was apparent that he was rapidly sinking, and he was informed that he was dying. The intelligence was received with no expression of disappointment or anxiety on the part of the dying hero; his only response was, "It is all right," which was repeated. He had previously said that he considered his wounds "a blessing," as Providence had always a good design in whatever it ordained, and to that Providence in which he had always trusted he committed himself with uninterrupted confidence. But once he regretted his early fall, and that was with reference to the immediate fortunes of the field. He said, "If I had not been wounded, or had had an hour more of daylight, I would have cut off the enemy from the road to the United States Ford, and we would have had them entirely surrounded, and they would have been obliged to surrender or cut their way out; they had no other alternative. My troops sometimes may fail in driving the enemy from a position, but the enemy always fail to drive my men from a position." This was said with a sort of smiling playfulness.

The following account of the dying moments of the hero is taken from the authentic testimony of a religious friend and companion:

"He endeavoured to cheer those who were around him. Noticing the sadness of his beloved wife, he said to her tenderly, 'I know you would gladly give your life for me, but I am perfectly resigned. Do not be sad—I hope I shall recover. Pray for me, but always remember in your prayer to use the petition, Thy will be done.' Those who were around him noticed a remarkable development of tenderness in his manner and feelings during his illness, that was a beautiful mellowing of that iron sternness and imperturbable calm that characterized him in his military operations. Advising his wife, in the event of his death, to return to her father's house, he remarked, 'You have a kind and good father. But there is no one so kind and good as your Heavenly Father.' When she told him that the doctors did not think he could live two hours, although he did not himself expect to die, he replied, 'It will be infinite gain to be translated to Heaven and be with Jesus.' He then said he had much to say to her, but was too weak.

"He had always desired to die, if it were God's will, on the Sabbath, and seemed to greet its light that day with peculiar pleasure, saying, with evident delight, 'It is the Lord's day;' and inquired anxiously what provision had been made for preaching to the army; and having ascertained that arrangements were made, he was contented. Delirium, which occasionally manifested itself during the last two days, prevented some of the utterances of his faith, which would otherwise have doubtless been made. His thoughts vibrated between religious subjects and the battle-field; now asking some questions about the Bible or church history, and then giving an order—'Pass the infantry to the front.' 'Tell Major Hawks to send forward provisions to the men.' 'Let us cross over the river, and rest under the shade of the trees'—until at last his gallant spirit gently passed over the dark river and entered on its rest."

It is not proposed here, nor could space be found within the limits of a supplementary chapter to make a record of the life and services of General Jackson. A very brief sketch is all that is possible; and indeed it is scarcely necessary to do more, as so much of his military life is already spread on the pages of this volume and intermixed with the general narrative of the war.

General Thomas Jonathan Jackson was born in Harrison county, Virginia, in 1825, and graduated at West Point in 1846. His first military services were in the Mexican war, and he behaved so well that he was brevetted major for his services. The Army Register and the actual history and facts of the Mexican war do not furnish the name of another person entering the war without position or office who attained the high rank of major in the brief campaign and series of battles from Vera Cruz to the city of Mexico.

At the close of the Mexican war, Jackson resigned his position in the army and obtained a professorship in the Virginia Military Institute. His services were not conspicuous here; Colonel Gilham was considered as the military genius of the school, and Thomas Jackson was but little thought of by the small hero-worshippers of Lexington. The cadets had but little partiality for the taciturn, praying professor.

Perhaps none of the acquaintances of Jackson were more surprised at his brilliant exhibitions of genius in this war, than those who knew his blank life at the Institute, and were familiar with the stiff and uninteresting figure that was to be seen every Sunday in a pew of the Presbyterian Church at Lexington. But true genius awaits occasion commensurate with its power and aspiration. The spirit of Jackson was trained in another school than that of West Point or Lexington, and had it been confined there, it never would have illuminated the page of history.

In the early periods of the war, Jackson, commissioned Colonel by the Governor of Virginia, was attached to General Johnston's command on the Upper Potomac. At Falling Waters, on the 2d of July, 1861, he engaged the advance of Patterson, and gave the Yankees one of the first exemplifications of his ready-witted strategy; as Patterson never knew that, for several hours, he was fighting an insignificant force, skillfully disposed to conceal their weakness, while Johnston was making his dispositions in the rear.

The first conspicuous services of Jackson in this war were rendered at Manassas in 1861; although the marks of active determination he had shown on the Upper Potomac, and the affair of Falling Waters, had already secured for him promotion to a Brigadier-Generalship. The author recollects some paragraphs in a Southern newspaper expressing great merriment at the first apparition of the future hero on the battle-field. His queer figure on horseback, and the habit of settling his chin in his stock, were very amusing to some correspondents, who made a flippant jest in some of the Southern newspapers of the military specimen of the Old Dominion. The jest is forgiven and forgotten in the tributes of admiration and love which were to ensue to the popular hero of the war.

We have already given in another part of this work (the first volume) an account of the remarkable expedition of Jackson in the depth of the winter of 1861-2 to Winchester, where he had been sent from Gen. Johnston's lines. The expedition was successful, and the march was made through an almost blinding storm of snow and sleet, our troops bivouacking at night in the forest, where many died from cold and exhaustion.

Without doubt, the most brilliant and extraordinary passage in the military life of General Jackson was the ever famous campaign of the summer of 1862 in the Valley of Virginia. From the Valley he reached by rapid marches the lines of the Chickahominy in time to play a conspicuous part in the splendid conclusion of the campaign of the Peninsula.

Since the battles of the Chickahominy, the military services of General Jackson are comparatively fresh in the recollections of the public. We have already seen in these pages that the most substantial achievements and brilliant successes of last summer's campaign in Virginia are to be attributed to him.

The participation of Jackson in the campaign of Maryland, and that of the Rappahannock, shared their glory, but without occasion for observation on those distinct and independent movements which were his *forte*, and for the display of which he had room in the Valley campaign, and that against Pope.

The most noble testimony of the services of the departed hero in the battle of Chancellorsville is to be found in the note of Gen. Lee, which is characteristic of his own generosity and worth. Gen. Lee wrote him:

"General: I have just received your note informing me that you were wounded. I cannot express my regret at the occurrence. Could I have dictated events, I should have chosen for the good of the country to have been disabled in your stead.

"I congratulate you upon the victory which is due to your skill and energy."

Jackson's response to his attendants on hearing the note read is said to have been, "Gen. Lee should give the glory to God." It was an expression of his modesty and reverence.

A friend relates that a few nights before this battle, an equally characteristic incident occurred that is worthy of record. He was discussing with one of his aids the probability and issue of a battle, when he became unusually excited. After talking it over fully, he paused, and with deep humility and reverence said, "My trust is in God;" then, as if the sound of battle was in his ear, he raised himself to his tallest stature, and with flashing eyes and a face all blazoned with the fire of the conflict, he exclaimed, "I wish they would come."

A strong religious sentiment combined with practical energy, and an apparent dash of purpose qualified by the silent calculations of genius, were the remarkable traits of the character of Jackson. It was his humble Christian faith combined with the spirit of the warrior that made that rare and lofty type of martial prowess that has shrined Jackson among the great heroes of the age.

From all parts of the living world have come tributes to his fame. "He was," says the London *Times*, "one of the most consummate Generals that "this century has produced. \* \* \* That mixture of daring and judg-"ment which is the mark of 'Heaven-born' Generals, distinguished him be-"yond any man of his time. Although the young Confederacy has been "illustrated by a number of eminent soldiers, yet the applause and devotion "of his countrymen, confirmed by the judgment of European nations, have given the first place to Gen. Jackson. The military feats he accomplished moved the minds of the people with astonishment, which it is only given to the highest genius to produce. The blows he struck at the enemy were as terrible and decisive as those of Bonaparte himself."

It is proposed already that the State of Virginia shall build for him a stately tomb, and strike a medal to secure the memory of his name. These expressions of a nation's gratitude may serve its own pleasure. But otherwise they are unnecessary.

> "Dear son of memory, great heir of fame,
> What need'st thou such weak witness of thy name?"

## CHAPTER XII.

A Period of Disasters*,DEPARTMENT OF THE MISSISSIPPI...Grant's March
Upon Vicksburg...Its Steps and Incidents...The Engagement of Port Gibson...
The Evacuation of Jackson...The Battle of Baker's Creek...Pemberton's
Declarations as to the Defence of Vicksburg...A Grand Assault upon "the
Heroic City"...Its Repulse...*The Final Surrender of Vicksburg*...How the Public Mind of the South was Shocked...Consequences of the Disaster...How it
Involved Affairs on the Lower Mississippi...Other Theatres of the War...THE
CAMPAIGN IN PENNSYLVANIA AND MARYLAND...Hooker Manouvred Out of Virginia...The Recapture of Winchester...The Second Invasion of the Northern
Territory...The Alarm of the North...General Lee's Object in the Invasion of
Maryland and Pennsylvania...His Essays at Conciliation...The Errour of Such
Policy...The Advance of his Lines into Pennsylvania...The Battle of Gettysburg...The Three Days' Engagements...Death of Barksdale...Pickett's Splendid Charge on the Batteries...Repulse of the Confederates...Anxiety and
Alarm in Richmond...Lee's Safe Retreat into Virginia...Mystery of his
Movement...Recovery of the Confidence of the South * * * * * Review
of the Present Aspects of the War...Comparison Between the Disasters of
1862 and those of 1863...The Vitals of the Confederacy yet Untouched...
Review of the Civil Administration...President Davis, his Cabinet and his
Favourites...His Private Quarrels...His Deference to European Opinion...
Decline of the Finances of the Confederacy...Reasons of this Decline—The
Confederate Brokers...The Blockade-Runners...The Disaffections of Property-
Holders...The Spirit of the Army...The Moral Resolution of the Confederacy...How the Enemy has Strengthened it...The Prospects of the Future.

We find it necessary to give another chapter to the extension of our narrative beyond its appropriate limit. We shall proceed rapidly with a general reference to such events as may exhibit the condition of the Confederacy at the time of this writing, reserving details for another volume that will properly cover the period of the *third* year of the War. That year has opened with disasters, at which we can now glance only imperfectly, for upon them the lights of time have scarcely yet developed.

## DEPARTMENT OF THE MISSISSIPPI.

As the attention of the reader returns to the busy scenes of the war, it is taken by one of those sudden translations, so common in this history, from Virginia to the distant theatres of the West. The smoke of battle yet lingered on the Rappahannock, when the attention of the public was suddenly drawn to the Valley of the Mississippi by the startling announcement that an army of the enemy was on the overland march against Vicksburg, that had so long defied an attack from the water.

We have at this time only very uncertain materials for the history of the campaign in Mississippi. We must at present trust ourselves to a very general outline that will exclude any considerable extent of comment; satisfied that what we can do at present to interest the reader is simply to put certain leading occurrences of the campaign in their natural succession, and make a compact resume of events which, up to this time, have been related in a very confused and scattering style.

By running the gauntlet of our batteries at Vicksburg with his transports, Grant avoided the necessity of the completion of the canal, and secured a passage of the river, after leading his troops over the narrow peninsula below Vicksburg, at any point above Port Hudson which he might select. It appears that the defences at Grand Gulf, twenty-two miles south of Warrenton, at the mouth of Black River, were only constructed after the enemy had succeeded in getting some of his vessels between Port Hudson and Vicksburg. The Black River being navigable for some distance, they were intended to obstruct the passage of a force to the rear of Vicksburg by this route.

The abandonment of our works there after a severe bombardment, opened the door to the enemy, and the battle of Port Gibson, fought on the first day of May, put them still further on their way to Vicksburg. The evacuation of Port Gibson by General Bowen was followed by that of Bayou Pierre, and his forces were withdrawn across the Big Black, within twenty miles of Vicksburg.

So far in the campaign the enemy had a remarkable advantage. Our generals were wholly unable to penetrate his designs, and were compelled to wait the progressive steps of their development.

It was impossible to foresee the precise point at which the blow would be struck, or to form any probable conjecture of the immediate objects of the enemy's enterprise. When Grant's transports had succeeded in passing the batteries at Vicksburg, he had a river front of more than a hundred miles where he could land. The point of his landing having been determined at Grand Gulf, it was still uncertain whether he meant to approach Vicksburg by the river, under cover of his gunboats, or whether he would attempt to circumscribe the place and cut our communications east. It subsequently appeared that the latter enterprise was selected by the enemy, and that Jackson was the immediate point of attack.

On the 14th of May the enemy took possession of Jackson. Gen. Johnston was entrusted with the active command of the Confederate forces in the Southwest too late to save those disastrous results which had already occurred; and the very first step to which he was forced by existing circumstances, was the evacuation of Jackson. But the enemy's occupation of the capital of Mississippi seems to have been but an unimportant incident, and it is probable that, even with inferiour forces on our side, a battle would have been risked there if Jackson had been of greater importance than as a point of railroad in possession of the enemy.

Although Gen. Bowen, in the engagement of Port Gibson, failed to check the rapid advance of the enemy, it was understood that he had been able to evacuate in good order his position south of the Big Black, and establish a line of defence, extending along that stream east from the Mississippi, so as to secure Vicksburg against assault from the south. This, the main line of our defence, was occupied by General Pemberton with heavy reinforcements from Vicksburg.

On the 16th of May occurred the bloody battle of Baker's Creek, (on the Jackson and Vicksburg road,) in which the force under Pemberton was defeated with considerable loss of artillery. On the following day the Confederates again sustained a disaster at Big Black Bridge; and on the 18th Vicksburg was closely invested by the enemy, and the right of his army rested on the river above the town.

It is probable that it was to give time for reinforcements to arrive in the enemy's rear, who, flushed with victory at Grand Gulf, Port Gibson and Jackson, had turned back from the latter on the rear defences of Vicksburg, that Gen. Pemberton, perhaps, unwisely, advanced from his works to meet Grant in the open field and hold him in check, and thus, from greatly inadequate forces, suffered the disheartening disasters of Baker's Creek and Big Black Bridge. As a last resort he retired behind his works with a weakened and somewhat dispirited but still glorious little army. The unfortunate commander appeased the clamour against himself by an apparently noble candour and memorable words of heroism. He said that it had been declared that he would sell Vicksburg, and exhorted his soldiers to follow him to see the price at which he would sell it, for it would not be less than his own life and that of every man in his command. Those words were not idle utterances; they deserve to be commemorated; they were heroic only in proportion as they were fulfilled and translated into action.

The events of the 19th, 20th and 21st of May wearied the Yankees, who imagined that they saw in their grasp the palm of the Mississippi. So fully assured were they of victory, that they posponed it from day to day. To storm the works was to take Vicksburg, in their opinion, and when it was known on the morning of the 21st that at ten o'clock next morning the whole line of Confederate works would be assaulted, the credulous and vain enemy accounted success so certain that it was already given to the wings of the telegraph.

Indeed, there is no doubt that at one hour of this famous day, McClernand, the Yankee General who made the assault on the left, sent a dispatch to Grant that he had taken three forts and would soon be in possession of the city. But the success was a deceitful one. The redoubts carried by the enemy brought him within the pale of a devouring fire. At every point he was repulsed; and with reference to completeness of victory, exhibitions of a devoted courage, and the carnage accomplished in the ranks of the enemy, these battles of Vicksburg must be accounted among the most famous in the annals of the war.

But despite the discouragements of the repulse, there still remained to the enemy the prospects of a siege under circumstances of peculiar and extraordinary advantage. Although Grant's attack was made from Grand Gulf, that place was not long his base; and when he gained Haines' Bluff and the Yazoo, all communication with it was abandoned. He was enabled to rely on Memphis and the river above Vicksburg for food and reinforcements; his communications were open with the entire West; and the Northern newspapers urgently demanded that the utmost support should be given to a favourite general, and that the Trans-Mississippi should be stripped of troops to supply him with reinforcements.

But the South still entertained hopes of the safety of Vicksburg. It was stated in Richmond by those who should have been well informed, that the garrison numbered considerably more than twenty thousand men, and was provisioned for a siege of six months. Nearly every day the telegraph had some extravagance to tell concerning the supreme safety of Vicksburg and the confidence of the garrison. The heroic promise of Pemberton that the city should not fall until the last man had fallen in the last ditch was called to the popular remembrance. The confidence of the South was swollen even to insolence by these causes; and although a few of the intelligent doubted the extravagant assurances of the safety of

Vicksburg, the people at large received them with an unhesitating and exultant faith.

Under these circumstances the surprise and consternation of the people of the South may be imagined, when, without the least premonition, the announcement came that the select anniversary of *the Fourth of July* had been signalized by the capitulation of Vicksburg, without a fight; the surrender of twenty odd thousand troops as prisoners; and the abandonment to the Yankees of one of the greatest prizes of artillery that had yet been made in the war. The news fell upon Richmond like a thunder-clap from clear skies. The day of our humiliation at Vicksburg had been ill-selected. But it was said that Gen. Pemberton was advised that the enemy intended to make a formidable assault on the next day, and that he was unwilling to await it with an enfeebled garrison, many of whom were too weak to bear arms in their hands. The condition of the garrison, although certainly not as extreme as that which Pemberton had heroically prefigured as the alternative of surrender, and although holding no honourable comparison with the amount of privation and suffering borne in other sieges recorded in history, was yet deplorable.* Our troops had suffered more from exhausting labours than from hunger; and their spirit had been distressed by the melancholy isolation of a siege in which they were cut off from communication with their homes, and perhaps by other causes which are not now certainly known. Patience is not a virtue of Southern soldiers; and for it at least the garrison of Vicksburg will not be conspicuous in history.

It is not possible at this time to determine the consequences of the fall of Vicksburg. That it was the ostensible key to a vast amount of disputed territory in the West, and that it involved a network of important positions, were universally admitted in the South. But this estimate of its importance is intricate and uncertain, and awaits the development of events. The army of Johnston was saved, instead of being risked in an attack on Grant's rear at Vicksburg, and is still disputing the enemy's encroachments in the Southwest. We must leave its movements to more convenient and future narration.

But we must recognize the fact of various disasters which have immediately ensued from the fall of Vicksburg. It compelled the surrender of Port Hudson as its necessary consequence.* It neutralized in a great measure a remarkable

---

* The fall of Port Hudson did not take place until after a prolonged and gallant resistance, the facts of which may be briefly commemorated here. On the morning of the 22d May, the enemy, under command of Gen. Banks, pushed his infantry forward within a mile of our breastworks. Having taken his position for the investment of our works, he advanced with his whole force against the breastworks, directing his main attack against the left, commanded by Col. Steadman. Vigourous assaults were also made against the extreme left of Col. Miles and Gen. Beale, the former of whom commanded on the centre, the latter on the right. On the left the attack was made by a brigade of negroes, composing about three regiments, together with the same force of white Yankees across a bridge which had been built over Sandy creek. About five hundred negroes in front advanced at double-quick within one hundred and fifty yards of the works, when the artillery on the river bluff, and two light pieces on our left, opened upon them, and at the same time they were received with volleys of musketry. The negroes fled every way in perfect confusion, and, according to the enemy's report, six hundred of them perished. The repulse on Miles' left was decisive.

On the 13th of June a communication was received from Gen. Banks, demanding the unconditional surrender of the post. He complimented the garrison in high terms for their endurance. He stated that his artillery was equal to any in extent and efficiency; that his men outnumbered ours five to one; and that he demanded the surrender in the name of humanity, to prevent a useless sacrifice of life. Gen. Gardner replied that his duty required him to defend the post, and he must refuse to entertain any such proposition.

On the morning of the 14th, just before day, the fleet and all the land batteries, which the enemy had succeeded in erecting at one hundred to three hundred yards from our breastworks, opened fire at the same time. About daylight, under cover of the smoke, the enemy advanced along the whole line, and in many places approached within ten feet of our works. Our brave soldiers were wide awake, and, opening upon them, drove them back in confusion, a great number of them being left dead in the ditches. One entire division and a brigade were ordered to charge the position of the 1st Mississippi and the 9th Alabama, and by the mere physical pressure of numbers some of them got within the works, but all these were immediately killed. After a sharp contest of two hours, the enemy were every where repulsed, and withdrew to their old lines.

During the remainder of the month of June, there was heavy skirmishing daily, with constant firing night and day from the gun and mortar boats. Du-

series of successes on the Lower Mississippi, including the victory of Gen. Taylor at Ashland, Louisiana, which broke one of the points of investment around Vicksburg, and his still more glorious achievement in the capture of Brashear City. The defence of the cherished citadel of the Mississippi had involved exposure and weakness in other quarters. It had almost stripped Charleston of troops; it had taken many thousand men from Bragg's army; and it had made such requisitions on his force for the newly organized lines in Mississippi, that that General was compelled or induced, wisely or unwisely, to fall back from Tullahoma, to give up the country on the Memphis and Charleston railroad, and practically to abandon the defence of Middle Tennessee.

While people in Richmond were discussing the story of Vicksburg, the grief and anxiety of that disaster were suddenly swallowed up by what was thought to be even more painful news from the army of Gen. Lee. For once it appeared to the popular imagination that a great disaster in the West had a companion in the East. The fall of Vicksburg was preceded but one day by the battle of Gettysburg. To that bat-

---

ring the siege of six weeks, from May 27th to July 7th, inclusive, the enemy must have fired from fifty to seventy-five thousand shot and shell, yet not more than twenty-five men were killed by these projectiles. They had worse dangers than these to contend against.

About the 29th or 30th of June, the garrison's supply of meat gave out, when Gen. Gardner ordered the mules to be butchered, after ascertaining that the men were willing to eat them. At the same time the supply of ammunition was becoming exhausted, and at the time of the surrender there were only twenty rounds of cartridges left, with a small supply for artillery.

On Tuesday, July 7th, salutes were fired from the enemy's batteries and gunboats, and loud cheering was heard along the entire line, and Yankees who were in conversing distance of our men told them that Vicksburg had fallen. That night about ten o'clock Gen. Gardner summoned a council of war, who, without exception, decided that it was impossible to hold out longer, considering that the provisions of the garrison were exhausted, the ammunition almost expended, and a large proportion of the men sick or so exhausted as to be unfit for duty. The surrender was accomplished on the morning of the 9th. The number of the garrison which surrendered was between five and six thousand, of whom not more than half were effective men for duty.

tle-field we must translate the reader by a very rapid summary of the operations which led to it.

### THE CAMPAIGN IN PENNSYLVANIA AND MARYLAND.

By a series of rapid movements, Gen. Lee had succeeded in manœuvreing Hooker out of Virginia. On the extreme left, Jenkins, with his cavalry, began the movement by threatening Milroy at Winchester, while under the dust of Stuart's noisy cavalry reviews, designed to engage the attention of the enemy, Ewell's infantry marched into the valley by the way of Front Royal. Advancing by rapid marches across the Blue Ridge, Gen. Ewell, the successor to Jackson's command, fell like a thunder-bolt upon Milroy at Winchester and Martinsburg, capturing the greater part of his forces, many guns, and heavy supplies of grain, ammunition and other military stores. The Yankees' own account of their disaster indicated the magnitude of our success. The New York *Herald* declared, "not "a thing was saved except that which was worn or carried "upon the persons of the troops. Three entire batteries of "field artillery and one battery of siege guns—all the artillery "of the command in fact—about two hundred and eighty wag- "ons, over twelve hundred horses and mules, all the commis- "sary and quartermaster's stores, and ammunition of all "kinds, over six thousand muskets, and small arms without "stint, the private baggage of the officers and men, all fell "into the hands of the enemy. Of the seven thousand men "of the command, but from sixteen hundred to two thousand "have as yet arrived here, leaving to be accounted for five "thousand men."

After accomplishing his victory at Winchester, Gen. Ewell moved promptly up to the Potomac, and occupied such fords as we might desire to use, in the event it should be deemed proper to advance into the enemy's country. The sudden appearance of Ewell in the Valley of the Shenandoah, coupled with the demonstration at Culpeper, made it necessary for Hooker to abandon Fredericksburg entirely, and to occupy the strong positions at Centreville and Manassas, so as to interpose his army between us and Washington, and thus prevent a sudden descent from the Blue Ridge by Gen. Lee upon the Yankee capital. Meanwhile, Longstreet and Hill were following fast upon Ewell's track, the former reaching Ashby's and Snicker's Gaps in time to prevent any movement upon Ewell's rear, and the latter (Hill) getting to Culpeper in good season to protect Longstreet's rear, or to co-operate with him in the event of an attack upon his flank, or to guard against any demonstration in the direction of Richmond.

Having gained over the Yankee commander the important advantage of the military initiative, and firmly established his communications in the rear of his base of operations on the other side of the Potomac, Gen. Lee was in a position to hurl his forces wherever he might desire; and it was soon announced in the North that Hooker had declined a battle in Virginia, and that the second invasion of the Northern territory had been commenced by the Confederates under auspices that had not attended the first. It was soon known that the light-horsemen of Lee had appeared upon his war path in the southern region of Pennsylvania. For weeks the dashing and adventurous cavalry of Jenkins and Imboden were persistently busy in scouring the country between the Susquehannah and the Alleghanies, the Monocacy and the Potomac, and from the lines before Harrisburg to the very gates of Washington and Baltimore their trumpets had sounded.

The North was thrown into paroxysms of terrour. At the first news of the invasion, Lincoln had called for a hundred thousand men to defend Washington. Governor Andrews offered the whole military strength of Massachusetts in the terrible crisis. Governor Seymour, of New York, summoned McClellan to grave consultations respecting the defences of Pennsylvania. The bells were set to ringing in Brooklyn. Regiment after regiment was sent off from New York to Philadelphia. The famous Seventh regiment took the field and proceeded to Harrisburg. The Dutch farmers in the valley drove their cattle to the mountains, and the archives were removed from Harrisburg.

Nor did the alarm exceed the occasion for it. It was obvious to the intelligent in the North that their army of the Potomac was the only real obstacle which could impede the triumphant march of the army of Lee into the very heart of the Yankee States, and in whatever direction he might choose to push his campaign. The press attempted some ridiculous comfort by writing vaguely of thousands of militia springing to arms. But the history of modern warfare afforded better instruction, for it taught clearly enough that an invading army of regular and victorious troops could only be effectively checked by the resistance of a similar army in the field, or of fortified places strong enough to compel a regular siege. In certain circumstances, a single battle had often decided the fate of a long war; and the South easily indulging the prospect of the defeat of Hooker's forces, was elated with renewed anticipations of an early peace.

While the destruction of Hooker's army was the paramount object of Gen. Lee's campaign, he had unfortunately fallen into the errour of attempting to conciliate the people of the North and to court the opinions of Europe by forswearing all acts of retaliation and omitting even the devastation of the enemy's country. The fertile acres of the Pennsylvania Valley were untouched by violent hands; all requisitions for supplies were paid for in Confederate money; and a protection was given to the private property of the enemy, which had never been afforded even to that of our own citizens. So far as the orders of Gen. Lee on these subjects restrained pillage and private outrage, they were sustained by public sentiment in the South, which, in fact, never desired that we should rotaliate upon the Yankees by a precise imitation of their enormities and crimes. But retaliation is not only the work of pillagers and marauders. Its ends might have been accomplished, as far as the people of the South desired, by inflicting upon the enemy some injury commensurate with what they had suffered at his hands; the smallest measure of which would have been the devastation of the country, which, done by our army in line of battle, would neither have risked demoralization nor detracted from discipline. Such a return for the outrages which the South had suffered from invading hordes of the Yankees, would in fact have been short of justice, and so far have possessed the merit of magnanimity. But Gen. Lee was resolved on more excessive magnanimity; and at the time the Yankee armies, particularly in the Southwestern portion of the Confederacy, were enacting outrages which recalled the darkest days of mediæval warfare, our forces in the Pennsylvania Valley were protecting the private property of Yankees, composing their alarm, and making a display of stilted chivalry to the amusement of the Dutch farmers and to the intense disgust of our own people.*

---

* A letter from our lines in Mississippi thus describes the outrages of the enemy there, which were cotemporary with Lee's civilities in Pennsylvania:

"I thought the condition of Northern Mississippi, and the country around my own home in Memphis, deplorable. There robberies were committed, houses were burned, and occasionally a helpless man or woman was murdered; but here, around Jackson and Vicksburg, there are no terms used in all the calendar of crimes which could convey any adequate conception of the revolting enormities perpetrated by our foes. Women have been robbed of their jewelry and wearing apparel—stripped almost to nakedness in the presence of jeering Dutch; ear-rings have been torn from their ears, and rings from bleeding fingers. Every house has been pillaged, and thousands burned. The whole country between the Big Black and the Mississippi, and all that district through which Grant's army passed, is one endless scene of desolation. This is not the worst; robbery and murder are surely bad enough, but worse than all this, women have been subjected to enormities worse than death.

"Negroes, men and women, who can leave their homes, are forced or enticed away. The children alone are left. Barns and all descriptions of farmhouses have been burned. All supplies, bacon and flour, are seized for the use of the invading army, and the wretched inhabitants left to starve. The roads along which Grant's army has moved, are strewn with all descriptions of furniture, wearing apparel and private property. In many instances husbands have been arrested and threatened with instant death by the hangman's rope, in order to make their wives reveal the places of concealment of their valuable effects. The poor women are made to ransom their sons, daughters and husbands. The worst slaves are selected to insult, taunt and revile their masters, and the wives and daughters of their masters."

If Gen. Lee had supposed that his moderate warfare would conciliate the Yankees, he was greatly mistaken; for it is precisely this warfare which irritates a people without intimidating them. The simple object of his campaign appears to have been the defeat of Hooker, which would uncover Washington and Baltimore. The critical conjuncture which had been so long sought was the battle of Gettysburg.

We must spare here many of the details of those movements which brought the two armies in contact, and trust ourselves to a brief and general account of this great engagement in Pennsylvania, followed, as it is, by a rapid current of events there and elsewhere.

Having crossed the Potomac at or near Williamsport, the Confederates marched to Hagerstown, to Greencastle and thence to Chambersburg. Ewell, who held the advance, went as far as Carlisle, some twelve miles from Harrisburg. Meanwhile, Hooker, having withdrawn his forces from Stafford, moved to and across the Potomac, and took up a line extending from Washington to Baltimore, expecting General Lee to offer him battle in Maryland. Finding himself disappointed in this, and compelled by pride or by his superiours, he relinquished his command to Meade, who, finding out that Lee had deflected in his march through Pennsylvania, and was moving down the Baltimore turnpike from Chambersburg, moved from Baltimore on the same road to meet him. The two armies which had ceased to confront each other since the breaking up of the Fredericksburg lines, found themselves again face to face near Gettysburg on Wednesday, July 1st.

The action of the 1st July was brought on by General Reynolds, who held the enemy's advance, and who thought himself in superiour force to the Confederates. He paid the penalty of his temerity by a defeat; he was overpowered and outflanked, and fell mortally wounded on the field.

In this fight the corps of A. P. Hill was generally engaged; but, about one hour after its opening, General Ewell, who was moving from the direction of Carlisle, came up and took a position on our extreme left. Two divisions of this corps, Rhodes' and Early's, advanced upon and engaged the enemy in front. Longstreet, who was not engaged in the fight of the first day, swung around his column to A. P. Hill's right, but did not take position for action until Thursday morning. The result of the first day was that the enemy was repulsed at all points of the line engaged, and driven over the range of hills to the south of Gettysburg, through the town and about half a mile beyond. At this point is a mountain which commands the ground in front for a mile on all sides. This the enemy retreated to after their repulse, and immediately fortified, their line occupying the mountain, and extending on the right and left of it.

The early part of Thursday, the 22d of July, wore away without any positive demonstration of attack on either side. Late in the afternoon an artillery attack was made by our forces on the left and centre of the enemy, which was rapidly followed by the advance of our infantry, Longstreet's corps on our side being principally engaged. A fearful but indecisive conflict ensued, and for four hours the sound of musketry was incessant. In the fight we lost a number of officers, among them Gen. Barksdale of Mississippi, whose brave and generous spirit expired, where he preferred to die, on the ensanguined field of battle. Of this "haughty rebel," who had fallen within their lines, the Yankees told with devilish satisfaction the story that his end was that of extreme agony, and his last words were to crave as a dying boon a cup of water and a stretcher from an ambulance boy. The letter of a Yankee officer testifies that the brave and suffering hero declared with his last breath that he was proud of the cause he died fighting for; proud of the manner in which he received his death; and confident that his countrymen were invincible.

The third day's battle was commenced by the Confederates. The enemy's position on the mountain was apparently impregnable, for there was no conceivable advance or approach that could not be raked and crossed with the artillery. The reserve artillery and all the essentials to insure victory to the Yankees were in position at the right time. All the heights and every advantageous position along the entire line where artillery could be massed or a battery planted, frowned down on the Confederates through brows of brass and iron. On the slopes of this mountain occurred one of the most terrific combats of modern times, in which three hundred cannon were belching forth their thunders at one time, and nearly two hundred thousand muskets were being discharged as rapidly as men hurried with excitement and passion could load them.

The battle of Friday had commenced early in the morning. With the exception from ten o'clock in the morning to one in in the afternoon, it lasted all day. The Confederates did not succeed in holding any of the crests, although one or two were reached; and night again closed on the smoke-wrapped field.

The most glorious incident of Gettysburg, and the one upon which the eye of history will beam, was the charge of our devoted men upon the deadly heights where turned the tide of battle. The principal stronghold of the enemy was known as McPherson's Heights, where his centre rested. In Thursday's fight this important position had for a short time been in possession of a single one of our brigades—Wright's noble Georgians—who had charged it with the bayonet and captured the heavy batteries on the crest, but were unable to hold it for want of timely support.

In Friday's contest, a more formidable and elaborate attempt was to be made to wrest from the enemy the crest which was the key of his position. Pickett's division being in the advance, was supported on the right by Wilson's brigade, and on the left by Heth's division, commanded by Pettigrew. The steady movement of Pickett's men into the tempest of fire and steel, against a mountain bristling with guns, had nothing to exceed it in sublimity on any of the battle-fields of the revolution. Into the sheets of artillery fire advanced the unbroken lines of our men. The devoted Confederates are struggling not only against the enemy's artillery, but against a severe fire from heavy masses of his infantry, posted behind a stone fence. But nothing checks their advance; they storm the fence, they shoot the gunners, and Kemper's and Armistead's banners are already planted on the enemy's works.

There is no doubt but that at this auspicious moment a proper amount of support to Pickett would have secured his position, and carried the fortunes of the day. But that support was not at hand. Pettigrew's division had faltered, and that gallant commander in vain strove to rally the raw troops. In the meantime, the enemy had moved around strong flanking bodies of infantry, and was rapidly gaining Pickett's rear. With overwhelming numbers in our font, almost hemmed in by the enemy, the order is given to fall back. The retreating line is pressed heavily. It does not give way. But many noble spirits who had passed safely through the fiery ordeal of the advance and charge, now fall on the right and on the left.

In this great battle, though unfavorable to us, the enemy's loss probably exceeded our own, as the Yankees were closely crowded on the hills, and devoured by our artillery fire. The information of the enemy's loss is perhaps most accurately obtained from the bulletin furnished by his Surgeon General, which stated that he had something over 12,000 Yankee wounded under his control. Counting one killed for four wounded, and making some allowance for a large class of wounded men who had not come under the control of the official referred to, we are justified in stating the enemy's loss in casualties at Gettysburg, as somewhere between fifteen and eighteen thousand. Our loss, slighter by many thousands in comparison, was yet frightful enough. On our side, Pickett's division had been engaged in the hottest work of the day, and the havoc in its ranks was appalling. Its losses on this day are famous, and should be commemorated in detail. Every Brigadier in the division was killed or wounded. Out of twenty-four regimental officers, only two escaped unhurt. The Colonels of five Virginia regiments were killed. The 9th Virginia went in two hundred and fifty strong, and came out with only thirty-eight men; while the equally gallant 19th rivaled the terrible glory of such devoted courage.

The recoil at Gettysburg was fatal, not necessarily, but by the course of events, to Gen. Lee's campaign; and the return of his army to its defensive lines in Virginia, was justly regarded in the South as a reverse in the general fortunes of the contest. Yet the immediate results of the battle of Gettysburg must be declared to have been to a great extent negative. The Confederates did not gain a victory, neither did the enemy. The general story of the contest is simple. Lee had been unable to prevent the enemy from taking the highlands, many of them with very steep declivities, and nearly a mile in slope. The battle was an effort of the Confederates to take those heights. The right flank, the left flank, the centre were successively the aim of determined and concentrated assaults. The Yankee lines were broken and driven repeatedly. But inexhaustible reserves and a preponderant artillery, advantageously placed, saved them from rout.

The first news received in Richmond of Gen. Lee's retreat, was from Yankee sources, which represented his army as a disorganized mass of fugitives unable to cross the Potomac on account of recent floods, and at the mercy of an enemy immensely superiour in numbers and flushed with victory. This news and that of the fall of Vicksburg reached the Confederate Capital the same day. Twenty-four hours served to dash the hope of an early peace, and to overcloud the horizon of the war. The temptation of despair was again whispered to weak minds. It was the second period of great disaster to the South, and renewed a grief similar to what had been expended a year ago upon the sorrowful stories of Donelson and New Orleans.

But happily in this instance the public despondency was of short duration. A few days brought news from our lines, which exploded the falsehoods of the Yankees, and assured the people of the South that the engagements of Gettysburg had resulted in worsting the enemy, in killing and wounding a number exceeding our own, and in the capture of a large number of prisoners. The public was yet further satisfied that the falling back of our army, at least as far as Hagerstown, was a movement dictated by general considerations of strategy and prudence. It consoled itself that the subsequent retirement of our forces into Virginia was the excess of safety; and it found reason for congratulation that the retreat of Lee to his old lines was accomplished with a dexterity and success that foiled the enemy, and disappointed the greater portion of his triumph.

But notwithstanding these causes of moderate thankfulness, it must be confessed that the retreat from Hagerstown across the Potomac was an inconsequence and a mystery to the intelligent public. Lee's position there was strong; his force was certainly adequate for another battle; preparations were made for aggressive movements; and in the midst of all came a sudden renouncement of the campaign, and the retreat into Virginia. The history of this untimely retreat has not been developed; but there is one fact to assist the explanation of it, and that is that the authorities at Richmond were much more alarmed than Gen. Lee, and much less capable than the commander, himself of judging the military situation from which his army was recalled. The troops availed themselves of no other refuge than that of their own soil; they had not been defeated or seriously worsted; and so far the public had its secondary wish for the safety of the army. But this did not exclude mortification on the part of those who believed that Gen. Lee had abandoned the enemy's territory, not as a consequence of defeat, but from the undue timidity or the arrogant disposition of the authorities who controlled him. The grounds of such a belief are not certainly stated; but its existence in the public mind is a fact to be recognized by the historian, and to be determined by evidence when time and occasion shall produce it.

\* \* \* \* \* \* \* \* \*

The check at Gettysburg and the fall of Vicksburg, which

we have seized upon as the prominent events of the summer of 1863, and of which we hope hereafter, in another volume, to give a more minute and faithful account, in connection with many cotemporary or closely consequent events, which are here omitted, afford a natural pause in which we may well review the events of the revolution, and speculate on its distant or ultimate future.

The disasters to which we have briefly referred, although considerable, were far from being desperate, and were scarcely occasions of any serious alarm in the South, as to the ultimate issue of the struggle. The military condition of the country was certainly far better than at the former unhappy period of the spring of 1862. Then our armies were feeble, and, in a great measure, disorganized; the conscription law had not gone into operation, and our reduced forces were scattered along an extended frontier. Now well disciplined and seasoned armies hold with compact forces the critical positions in the Confederacy. The loss of territory, which in a European campaign, where inland fortresses and great cities give convenient footholds to an invading army, would have been estimated as a fatal disadvantage, had a very different signification in a war between the two great American powers. Indeed it may be said that the armies of our enemy scarcely did more than hold the ground they stood upon, and that in a war now passing into its third year, they had failed to touch the vitals of the Confederacy. The temporary cession of large bodies of territory to them, was really to their disadvantage in military respects; for it occasioned the necessity of extending their lines of communication, exposing their rear, and subjecting themselves, on every side, to the dangers of a hostile country, where there were no great fortresses or citadels to protect them.

But it must be confessed that there were to be found at this time but few subjects of congratulation in the internal condition of the Confederacy. The civil administration, in many of the departments, was ignorant, defective and, in some instances, oppressive. The appendage of Congress might well have been dispensed with in our revolution, for it accomplished nothing; all its legislation was patch-work, and its measures but the weak echoes of the newspapers. The extraordinary cabinet of Mr. Davis still survived as a ridiculous cypher; for its members never dared to raise their voices on any public measure, or to assert their existence beyond signing their names to certify the laws and orders of the government or the will of the President.

The military pragmatism of the President was his worst failing. He had treated Price, among the earliest heroes of the war, with cold and insolent neglect. He had constrained Gustavus Smith to resign, and deprived the country of one of its most brilliant Generals. He had taken the unfair opportunity of a sick furlough on the part of Beauregard to deprive him of his command in the West and give it to a favourite. He had even attempted to put Jackson in leading strings; for it was the Presidential order that set bounds to his famous Winchester expedition, and that would have timidly recalled him from his splendid campaign in the Valley. Nor was this all. There was reason to suppose that Lee's return from the territory of the North was constrained by the views of the Executive, and that the President, who had once defeated the capture of Washington by his interference at the first field of Manassas, had again repeated his intermeddling, removed a decisive victory from the grasp of our army, and turned back the war for years.

While such was the envious or ignorant interference of the President with our most meritorious Generals, he was not without favourites. While he quarreled with such men as Price, Beauregard, Gustavus Smith and Johnston, he maintained such favourites as Holmes, Heth, Lovell and Pemberton. No man was ever more sovereign in his likes and dislikes. Favourites were elevated to power and the noblest spirits consigned to obscurity by the fiat of a single man in the Confederacy, and that man one of the strongest prejudices, the harshest obstinacy, and the most ungovernable fondness for parasites.

In this war Mr. Davis has evidently been anxious to appear in the eyes of Europe as the military genius of the Confederacy, as well as the head of its civil administration. He has been careless of public opinion at home. But this has been no proof of stoicism or of greatness; it has merely shown his conceit to be in a different direction. This conceit has been that of "provincialism"—the courting of that second-hand public opinion which is obtained from the politicians and journalists of Europe; the bane of political and civil society in the South. No man of equal public station on this continent has ever courted the opinions of Europe more assiduously than the President of this Confederacy. The proclamations of the Executive, the general orders of the army, the pronunciamentoes of chivalry which have denied the rights of retaliation, bilked the national conscience, and nursed a viperous enemy with the milk of kindness, have all been composed with an eye to European effect. Compromises of dignity and self-respect have been made to conciliate foreign nations. Consuls drawing their *exequaturs* from the Washington government—a standing derogation to the Confederacy which has received them—have been sheltered and endured here; and Europe, which denies our rights over our territory, has received at our hands the safety of her citizens.

We have referred in other pages to the low condition of the finances of the Confederacy in the opening months of this year. It had since declined much further. In February, 1862, President Davis had made the most extravagant congratulations to the country on our financial condition, and pointed with an air of triumph to the failing fortunes of the enemy's treasury. In less than eighteen months thereafter, when gold was quoted in New York at twenty-five per cent. premium, it was selling in Richmond at nine hundred per cent. premium! Such have been the results of the financial wisdom of the Confederacy, dictated by the President, who advised Congress to authorize illimitable issues of treasury notes, and aggravated no doubt by the ignorance of his Secretary, who invented a legerdemain of funding which succeeded not only in depreciating the currency, but also in dishonouring the government.

The experiments of Mr. Memminger on the currency was the signal of multiplied and rapid depreciation. While the eccentric and pious Secretary was figuring out impossible schemes of making money, or ransacking the book-stores for works on religious controversy, unprincipled brokers in the Confederacy were undermining the currency with a zeal for the destruction of their country not less than that of the Yankees. The assertion admits of some qualification. Sweeping remarks in history are generally unjust. Among those engaged in the business of banking and exchange in the South, there were undoubtedly some enlightened and public-spirited men who had been seduced by the example or constrained by the competition of meaner and more avaricious men of the same profession, to array themselves against the currency, and to commit offences from which they would have shrunk in horrour, had they not been disguised by the casuistry of commerce and gain.

It was generally thought in the South reprehensible to refuse the national currency in the payment of debts. Yet the broker, who demanded ten dollars in this currency for one in gold, really was guilty of nine times refusing the Confederate money. It was accounted shocking for citizens in the South to speculate in soldiers' clothing and bread. Yet the broker, who demanded nine or ten prices for gold, the representative of all values, speculated alike in every necessary in the country. Nor was this the greatest of their offences. With unsurpassed shamelessness brokers in the Confederacy exposed the currency of the North for sale and demanded for it four hundred per cent. premium over that of the Confederacy! This act of benefit to the Yankees was openly allowed by the government. A bill had been introduced in Congress to prohibit this traffic and to extirpate this infamous anomaly in our history; but it failed of enactment, and its failure can only be attributed to the grossest stupidity, or to sinister influences of the most dishonourable kind. The traffiic was immensely profitable. State bonds and bank bills to the amount of many millions were sent North by the brokers, and the rates of discount were readily submitted to when the returns were made in Yankee paper money, which, in the Richmond shops, was worth in Confederate notes five dollars for one.

One—but only one—cause of the depreciation of the Confederate currency was illicit trade. It had done more to demoralize the Confederacy than anything else. The inception of this trade was easily winked at by the Confederate authorities; it commenced with paltry importations across the Potomac; it was said that the country wanted medicines, surgical instruments and a number of trifles, and that trade with the Yankees in these could result in no serious harm. But by the enlarged license of the government it soon became an infamy and a curse to the Confederacy. What was a petty traffic in its commencement soon expanded into a shameless trade, which corrupted the patriotism of the country, constituted an anomaly in the history of belligerents, and reflected lasting disgrace upon the honesty and good sense of our government. The country had taken a solemn resolution to burn the cotton in advance of the enemy; but the conflagration of this staple soon came to be a rare event; instead of being committed to the flames it was spirited to Yankee markets. Nor were these operations always disguised. Some commercial houses in the Confederacy counted their gains by millions of dollars since the war, through the favour of the government in allowing them to export cotton at pleasure. The beneficiaries of this trade contributed freely to public charities and did certain favours to the government; but their gifts were but the parings of immense gains; and often those who were named by weak and credulous people or by interested flatterers as public-spirited citizens and patriotic donors, were, in fact, the most unmitigated extortioners and the vilest leeches on the body politic.

In this war we owe to the cause of truth some humiliating confessions. Whatever diminution of spirit there may have been in the South since the commencement of her struggle, it has been on the part of those pretentious classes of the wealthy, who, in peace, were at once the most zealous "secessionists" and the best customers of the Yankees, and who, now, in war, are naturally the sneaks and tools of the enemy. The cotton and sugar planters of the extreme South who prior to the war were loudest for secession, were at the same time known to buy every article of their consumption in Yankee markets, and to cherish an ambition of shining in the society of Northern hotels. It is not surprising that many of these affected patriots have found congenial occupation in this war in planting in copartnership with the enemy, or in smuggling cotton into his lines. The North is said to have obtained in the progress of this war, from the Southwest and Charleston, enough cotton at present prices to uphold its whole system of currency—a damning testimony of the avarice of the planter. Yet it is nothing more than a convincing proof, in general, that property, though very pretentious of patriotism, when identified with selfishness, is one of the most weak and cowardly things in revolutions and the first to succumb under the horrours of war.

It is pleasing to turn from the exhibition of ignorance and weakness in the government, and the vile passions of its favourites, to the contemplation of that patriotic spirit which yet survives in the masses of the people and keeps alive the sacred animosities of the war. We rejoice to believe that the masses are not only yet true, but that a haughtier and fiercer spirit than ever animates the demand of our people for independence, and insures their efforts to obtain it. The noble people and army who have sustained and fought this war will have cause to rejoice. Society in the South is being upheaved by this war, and with our independence will be re-established on new orders of merit. The insolent and pampered slaveholding interest of the South; the planters' aristocracy blown with conceit and vulgar airs of patronage; the boast of lands and kin give way before new aspirants to honour. The republic gives new titles to greatness. Many of those who were esteemed great politicians before the war are now well-nigh forgotten. The honours of State, the worship of society, the rewards of affection are for the patriots of the revolution that will date our existence. Such are the great prizes, intertwined with that of independence, which stir our people and army with noble desires and beckon them to victory.

It is not only in the present external situation of the war that encouragement is to be found for the South. With considerable additions to her material elements of success, the South has in the second year of the war abated none of that moral resolution which is the vital and essential principle of victory, whatever co-operation and assistance it may derive from external conditions. That resolution has been strengthened by recent developments; for as the war has progressed, the enemy has made a full exposure of his cruel and savage purposes, and has indicated consequences of subjugation more terrible than death.

He has, by the hideous array of the instruments of torture which he has prepared for a new inauguration of his authority among those who have disputed it, not only excited the zeal of a devoted patriotism to war with him, but has summoned even the mean but strong passions of selfishness to oppose him. The surrender to an enemy as base as the Yankee, might well attract the scorn of the world and consign the South to despair. The portions of such a fate for the South are gibbets, confiscation, foreign rule, the tutelage of New England, the outlawry of the negro, the pangs of universal poverty, and the contempt of mankind.

War is a thing of death, of mutilation and fire; but it has its law of order; and when that law is not observed, it fails in effecting the purpose for which it is waged, and the curse it would inflict recoils upon itself. It is remarkable in the present war, that the policy of the Washington government has been an increase in every feature of the first cause of the revolt. But this has been fortunate for the South. The consequences of such despotic and savage violences, as the emancipation proclamation, the arming of slaves and the legalization of plunder, have been the growth of new hostility to the Union, and an important and obvious vindication to the world of the motives of the South and the virtues of her cause.

Regarding the condition of events in which this record closes; the broad lustre of victories covering the space of so many months; the numbers of our forces in the field, unequalled at any other period of the war; and the spirit animated by the recollections of victorious arms and stung by the fresh cruelties of an atrocious enemy, we may well persuade ourselves that there is no such word as "fail" in this struggle. Even beneath the pall of disaster, there is no place for such a word. The banners of the Confederacy do not bear the mottoes and devices of a doubtful contest. That brave phrase we may apply to ourselves, which is the law of progress and success; which summons the energies of mankind and works out the problems of human existence; which is at once an expression of the will of the Creator and the power of the creature; and which beautifully harmonizes the dispensations of Providence with the agency of men—"FORTUNA FORTIBUS."

# CHAPTER XIII.

### REVIEW—POLITICAL IDEAS IN THE NORTH, &c.

The Dogma of Numerical Majorities...Its Date in the Yankee Mind... Demoralization of the Idea of the Sovereignty of Numbers...Experience of Minorities in American Politics...Source of the Doctrine of "CONSOLIDATION"...The Slavery Question the Logical Result of Consolidation...Another Aspect of Consolidation in the Tariff...Summary of the Legislation on the Tariff...A Yankee Picture of the Poverty of the South...John C. Calhoun... President Davis' Opinion of his School of Politics..."Nullification," as a Union Measure...Mr. Webster's "Four Exhaustive Propositions"...The True Interpretation of the Present Struggle of the South...The Northern Idea of the Sovereignty of Numbers...Its Results in this War...President Lincoln's Office...The Revenge of the Yankee Congress Upon the People...The Easy Surrender of their Liberties by the Yankees...Lincoln and Cromwell...Explanation of the Political Subserviency in the North...Superficial Political Education of the Yankee...His "Civilization "...The Moral Nature of the Yankee Unmasked by the War...His New Political System...Burnside's "Death Order"...A Bid for Confederate Scalps...A New Interpretation of the War... The North as a Parasite...The Foundations of the National Independence of the South...Present Aspects of the War...Its External Condition and Morals... The Spirit of the South and the Promises of the Future.

The chief value of history is the moral discoveries it makes. What is discovered in the records of the old Union and the events of the present war, of that portion of the American people commonly known as the Yankees, furnishes not only food for curiosity, but a valuable fund of philosophy.

In exploring the character and political experience of the people of the North, much of what is generally thought to be a confusion of vices may be traced to the peculiar idea that people have of the nature and offices of government. Their idea of government may be briefly stated as the *sovereignty of numbers*. This conception of political authority is of no late date with the people of the North; it came in their blood and in their traditions for centuries; it was part of the Puritanical idea; it was manifest in the Revolution of 1776 (the issues of which were saved by the conservatism of the South); and it is to-day exhibited in the passionate and despotic populace that wages war upon the Confederacy.

The peculiarities of this idea of government are very interesting, and its consequences are visible in every part and fibre of the society of the North. It excludes all the elements of virtue and wisdom in the regulation of political authority; it regards numbers as the great element of free government; it represents a numerical majority as infallible and omnipotent; and it gives opportunity to the flattery of demagogues to proclaim the divine rights and sagacity of numbers, and to denounce all constitutions which restrict liberty as most unrighteous inventions.

It is unnecessary to comment at length upon the errour and coarseness of this idea of government. According to the interpretation of the Yankees, the body politic ought simply to have a political organization to bring out and enforce the will of the majority; and such an organization was supposed to be the general government made by our forefathers. But while it is unnecessary to discuss the fallacy of this view, it is entertaining and instructive to observe the train of demoralization it introduced into the society of the North and the consequences it involved.

The Northern idea of government was materialistic; it degraded political authority because it despoiled it of its moral offices and represented it as an accident determined by a comparison of numbers. It destroyed the virtue of minorities; compelled them to servile acquiescence; and explains that constant and curious phenomenon in much of American politics—the rapid absorption of minorities after the elections. It laid the foundations of a despotism more terrible than that of any single tyrant; destroyed moral courage in the people; broke down all the barriers of conservatism; and substituted the phrase, "*the majority must govern,*" for the conscience and justice of society.

This idea, carried out in the early political government of America, soon attained a remarkable development. This development was the absurd doctrine of CONSOLIDATION. It denied the rights of the States; refused to interpret the Union from the authority of cotemporaries or from the nature of the circumstances in which it was formed, or from the objects which it contemplated; and represented it as a central political organization to enforce the divine pleasure of a numerical majority. The Union was thus converted, though with difficulty, into a remorseless despotism, and the various and conflicting interests and pursuits of one of the vastest political bodies in the world were entrusted to the arrogant and reckless majority of numbers.

The slavery question was the logical and inevitable result of Consolidation. It is remarkable how many minds in America have proceeded on the supposition that this agitation was accidental and have distracted themselves with the foolish inquiry why the Yankees assailed the domestic institutions of the South while they neglected to attack the similar institutions of Cuba and Brazil. These minds do not appreciate the fact that the slavery agitation was a *necessity* of the Northern theory of government. Duty is the correlative of power; and if the government at Washington in Yankee estimation was a consolidated organization, with power to promote the general welfare by any means it might deem expedient, it was proper that it should overthrow the hated institution of slavery in the South. The central government was responsible for its continuance or existence in proportion to its power over it. Under these circumstances the duty of acting upon the subject of slavery was imperious and amounted to a moral necessity.

But the slavery agitation was not the only remarkable consequence of the Northern idea of the divine rights of majorities. It may be said that every political maxim of the North has its practical and selfish application as well as its moral and sentimental aspect. The same idea of the power of numerical majorities that kindled the slavery disputes gave birth to the tariff and other schemes of legislation to make the Southern minority subservient and profitable to those who were their masters by the virtue of numbers.

The slavery and tariff issues are singularly associated in American politics; for one at least was an important auxiliary to the other. It was necessary for the Northern people to make their numerical power available to rule the Union; and as slavery was strictly a sectional interest, it only had to be made the criterion of the parties at the North to unite this section and make it master of the Union. When the power of the North could thus be united, it was easy to carry out its measures of sectional ambition, encroachment and aggrandizement. The history of the enormous despotism of Yankee tariffs is easily summed up.

The war of 1812 left the United States with a debt of one hundred and thirty millions. To provide for the payment of this debt, heavy duties were laid on foreign goods; and as in the exigencies of the war some home manufactures had sprung up, which were useful and deserving, and which were in danger of sinking under foreign competition, on the return of peace it was proposed to regulate the tariff so as to afford them some assistance. Protection was an incidental feature in the tariff of 1816, and as such was zealously recommended even by John C. Calhoun, who was a conspicuous advocate of the bill. But the principle of protection once admitted, maintained its hold and enlarged its demands. In the tariffs of 1820, '24 and '28, it was successively carried further; the demand of the North for premiums to its manufacturing interests becoming more exacting and insolent.

In 1831 the public debt had been so far diminished as to render it certain that, at the existing rate of revenue, in three years the last dollar would be paid. The government had been collecting about twice as much revenue as its usual expenditures required, and it was calculated that if the existing tariff continued in operation, there would be after three years an annual surplus in the treasury of twelve or thirteen millions. Under these circumstances, the reduction of the tariff was a plain matter of justice and prudence; but it was resisted by the North with brazen defiance. Unfortunately, Mr. Clay was weak enough to court popularity in the North by legislative bribes, and it was mainly through his exertions that enough was saved of the protection principle to satisfy the rapacity of the Yankee; for which the statesman of Kentucky enjoyed a brief and indecent triumph in the North.

As an engine of oppression of the South, the tariff did its work well; for it not only impoverished her, but fixed on her a badge of inferiority which was an unfailing mark for Yankee derision. The South had no great cities. Their growth was paralyzed, and they were scarcely more than the suburbs of Northern cities. The agricultural productions of the South were the basis of the foreign commerce of the United States; yet Southern cities did not carry it on. The resources of this unhappy part of the country were taxed for the benefit of the Northern people, and for forty years every tax imposed by Congress was laid with a view of subserving the interests of the North.

The blight of such legislation on the South was a source of varied gratification to the Yankee; especially that it gave him the conceit that the South was an inferiour. The contrast between the slow and limited prosperity of the South and the swift and noisy progress of the North, was never more remarkable than at the period of the great tariff controversy of 1831-2. The condition of the country at this time is described by Parton, the Yankee biographer of Andrew Jackson, with flippant self-complacency. He says:

" The North was rushing on like a Western high-pressure
" steamboat, with rosin in the furnace and a man on the safety
" valve. All through Western New York, Ohio, Indiana and
" Illinois, the primeval wilderness was vanishing like a mist,
" and towns were springing into existence with a rapidity that
" rendered necessary a new map every month, and spoiled the

"gazetteers as fast as they were printed. The city of New
"York began already to feel itself the London of the New
"World, and to calculate how many years must elapse before
"it would be the London of the World.

"The South meanwhile was depressed and anxious. Cotton
"was down, tobacco was down. Corn, wheat and pork were
"down. For several years the chief products of the South
"had either been inclining downward, or else had risen in
"price too slowly to make up for the (alleged) increased price
"of the commodities which the South was compelled to buy.
"Few new towns changed the Southern map. Charleston
"languished, or seemed to languish, certainly did not keep
"pace with New York, Boston and Philadelphia. No Cincin-
"nati of the South became the world's talk by the startling
"rapidity of its growth. No Southern river exhibited at
"every bend and coyne of vantage a rising village. No
"Southern mind, distracted with the impossibility of devising
"suitable names for a thousand new places per annum, fell
"back in despair upon the map of the old world, and selected
"at random any convenient name that presented itself, bestow-
"ing upon clusters of log huts such titles as Utica, Rome, Pa-
"lermo, Naples, Russia, Egypt, Madrid, Paris, Elba and
"Berlin. No Southern commissioner, compelled to find names
"for a hundred streets at once, had seized upon the letters of
"the alphabet and the figures of arithmetic, and called the
"avenues A, B, C and D, and, instead of naming his cross
"streets, numbered them."

For forty years the North reaped the fruits of partial legislation, while the South tasted the bitterness of oppression.
The shoemakers, the iron men, the sailmakers, and the cotton
and woolen spinners in the North clamoured for protection
against their English, Swedish and Russian competitors, and
easily obtained it. The South paid duties upon all articles
that the tariff kept out of the country; but these duties, instead of going into the treasury as revenue, went into the
purses of manufacturers as bounty. After paying this tribute,

money to the North, the South had then to pay her quota for the support of the government. The North, for there was perfect free trade between the States, had a preference over all the world for its wares in the markets of the South. This preference amounted to 20 or 30 or 40 or 50 per cent., and even more, according to the article and the existing tariff. It extended over a country having twelve millions of customers. The sum of the Yankee profits out of the tariff was thus enormous. Had the South submitted to the "Morrill tariff," it would have exacted from her something like one hundred million dollars as an annual tribute to the North. But submission has some final period, and the South has no longer a lot in the legislation at Washington.

In the tariff controversy of 1831-2, we find the premonitions of the present revolution. It is a curious circumstance that in the excitement of that period some medals were secretly struck, bearing the inscription, "*John C. Calhoun, First President of the Southern Confederacy.*" The name of the new power was correctly told. But the times were not ripe for a declaration of Southern independence, and even the public opinions of Mr. Calhoun resisted the suggestion of a dissolution of the Union.

The "nullification" doctrine of the statesman of North Carolina is one of the most interesting political studies of America; for it illustrates the long and severe contest in the hearts of the Southern people between devotion to the Union and the sense of wrong and injustice. Mr. Calhoun either did not dare to offend the popular idolatry, or was sincerely attached to the Union; but at the same time he was deeply sensible of the oppression it devolved upon the South. Nullification was simply an attempt to accommodate these two facts. It professed to find a remedy for the grievances of States without disturbing the Union; and the nullification of an unconstitutional law within the local jurisdiction of a State was proposed as the process for referring the matter to some constitutional tribunal other than the Supreme court, whose judgments should be above all influences of political party. It was a crude scheme, and only remarkable as a sacrifice to that peculiar idolatry in American politics which worshipped the name of the Union.

The present President of the Southern Confederacy—Mr. Jefferson Davis—has referred to the political principles of Mr. Calhoun in some acute remarks made on the interesting occasion of his farewell to the old Senate at Washington. He says:

"A great man, who now reposes with his fathers, and who has often been arraigned for a want of fealty to the Union, advocated the doctrine of nullification because it preserved the Union. It was because of his deep-seated attachment to the Union; his determination to find some remedy for existing ills short of a severance of the ties which bound South Carolina to the other States, that Mr. Calhoun advocated the doctrine of Nullification, which he proclaimed to be peaceful; to be within the limits of State power, not to disturb the Union, but only to be a means of bringing the agent before the tribunal of the States for their judgment."

In defending in the speech referred to the action of the State of Mississippi in separating herself from the Union, Mr. Davis remarks with justice, that Secession belongs to another class of remedies than that proposed by the great South Carolinian. The Kentucky and Virginia resolutions of 1798, long the political text of the South, bore the seeds of the present revolution, for they laid the foundation for the right of secession in the sovereignty of the States; and Mr. Calhoun's deduction from them of his doctrine of nullification was narrow and incomplete.

But we shall not renew here vexed political questions. We have referred at some length to the details of the old United States tariffs and the incidental controversies of parties, because we shall find here a peculiar development of the political ideas of the North. To all the ingenious philosophy of State rights; to the disquisitions of Mr. Calhoun and Mr. Tyler; to the discussions of the moral duties of the government, the North had but one invariable reply, and that was the sovereignty of the will of the majority. It recognized no sovereign but numbers, and it was thought to be a sufficient defence of the tariff and other legislation unequal to the South that it was the work and will of the majority.

It was during the agitation of the tariff that the consolidation school became firmly established. Mr. Webster, the mouth-piece of the manufacturing interest in the North, attempted by expositions of the Constitution to represent the government as a central organization of numbers, without any feature of originality to distinguish it from other rude democracies of the world. In his attempt to simplify it, he degraded it to the common-place of simple democracy, and insulted the wisdom of those who had made it. The political opinions of Mr. Webster were summed up in what he arrogantly called "Four Exhaustive Propositions." These propositions were famous in the newspapers of his day, and may be reproduced here as a very just summary of the political ideas of the North:

MR. WEBSTER'S FOUR EXHAUSTIVE PROPOSITIONS.

1. "That the Constitution of the United States is not a "league, confederacy or compact between the people of the "several States in their sovereign capacity; but a government "founded on the adoption of the people, and creating direct "relations between itself and individuals."

2. "That no State authority has power to dissolve these re- "lations; that nothing can dissolve them but revolution; and "that, consequently, there can be no such thing as secession "without revolution."

3. "That there is a supreme law, consisting of the Consti- "tution of the United States, acts of Congress passed in pur- "suance of it, and treaties; and that in cases not capable of "assuming the character of a suit in law or equity, Congress "must judge of and finally interpret this supreme law, as

"often as it has occasion to pass acts of legislation; and in cases capable of assuming the character of a suit, the Supreme Court of the United States is the first interpreter."

4. "That the attempt by a State to abrogate, annul or nullify an act of Congress, or to arrest its operation within her limits, on the ground that, in her opinion, such law is unconstitutional, is a direct usurpation on the just powers of the general government, and on the equal rights of other States; a plain violation of the Constitution; and a proceeding essentially revolutionary in its character and tendency."

It is in the light of these propositions that the present assertion of the independence of the South is denounced by the North as rebellion. And it is with reference to them and their savage doctrine of the power of numbers in a union of sovereign States, that we may in turn challenge the world to declare if the South in this struggle is not enlisted in the cause of free government, which is more important to the world than "the Union" which has disappeared beneath the wave of history.

In the present war the North has given faithful and constant indications of its dominant idea of the political sovereignty, as well as the military omnipotence, of numbers. It is absurd to refer to the person of Abraham Lincoln as the political master of the North; he is the puppet of the vile despotism that rules by brute numbers. We have already referred to some of the characteristics of such despotism. We shall see others in this war in the timidity and subservient hesitation to which such a government reduces party minorities and in that destitution of honour which invariably characterizes the many-headed despotism of the people.

Mr. Lincoln was elected on a principle of deadly antagonism to the social order. His party found him subservient to their passions, and with the President in the hollow of their hand, for two years they have reigned triumphantly in the Congress at Washington. Such has been the stupendous lunacy and knavery of this body, that it will be regarded in all coming time as a blotch on civilization and a disgrace to the common humanity of the age.

There are some minds in the South which are prejudiced by the impression that the power of the Lincoln party was broken by the fall elections of 1862; that it has lost the majority of numbers in the North; and that thereby the despotism which we have described as characteristic of the North is rapidly approaching the period of its dissolution or an era of reaction. But this reply to our theory does not take into account all the facts. The Republican party in the North still has the *majority of force*—a majority more dangerous and appalling than that of numbers, as it finds more numerous objects of revenge among its own people.

The Yankee Congress rejected at the polls has taken fearful revenge on the people who ventured an opinion hostile to the ruling dynasty. They have passed the bank, conscription and *habeas corpus* suspension bills, thus placing every life and every dollar, and, indeed, every right of twenty millions of freeborn people at the absolute mercy of Abraham Lincoln. They have abated none of their legislation against the interests of humanity and the written and unwritten law of civilization in this war. They have added to it. They are organizing insurrections in South Carolina; they have sent a negro army into Florida: they are organizing black regiments in Tennessee. But a few months ago the infamous law was passed at Washington known as "the Plunder Act," in which the Secretary of the Treasury was authorized to appoint agents to go South, collect all property, send it North and have it sold. In different parts of the Confederacy the Yankee troops are now destroying all farming implements, seizing all provisions, and preventing the planting of crops, with the avowed determination of starving the Southern people into submission. Such a warfare contemplates the extermination of women and children as well as men, and proposes to inflict a revenge more terrible to or tolerate the assaults of the Washington government on than the tortures of savages and the modern atrocities of the Sepoys.

It is, perhaps, not greatly to be wondered at that a people like the Yankees should show a brutal rage in warfare upon an enemy who has chastised their insolence and exasperated their pride, and that they should therefore be generally ready to give their adhesion to any train of measures calculated for revenge upon the South. But it is a matter of grave and solicitous inquiry that this people should so easily tolerate measures in the government which have been plainly directed against their own liberties and which, while they have been applauding a "vigorous prosecution of the war," have established a savage despotism at home. It is yet more remarkable that the erection of this despotism should be hailed with a certain applause by its own victims. History has some instances of the servile and unnatural joys of a people in the surrender of their liberties; but none grosser than that in which has been inaugurated the throne of Abraham Lincoln at Washington.

There are numerous examples in history where great abilities or some scattered virtues in the character of a despot have won the flattery of minds not ignoble and unconscious of their humiliation. Milton in his Latin superlatives spoke of Cromwell very much after the same manner in which Mr. Lincoln is spoken of in Yankee vernacular. *Eum te agnoscunt omnes, Cromuelle, ea tu civis maximus et gloriosissimus, dux publici consilii, exercitum, fortissimorum imperator, pater patriæ gessisti.* But the Western lawyer and tavern-jester is not a Cromwell. No attractions of genius are to be found in the personal composition of Abraham Lincoln. His person in fact is utterly unimportant. He holds the reins for a higher power; and that power is the many-headed monster of Fanaticism, which by numbers or by force constrains the popular will and rules with the rod of iron.

The disposition generally of the Northern people to submit

their own liberties and the destruction of their civil rights, must proceed from permanent and well-defined causes. We have already hinted in these pages an explanation of this servile acquiescence in the acts of the government. It is doubtless the fruit of the false political education in the North that gives none other but materialistic ideas of government and inculcates the virtue of time-serving with all political majorities. It is to be attributed to the demoralization of the Yankee; to the servile habit of his mind; to his long practice of submission to the wild democracy of numbers—all proceeding from that false idea of government which recognizes it only as the organ of an accidental party, and not as a self-existent principle of right and virtue. It is a melancholy fact that the people of the North have long ceased to love or to value liberty. They have ceased to esteem the political virtues; to take any account of the moral elements of government; or to look upon it else than as a physical power, to be exercised at the pleasure of a party, and to be endured until reversed by the accident of numbers.

The superficial political education of the people of the North explains much that is curious in their society. Time-serving of power gave them wealth, while it degraded their national character. In the old government they easily surrendered their political virtue for tariffs, bounties, &c.; and the little left of it is readily sacrificed on the devilish altars of this war. Their habit of material computation made them boastful of a "civilization" untouched by the spirits of virtue and humanity, consisting only of the rotten, material things which make up the externals and conveniences of life, and the outer garments of society. Their wealth was blazed out in arts and railroads; common schools, the nurseries of an insolent ignorance; and gilded churches, the temples of an impure religion. No people has ever established more decisively the fact of the worthlessness of what remains of "civilization," when the principle of liberty is subtracted, or more forcibly illustrated how much of phosphorescent rottenness there is in such a condition.

21

> "Their much-loved wealth imparts
> Convenience, plenty, elegance and arts;
> But view them closer, craft and fraud appear,
> Even liberty itself is bartered here,
> At gold's superiour charms all freedom flies,
> The needy sell it and the rich man buys;
> A land of tyrants and a den of slaves."

The present war has sufficiently demonstrated the mistake of the North in the measure of its civilization, and convinced the world that much of what it esteemed its former strength was "but plethoric ill." It has done more than this, for it has unmasked the moral nature of the Yankee. It has exposed to the detestation of the world a character which is the product of materialism in politics and materialism in religion—the spawn of the worship of power and the lust of gain. The Yankee who has followed up an extravagance of bluster by the vilest exhibitions of cowardice; who has falsified his prate of humanity by the deeds of a savage; who, in the South, has been in this war a robber, an assassin, a thief in the night and at home a slave fawning on the hand that manacles him, has secured for himself the everlasting contempt of the world. The characteristics of a people who boasted themselves the most enlightened of Christian nations, are seen in a castrated civilization; while the most remarkable qualities they have displayed in the war are illustrated by the coarse swagger and drunken fumes of such men as Butler, and the rouged lies of such "military authorities" as Halleck and Hooker.

All vestiges of constitutional liberty have long ago been lost in the North. The very term of "State rights" is mentioned with derision, and the States of the North have ceased to be more than geographical designations. No trace is left of the old political system but in the outward routine of the government. The Constitution of the United States is but "the skin of the immolated victim," and the forms and ceremonies of a republic are the disguises of a cruel and reckless despotism.

During the two miserable and disastrous years that Mr. Lincoln has held the presidency of the United States, he has made the institutions of his country but a name. The office of President is no longer recognized in its republican simplicity; it is overlaid with despotic powers and exceeds in reality the most famous imperial titles. Not a right secured by the Constitution but has been invaded; not a principle of freedom but has been overthrown; not a franchise but has been trampled under foot. The infamous "death order" published by Burnside, more bloody than the Draconian penalty and more cruel than the rude decrees of the savage, is without a parallel in the domestic rule or in the warfare of any people making the feeblest pretence to civilization. It assigns the penalty of death to "writers of letters sent by secret mails," and to all persons who "feed, clothe or in any manner aid" the soldiers of the Confederacy. This infamous decree will live in history; it is already associated with a memorable martyrdom—that of Clement Vallandigham.

It is remarkable that the North finds great difficulty in assigning to the world the objects of the present mad and inhuman war. The old pretences made by the Yankees of fighting for a constitutional Union, and contesting the cause of free government for the world, are too absurd and disgusting to be repeated. They are unwilling to admit that they are fighting for revenge, and prosecuting a war, otherwise hopeless, for the gratification of a blind and fanatical hate. They have recently changed the political phrases of the war, and the latest exposition of its object is that the North contends for "the life of the nation." If this means that a parasite is struggling for existence, and that the North desires the selfish aggrandizements of the Union, and its former tributes to its wealth, we shall not dispute the theory. But the plain question occurs, what right has the North to constrain the association of a people who have no benefit to derive from the partnership, and who, by the laws of nature and society, are free to consult their own happiness? The North has territory and numbers and physical resources enough for a separate existence, and if she has not virtue enough to sustain a national organization, she has no right to seek it in a compulsory union with a people who, sensible of their superiour endowments, have resolved to take their destinies in their own hands.

There is one sense, indeed, in which association with the South does imply the national welfare of the North. The South gave to the old government all its ideas of statesmanship; it leavened the political mass with its characteristic conservatism; and it combatted and, to some extent, controlled the brutal theory that represented numbers as the element of free government. The revolutionary and infidel society of the North was moderated by the piety and virtues of the South, and the old national life was in some degree purified by the political ideas and romantic character of that portion of the country now known as the Confederacy. It is in this sense that the Southern element is desirable to the North, and that the Union involves "the life of the nation;" and it is precisely in the same sense that an eternal dissociation and an independent national existence are objects to the South not only of desire, but of vital necessity.

We can never go back to the embraces of the North. There is blood and leprosy in the touch of our former associate. We can never again live with a people who have made of this war a huge assassination; who have persecuted us with savage and cowardly hate; who gloat over the fancies of starving women and children; who have appealed to the worst passions of the black heart of the negro to take revenge upon us; and who, not satisfied with the emancipation proclamation and its scheme of servile insurrection, have actually debated in their State Legislatures the policy of paying negroes premiums for the murder of white families in the South.*

---

\* The following is taken from an Abolition pamphlet (1863), entitled "Interesting Debate," &c., in the Senate of Pennsylvania. It is characteristic of the blasphemous fanaticism of the Yankee and his hideous lust for blood:

"Mr. Lowry—I believed then and now that He who watches over the sparrow will chastise us until we will be just towards ourselves and towards four millions of God's poor, down-cast prisoners of war. I said that I would arm

While we congratulate ourselves on the superiority of our political ideas over those of the North, and the purer life of our society, we do not forget that, although we have carried away much less of the territory and numbers of the old Union than have been left to our enemy, we still have a sufficiency of the material elements of a national existence.

The South has attempted to lay the foundations of national independence, with a territory as great as the whole of Europe, with the exception of Russia and Turkey; with a population four times that of the continental colonies; and with a capacity for commerce equivalent to nearly four-fifths of the exports of the old Union."

It is only necessary to glance at the cotemporary aspects of the war to re-assure our confidence in its destiny, and to renew our vows upon its altars. The hope of reconstruction is a vanity of the enemy. To mobocratic Yankees; to New England "majorities;" to the base crews of Infidelity and Abolitionism; to the savages who have taken upon their souls the curse of fratricidal blood and darkened an age of civilization with unutterable crime and outrage, the South can never surrender, giving up to such a people their name, their lands, their wealth, their traditions, their glories, their heroes newly dead, their victories, their hopes of the future. Such a fate is morally impossible. We have not paid a great price of life

---

the negro—that I would place him in the front of battle—and that I would invite his rebel master with his stolen arms to shoot his stolen ammunition into his stolen property at the rate of a thousand dollars a shot. I said further, that were I commander-in-chief, by virtue of the war power and in obedience to the customs of civilized nations and in accordance with the laws of civilized nations, I would confiscate every rebel's property, whether upon two legs or four, and that I would give to the slave who would bring me his master's disloyal scalp one hundred and sixty acres of his master's plantation; nor would I be at all exacting as to where the scalp was taken off, so that it was at some point between the bottom of the ears and the top of the loins. This, sir, was my language long before Fremont had issued his immortal proclamation. The logic of events is sanctifying daily these anointed truths. Father, forgive thou those who deride and vilify me, because I enunciated them: they know not what they do."

for nothing. We have not forgotten our dead. The flower of our youth and the strength of our manhood have not gone down to the grave in vain. We are not willing for the poor boon of a life dishonoured and joyless to barter our liberties, surrender our homes to the spoiler, exist as the vassals of Massachusetts or become exiles, whose title to pity will not exceed the penalty of contempt. Any contact, friendly or indifferent, with the Yankee, since the display of his vices, would be painful to a free and enlightened people. It would be vile and unnatural to the people of the South if extended across the bloody gulf of a cruel war, and unspeakably infamous if made in the attitude of submission.

www.ingramcontent.com/pod-product-compliance
Lightning Source LLC
Chambersburg PA
CBHW030755230426
43667CB00007B/983